INDIA BOOKVARSITY

LOTUS CHOICES

Editor: Mahendra Kulasrestha

Classics Revived
for an
Ultramodern World

The Golden Book of
R I G V E D A
Humanity's Oldest
Scripture

The first book of its kind
for the general reader

THE
GOLDEN
BOOK OF

R I G V E D A

Selected hymns,
rearranged subjectwise,
translated into easy-to-
understand English by
R.T.H. GRIFFITH
whose translations of all
the Vedas are equally
authentic and famous

Source:
Sacred Books of the East
Edited by F. Max Muller
and published by
Clarendon Press, Oxford, UK
in the 1880s

THE GOLDEN BOOK OF RIGVEDA

Published by:
LOTUS PRESS

4263/3, Ansari Road, Darya Ganj, New Delhi-110002
Ph: 30903912, 23290047
E-mail: lotus_press@sify.com

ISBN 81-8382-010-7

New First Edition 2006

Lasertypeset by: Computek System, Delhi-110032
Printed at: Gyan Sagar, New Delhi

The Veda belongs to the history of the world and India. As long as man continues to take an interest in the history of his race and as long as we collect in libraries and museums the relics of former ages, the first in that long row of books will belong for ever to the Rigveda.

—F. Max Muller

Mirror of a Fantastic Culture

Since my early childhood, I have been interested in the Vedas. My family was Arya Samaji, so I visited every Sunday the Arya Samaj Mandir at Meston Road, Kanpur, with Father, to participate in the Havan in the morning. We did not visit temples, the mainstream centres of worship of the Hindus. The Arya Samaj teaching that idol-worship was non-Aryan and non-Vedic, had an abiding effect on me, and I could not even develop a love for any kind of Puja and image and temple-centred culture of religious belief and worship. The Havan or Yajna-oriented performance was a sobering, dignified attraction, with the high sounding mantras filling up the atmosphere with herb-induced fragrance emitted by the loudly burning fire—the god Agni at the centre. The mantras, though difficult to pronounce, were quickly memorised, and stay in the mind till date—though the Havan is rarely performed these days.

No book of any of the Vedas was available at our homes, though very soon translations in chaste Hindi, of the various Puranas, illuminated with lots of coloured and black and white pictures, came to arrive every month in our homes courtesy the venerable Hanuman Prasad Poddar and Jai Dayal Goenka, who published *Kalyan*, a magazine no one belonging to those times will ever forget. It was a highly low priced magazine and we were told that Shri Goenka used to collect funds from the wealthy Marwaris for the purpose of publishing Puranic literature for general benefit. The annual numbers of *Kalyan* were always unbelievably huge, presenting one complete Purana, unabridged and illustrated from cover to cover. Being essentially stories, they were very readable; we ate and chewed the material with great relish. I feel grateful to these for my extensive knowledge of Hindu mythology.

Kalyan was not interested in the Vedas, not even the Upanishads; the *Gita* was its ultimate limit, of which it published a variety of editions. No one else published the Vedas, not even the Arya Samaj. What these super holy books of India contained, remained a mystery. Some Upanishads were published, specially the smaller ones, but the Brahmanas, Aranyakas etc. never came out. After some time Pandit Satvalekar of Maharashtra came out with his Hindi translations of the Vedas which became very popular, and are regarded till date as the best work on the ignored scriptures. The present writer organised his felicitations when he completed 90 years of his life dedicated to Vedic studies in 1957, in Bombay. The well known writer of historical fiction, Central minister during Shri Nehru's times, the leader of the famous Police Action against the Nizamate of Hyderabad, founder of Bharatiya Vidya Bhavan, K.M. Munshi, was the Chairman of the Committee, and I the Convener-Secretary.

The short-statured, soft-spoken Pt. Satvalekar was an artist, a painter of portraits, graduate of Sir J.J. School of Arts in Bombay, now Mumbai, who later on turned his attention to the study of the Vedas and took upon himself the onerous task of presenting the Vedas—the scriptures held in the highest regard by the masses in modern times. I visited his establishment at Valsad in Gujerat. A Sayana, he lived up to age 102.

The Vedas and related writings are different in concept, structure, content and presentation to any other religious literature in the world. Its non-availability, unlike the Bible, Quran, the Puranas, etc., is another great hurdle to their knowledge and understanding. Many Western scholars like Max Muller, Macdonell, Oldenburg, Roth, Bloomfield, Wilson, Griffith, etc., much attracted by their religio-cultural novelty and abundance, devoted lives after lives in studying, translating and interpreting them in many European languages, and as valued by-products developing new disciplines of linguistics, comparative philology, Sanskrit and oriental studies etc., which, in addition to extending the influence and reach of humanistic sciences, started changing the outlook of ancient as well as modern history.

Several translations and commentaries on the Vedas were published during the later years of nineteenth century. But they were not accorded the welcome they deserved in the country. Our pandits criticised them for not being authentic, though most of them were based on the only Sanskrit commentary made by Sayana, a minister in the Vijayanagar empire of South India, and that of Yaskacharya.

The celebrated ICS Scholar of the British times, Romesh C. Dutt, who also translated the *Ramayana* and the *Mahabharata* in English verse, made the first ever translation of the Rigveda in his mother tongue Bengali, but instead of welcoming it, the people hounded him for dishonouring the sacred work. This was the general attitude of the Indian people to work on the Vedas in those times.

The Arya Samaj insisted that the Vedas were purely philosophical and divine, and no human or historical reference could be attributed to them. Swami Dayanand had started translating the Vedas but was unable to work beyond a point, so the controversy could not be settled. After his passing away, this problem was ignored, perhaps as a matter of strategy. Acharya Vishwa Bandhu, an Arya Samaj Vedic scholar, who ran the Vedic Research Institute, an offshoot of the Samaj in pre partition Lahore, and later on in Hoshiarpur, Punjab (where the present writer also worked for many years), was of the view that the Vedas contained history. He got made a many-volume concordance of the Vedas and published it from the Institute, and though he wanted to translate them, he could not undertake the project.

The Vedas have been regarded as the source and the most sacred central point of all Hindu religious expressions but none, beyond paying a lip-service and reciting a few select mantras in their ceremonies, has cared to look into them with genuine interest and scholarship. Not only that, many of them have interpreted them to suit and support their own sectarian beliefs and rituals. I have come across a commentary, belonging to a sect, which brings out the story of Rama, the sect's idol, complete in most respects, from the Vedas.

A good translation of the Rigveda in Hindi, the present writer came across long ago, was by Pt. Ram Govind Trivedi and published by the well known Indian Press of Allahabad of those times. For the first time I could acquire a reasonably correct but most interesting knowledge of the Vedas. I wrote several articles based on it. These became quite popular. I had then the opportunity to work with the well-known V. Vedic Research Inst. of Punjab. An offshoot of the Arya Samaj movement, it had as its Director, Acharya Vishwa Bandhu, who had created a furore in the movement by insisting, as against the general Arya Samaj belief, that the Vedas did contain history.

●

Much has been written on the Vedas and their culture, which by all accounts, has been and is significant among the oldest world cultures. But it is most unfortunate that a section among ourselves takes pleasure in deriding it no end. Books like A.L. Basham's *The Wonder that was India* do present the subject in perspective. To be just to other cultures, one may say that most ancient cultures were wonders, fantastic in several respects. The Egyptian culture is another example, the only difference being that they have died out while Vedic-Aryan-Indian culture survives. Not only that, it has progressed from material to spiritual, from ideas to new and newer ideas, and ways of life, in its constant journey. Words, language, writing, has been its special features—as against the features of building, painting, sculpture of the Egyptian culture—which has given it the quality of thinking further, assimilating and moving on.

It is again a pity that the real picture of the Vedic life and culture is not known to many, as it has not been properly presented. The hymns are similar and repetitive and in themselves do not mean much of substance. Being simple collections of recitations by priestly families, they can't mean anything more. To serve this purpose, they need selective editing. What is important, is that they are honest, like the descriptions in the Bible, Koran, etc. What they, therefore reflect, is correct, and should be studied and judged in the context of those times. The reader will find them gripping, and unimaginably interesting, to say the least.

The present selection has been made with this concept in view. The selections have been placed in four clear and cut categories, and try to include samples of all kind of material, thought-related and mundane. The picture which emerges is of a growing culture, experimenting, accepting or rejecting and scintillating in the extreme.

There have been many translations of the Vedas, but the editor has preferred this one by Griffith because of its comparative simplicity and common-sense conclusions. He does not follow Sayana in all respects, as Wilson does, and discusses wherever needed. The modern reader will certainly appreciate it and find it helpful.

The culture developed on the basis of the Vedas grew into a humanistic culture. A.L. Basham in his famous work says about it:

'In no other part of the ancient world were the relations of man and man, and of man and the state, so fair and humane. In no other early civilisation were slaves so few in number, and in no other ancient law book are their rights so well protected as in the *Arthashastra*. No other ancient law giver proclaimed such noble ideals of fairplay in battle as in Manu, in all her history of warfare Hindu India has few tales to tell of cities put to the sword or of the massacre of non-combatants. The ghastly sadism of the kings of Assyria, who flayed their captives alive, is completely without parallel in ancient India. To us the most striking feature of ancient Indian civilisation is its humanity.'

Rigveda:
The oldest literary document in existence

This work is an attempt to bring within reach of all readers of English a translation of the Hymns of the Rigveda which while aiming especially at close fidelity to the letter and the spirit of the original, shall be as readable and intelligible as the nature of the subject and other circumstances permit.

Veda, meaning literally knowledge, is the name given to certain works which formed the foundation of the early religious belief of the Hindus. These are the Rigveda, the Samaveda, the Yajurveda, and the Atharvaveda; and of these the Rigveda—so called because its Samhita or collection of mantras or hymns consists of Richas or verses intended for loud recitation—is the oldest, the most important, and the most generally interesting, some of its hymns being rather Indo-European than Hindu, and representing the condition of the Aryans before their final settlement in India. These four Vedas are considered to be of divine origin and to have existed from all eternity, the Rishis or sacred poets to whom the hymns are ascribed being merely inspired seers who saw or received them by sight directly from the Supreme Creator. In accordance with this belief, these sacred books have been preserved and handed down with the most reverential care from generation to generation and have accompanied the great army of Aryan immigrants in their onward march from the Land of the Seven Rivers to the Indian Ocean and the Bay of Bengal.

Each of these four Vedas is divided into two distinct parts, one the Mantra containing prayer and praise, the other the Brahmana containing detailed directions for the performance of the ceremonies at which the Mantras were to be used, and explanations of the legends connected with them, the whole forming a vast body of sacred literature in verse and in prose, devotional, ceremonial, expository and theosophic.

The Samhita of the Rigveda is a collection of hymns and songs brought by the remote ancestors of the present Hindus from their ancient homes on the banks of the Indus where they had been first used in adoration of the Father of Heaven, of the Sun, of Dawn, of Agni or the god of fire, in prayers for health, wealth, long life, offspring, cattle, victory in battle, and freedom from the bonds of sin; and celebration of the ever-renewed warfare between the beneficent thunder-wielding Indra, the special champion of the Aryans, and the malevolent powers of darkness and the demons of drought who withheld the rain of heaven.

Of these hymns there are more than a thousand, arranged in ten Mandalas, Circles or Books, in accordance with an ancient tradition of what we should call authorship, the hymns ascribed to the same Rishi, inspired poet or seer or to the same school or family of Rishis being placed together. Within these divisions the hymns are generally more or less in the order of the deities to whom they are addressed. Agni and Indra are the gods most frequently invoked. Hymns to Agni generally come first, next come those addressed to Indra, and after them those of other deities or deified objects of adoration. The ninth Book is devoted almost entirely to Soma, the deified juice used in pouring libations to the gods, and the tenth forms a sort of appendix of peculiar and miscellaneous materials.

Independently of the evidence afforded by Indian tradition, there can be no reasonable doubt of the great antiquity of the Rigveda Samhita which with the exception of the Egyptian monumental records and papyrus rolls, and the Assyrian literature, is probably the oldest literary document in existence. But it seems impossible to fix, with anything approaching to certainty, any date for the composition of the hymns. In the first Hymn of Book I, ancient and recent or modern Rishis or seers are spoken of, and there is other internal evidence that some hymns are much older than others. Colebrooke came to the conclusion from astronomical calculations, that a certain Vedic calendar was composed in the fourteenth century before the Christian era; from which it would follow, that as this calendar must have been prepared after the arrangement of the Rigveda and the inclusion of the most modern hymn, the date of the earliest hymn might be carried back perhaps, some thousand years. The correctness of Colebrooke's conclusion, however, has been questioned, and some recent scholars consider that his calculations are of a very vague character and do not yield any such definite date.

In the absence of any direct evidence, the opinions of scholars vary and must continue to vary with regard to the age of the hymns of the Rigveda. "The reasons, however," to quote Professor Weber, "by which we are fully justified in regarding the literature of India as the most ancient literature of which written records of an extensive scale have been handed down to us are these:—"In the more ancient parts of the Rigveda Samhita, we find the Indian race settled on the north-western borders of India, in the Punjab, and even beyond the Punjab, on the Kubha, or Kophen in Kabul. The gradual spread of the race from these seats towards the east, beyond the Sarasvati and over Hindustan as far as the Ganges, can be traced in the later portions of the Vedic writings almost step by step. The writings of the following period, that of the epic, consist of accounts of the internal conflicts among the conquerors of Hindustan themselves, as, for instance, the Mahabharata; or of the farther spread of Brahminism towards the south, as for instance, the Ramayana. If we connect with this the first fairly accurate information about India which we have from a Greek source, viz., from Megasthenes, it becomes clear that at the time of this writer the Brahminising of Hindustan was already completed, while at the time of Periplus the very southernmost point of the Deccan had already become the seat of the worship of Gauri, the wife of Siva. What a series of years, of centuries, must necessarily have elapsed before this boundless tract of the country, inhabited by wild and vigorous tribes, could have been brought over to Brahminism!"

I must beg my European readers not to expect to find in these hymns and songs the sublime poetry that they meet with in Isaiah or Job, or the Psalms of David. Occasionally, we meet with fine outbursts of poetry, especially in the hymns addressed to Dawn, but these are never long sustained, and as a rule we find few grand similes or metaphors. The worst fault of all, in the collection regarded as a whole, is the intolerable monotony of a great number of the hymns, a monotony which reaches its climax in the ninth Book which consists almost entirely of invocations of Soma Pavamana, or the deified Soma juice in process of straining and purification.

The great interest of the Rigveda is, in fact, historical rather than poetical. As in its original language we see the roots and shoots of the languages of Greek and Latin, of Kelt, Teuton and Slavonian, so the deities, the myths, and the religious beliefs and practices of the Veda throw a flood of light upon the religions of all European countries before the introduction of Christianity. As the science of comparative philology could hardly have existed without the study of Sanskrit, so the comparative history of the religions of the world would have been impossible without the study of the Veda.

My translation, which follows the text of Max Muller's splendid six-volume edition, is partly based on the work of the great scholiast Sayana who was Prime Minister at the court of the King of Vijaynagar in the fourteenth century of our era. Sayana's commentary has been consulted and carefully considered for the general sense of every verse and for the meaning of every word, and his interpretation has been followed whenever it seemed rational, and consistent with the context, and with other passages in which the same word or words occur. With regard to Sayana's qualifications as an interpreter of the Veda there is, or was, a conflict of opinion among European scholars. Professor Wilson—whose translation of the Rigveda is rather a version of Sayana's paraphrase—was firmly persuaded that he had a "knowledge of his text far beyond the pretensions of any European scholar, and must have been in possession of all the interpretations which had been perpetuated by traditional teaching from the earliest times." Yet, as Dr. J. Muir has pointed out, Professor Wilson in the notes of his translation admits that he "occasionally failed to find in Sayana a perfectly satisfactory guide," that "the scholiast is evidently puzzled," and that his explanations are obscure.

On the other hand, Professor Roth—the author of the Vedic portion of the great *St. Petersburg Lexicon*—says in his preface to that work: "So far as regards one of the branches of Vedic literature, the treatise on theology and worship, we can desire no better guides than these commentators, so exact in all respects, who follow their texts word by word, who so long as even the semblance of a misconception might arise, are never weary of repeating what they have frequently said before, and who often appear as if they had been writing for us foreigners rather than for their own priestly alumni who had grown up in the midst of these conceptions and impressions. Here... they are in their proper ground. The case, however, is quite different when the same men assume the task of interpreting the ancient collections of hymns... Here were required not only quite different qualifications for interpretation but also a greater freedom of judgment and a greater breadth of view and of historical intuitions."

Professor Max Muller says: "As the authors of the Brahmanas were blinded by theology, the authors of the still later Niruktas were deceived by etymological fictions, and both conspired to mislead by their authority the later and more sensible commentators, such as Sayana. Where Sayana has no authority to mislead him, his commentary is at all events rational; but still his scholastic notions would never allow him to accept the free interpretation which comparative study of these venerable documents forces upon the unprejudiced scholar. We must therefore discover ourselves the real vestiges of these ancient poets."

Professor Benfey says: "Every one who has carefully studied the Indian interpretations is aware that absolutely no continuous tradition extending from the composition of the Veda to their explanation by Indian scholars, can be assumed; that, on the contrary, between the genuine poetic remains of Vedic antiquity and their interpretations a long-continued break in tradition must have intervened, out of which at most the comprehension of some particulars may have been rescued and handed down to later times by means of liturgical usages and words, formulae, and perhaps, also, poems connected therewith. Besides these remains of tradition, which must be estimated as very scanty, the interpreters of the Veda had, in the main, scarcely any other helps than those which, for the most part, are still at our command, the usage of the classical speech, and the grammatical and etymological-lexicographical investigation of words."

A very different opinion of the value of the Indian commenntators was held and expressed by Professor Goldstucker: "Without the vast information," he says, "which these commentators have disclosed to us,—without their method of explaining the obscurest text,—in one word, without their scholarship, we should still stand at the outer doors of Hindu antiquity." He ridicules the assertion that a European scholar can understand the Veda more correctly than Sayana, or arrive more nearly at the meaning which the Rishis gave to their own hymns, and yet even this staunch champion of the Indian commentators "cannot be altogether acquitted of a certain heretical tendency to deviate in practice from the interpretations of Sayana."

The last quotation which I shall make in connexion with this question is from Professor E.B. Cowell's Preface to his edition of Vol. V of Wilson's translation of the Rigveda Samhita: "This work does not pretend to give a complete translation of the Rigveda, but only a faithful image of that particular phase of its interpretation which the medieval Hindus, as represented by Sayana, have preserved." This view is in itself interesting and of an historical value; but far wider and deeper study is needed to pierce to the real meaning of these old hymns.

But it must not be supposed that European students and interpreters of the Veda claim anything like infallibility, completeness, or finality for the results to which their researches have led them. All modern scholars will allow that many hymns are dark as the darkest oracle, that, as Professor Max Muller says, there are whole verses which, as yet, yield no sense whatever, and words the meaning of which we can only guess. As in the interpretation of the more difficult books of the Old Testament and the Homeric poems, so in the explanation of the Veda complete success, if ever attainable, can be attained only by the labours of generations of scholars.

The Hymns are composed in various metres, some of which are exceedingly simple and others comparatively complex and elaborate, and two or more different metres are frequently found in the same Hymn; one Hymn, for instance, in Book I shows nine distinct varieties in the same number of verses. The verses or stanzas consist of three or more—generally three or four—Padas, semi-hemistichs or lines, each of which contains eight, eleven or twelve syllables, sometimes, but rarely, five, and still less frequently four or more than twelve. As regards quantity, the first syllables of the line are not strictly defined, but the last four are regular, the measure being iambic in the eight and twelve syllable verses and trochaic in those of eleven syllables. Partly by way of safeguard against the besetting temptation to paraphrase and expand, and partly in the hope of preserving, however imperfectly, something of the form of the Hymns, I have translated each verse by a verse syllabically commensurate with the original and generally divided into corresponding hemistichs.

Nilgiri, 1889   —R.T.H. Griffith

CONTENTS

-·-

THOUGHT

DEITIES

LIFE

EVENTS

THOUGHT

Kah: Who?

-.-

Hiranyagarbha

Kah (quis) meaning Who? that is, the Unknown God, has been applied as a name to Prajapati, and to other gods.

हिरण्यगर्भः समवर्तताग्रे भूतस्य जातं: पतिरेक आसीत्।
स दाधार पृथिवीं द्यामुतेमां कस्मै देवाय हविषा विधेम।।
य आत्मदा बलदा यस्य विश्व उपासते प्रशिषं यस्य देवा:।
यस्य छायामृतं यस्य मृत्यु: कस्मै देवाय हविषा विधेम।।
य: प्राणतो निमिषतो महित्वैक इद्राजा जगतो बभूव।
य ईशे अस्य द्विपदश्चतुष्पद: कस्मै देवाय हविषा विधेम।।
यस्येमे हिमवन्तो महित्वा यस्य समुद्रं रसया सहाहु:।
यस्येमा: प्रदिशो यस्य बाहू कस्मै देवाय हविषा विधेम।।
येन द्यौरुग्रा पृथिवी च दृळ्हा येन स्व: स्तभितं येन नाक:।
यो अन्तरिक्षे रजसो विमान: कस्मै देवाय हविषा विधेम।।
यं क्रन्दसी अवसा तस्तभाने अभ्यैक्षेतां मनसा रेजमाने।
यत्राधि सूर उदितो विभाति कस्मै देवाय हविषा विधेम।।
आपो ह यद्बृहतीर्विश्वमायन् गर्भ दधाना जनयन्तीरग्निम्।
ततो देवानां समवर्ततासुरेक: कस्मै देवाय हविषा विधेम।।

यश्चिदापो महिना पर्यपश्यद् दक्षं दधाना जनयन्तीर्यज्ञम्।
यो देवेष्वधि देव एक आसीत् कस्मै देवाय हविषा विधेम॥
मा नो हिंसीज्जनिता यः पृथिव्या यो वा दिवं सत्यधर्मा जजान।
यश्चापश्चन्द्रा बृहतीर्जजान कस्मै देवाय हविषा विधेम॥
प्रजापते न त्वदेतान्यन्यो विश्वा जातानि परि ता बभूव।
यत् कामास्ते जुहुमस्तन्नो अस्तु वयं स्याम पतयो रयीणाम्॥

1. In the beginning rose Hiranyagarbha, born Only Lord of all created beings.

    He fixed and holdeth up this earth and heaven. What God shall we adore with our oblation?

2. Giver of vital breath, of power and vigour, he whose commandments all the Gods acknowledge:

    The Lord of death, whose shade is life immortal. What God shall we adore with our oblation?

3. Who by his grandeur hath become Sole Ruler of all the moving world that breathes and slumbers;

    He who is Lord of men and Lord of cattle. What God shall we adore with our oblation?

4. His, through his might, are these snowcovered mountains, and men call sea and Rasa his possession:

    His arms are these, his are these heavenly regions. What God shall we adore with our oblation?

5. By him the heavens are strong and earth is steadfast, by him light's realm and sky-vault are supported:

    By him the regions in mid air were measured. What God shall we adore with our oblation?

6. To him, supported by his help, two armies embattled look while trembling in their spirit,

    When over them the risen Sun is shining. What God shall we adore with our oblation?

7. What time the mighty waters came, containing the universal germ, producing Agni,

   Thence sprang the Gods' one spirit into being. What God shall we adore with our oblation?

8. He in his might surveyed the floods containing productive force and generating Worship.

   He is the God of gods, and none beside him. What God shall we adore with our oblation?

9. Ne'er may he harm us who is earth's Begetter, nor he whose laws are sure, the heavens' Creator,

   He who brought forth the great and lucid waters. What God shall we adore with our oblation?

10. Prajapati! thou only comprehend all these created things, and none beside thee.

   Grant us our hearts' desire when we invoke thee: may we have store of riches in possession.

   (X/21)

Srishti: Creation

-.-

Prajapati

नासदासीन्नो सदासीत् तदानीं नासीद्रजो नो व्योम। परो यत्।
किमावरीव: कुह कस्य शर्मन्नम्भः किमासीद्गहनं गभीरम्॥
न मृत्युरासीदमृतं न तर्हि न रात्र्या अहन आसीत् प्रकेत:।
आनीदवातं स्वधया तदेकं तस्माद्धान्यन्न पर: किं चनास॥
तम आसीत् तमसा गूळ्हमग्रेऽप्रकेतं सलिलं सर्वमा इदम्।
तुच्छ्येनाभ्वपिहितं यदासीत् तपसस्तन्महिनाजायतैकम्॥
कामस्तदग्रे समवर्तताधि मनसो रेत: प्रथमं यदासीत्।

सतो बन्धुमसति निरविन्दन् हृदि प्रतीष्या कवयो मनीषा।।
तिरश्चीनो विततो रश्मिरेषा मध: स्विदासी३दुपरि स्विदासी३त्।
रेतोधा आसन् महिमान आसन् त्स्वधा अवस्तात् प्रयति: परस्तात्।।
को अद्धा वेद क इह प्र वोचत् कुत आजाता कुत इयं विसृष्टि:।
अर्वाग्देवा अस्य विसर्जनेनाऽथा को वेद यत आबभूव।।
इयं विसृष्टिर्यत आबभूव यदि वा दधे यदि वा न।
यो अस्याध्यक्ष: परमे व्योमन् त्सो अङ्ग वेद यदि वा न वेद।।

1. Then was not non-existent nor existent: there was no realm of air, no sky beyond it.

    What covered in, and where? and what gave shelter? Was water there, unfathomed depth of water?

2. Death was not then, nor was there aught immortal: no sign was there, the day's and night's divider.

    That One Thing, breathless, breathed by its own nature: apart from it was nothing whatsoever.

3. Darkness there was : at first concealed in darkness this All was indiscriminated chaos.

    All that existed then was void and formless: by the great power of Warmth was born that Unit.

4. Thereafter rose Desire in the beginning, Desire, the primal seed and germ of Spirit.

    Sages who searched with their heart's thought discovered the existent's kinship in the non-existent.

5. Transversely was their severing line extended: what was above it then, and what below it?

    There were begetters, there were nighty forces, free action here and energy up yonder.

6. Who verily knows and who can here declare it, whence it, was born and whence comes this creation?

The Gods are later than this world's Production.
Who knows then whence it first came into being?

7. He, the first origin of this creation, whether he formed
it all or did not form it,

Whose eye controls this world in highest heaven,
he verily knows it, or perhaps he knows not.

(X/129)

•

Madhuchchhanda

ऋतं च सत्यं चाभीद्धात् तपसोऽध्यंजायत। ततो रात्र्यंजायत ततः समुद्रो अर्णवः॥

समुद्रादर्णवादधि संवत्सरो अजायत। अहोरात्राणि विदधद्विश्वस्य भिषतो वशी॥

सूर्याचन्द्रमसौ धाता यथापूर्वमंकल्पयत्। द्विवं च पृथिवीं चाऽन्तरिक्षमथो स्वः॥

1. From Fervour kindled to its height
   Eternal Law and Truth were born:
   Thence was the Night produced, and thence the
   billowy flood of sea arose.

2. From that same billowy flood of sea the Year was
   afterwards produced,
   Ordainer of the days nights, Lord over all who close
   the eye.

3. Dhatar, the great Creator, then formed in due order
   Sun and Moon.
   He formed in order Heaven and Earth, the regions
   of the air, and light.

(X/190)

Purusa : The Universal Soul

Narayana

Purusa, embodied spirit, or Man personified and regarded as the soul and original source of the universe, the personal and life-giving principle in all animated beings, is said to have a thousand, that is, innumerable, heads, eyes, and feet, as being one with all created life. A space ten fingers wide: the region of the heart of man, wherein the soul was supposed to reside. Although as the Universal Soul he pervades the universe, as the Individual Soul he is enclosed in a space of narrow dimensions.

सहस्रशीर्षा पुरुष: सहस्राक्ष: सहस्रपात्।
स भूमि वि श्वतो वृत्वा ऽत्यतिष्ठद्दशांङ्गुलम्॥
पुरुष एवेदं सर्वं यद्भूतं यच्च भव्यम्।
उतामृतत्वस्येशानो यदन्नेनातिरोहति॥
एतावानस्य महिमा ऽतो ज्यायाँश्च पुरुष:।
पादोऽस्य वि श्वा भूतानि त्रिपादस्यामृतं दिवि॥
त्रिपादूर्ध्व उदैत् पुरुष: पादोऽस्येहाभवत् पुन:।
ततो विष्वङ् व्यक्रामत् साशनानशने अभि॥
तस्माद्विराळजायत विराजो अधि पूरुष:।
स जातो अत्यरिच्यत पश्र्वाद्भूमिमथो पुर:॥
यत पुरुषेण हविषा देवा यज्ञमतन्वत।
वसन्तो अस्यासीदाज्यं ग्रीष्म इध्म: शरद्धवि:॥
तं यज्ञं बर्हिषि प्रौक्षन् पुरुषं जातमग्रत:।
तेन देवा अयजन्त साध्या ऋषयश्च ये॥
तस्माद्यज्ञात सर्वहुत: संभृतं पृषदाज्यम्।
पशून् ताँश्चक्रे वायव्यानारण्यान् ग्राम्याश्च ये॥
तस्माद्यज्ञात सर्वहुत ऋच: सामानि जज्ञिरे।
छन्दांसि जज्ञिरे तस्माद्यजुस्तस्मादजायत॥

तस्माद श्वा अजायन्त ये के चोभयादतः।
गावो ह जज्ञिरे तस्मात् तस्माज्जाता अजावयः॥
यत् पुरुषं व्यदधुः कतिधा व्यकल्पयन्।
मुखं किमस्य कौ बाहू का ऊरू पादा उच्येते॥
ब्राह्मणोऽस्य मुखमासीद्बाहू राजन्यः कृतः।
ऊरू तदस्य यद्वैश्यः पद्भ्यां शूद्रो अजायत॥
चन्द्रमा मनसो जातश्चक्षोः सूर्यो अजायत।
मुखादिन्द्रश्चाग्निश्च प्राणाद्वायुरजायत॥
नाभ्या आसीदन्तरिक्षं शीर्ष्णो द्यौः समवर्तत।
पद्भ्यां भूमिर्दिशः श्रोत्रात् तथा लोकाँ अकल्पयन्॥
सप्तास्यासन् परिधयस्त्रिः सप्त समिधः कृताः।
देवा यद्यज्ञं तन्वाना अबध्नन् पुरुषं पशुम्॥
यज्ञेन यज्ञमयजन्त देवास्तानि धर्माणि प्रथमान्यासन्।
ते ह नाकं महिमानः सचन्त यत्र पूर्वे साध्याः सन्ति देवाः॥

1. A thousand heads hath Purusa, a thousand eyes, a thousand feet.

   On every side pervading earth he fills a space ten fingers wide.

2. This Purusa is all that yet hath been and all that is to be;

   The Lord of Immortality which waxes greater still by food.

3. So mighty is his greatness; yea, greater than this is Purusa.

   All creatures are one-fourth of him, three fourths eternal life in heaven.

4. With three-fourths Purusa went up: one-fourth of him again was here.

   Thence he strode out to every side over what eats not and what eats.

5. From him Viraj was born; again Purusa from Viraj was born.

   As soon as he was born he spread eastward and westward o'er the earth.

6. When Gods prepared the sacrifice with Purusa as their offering,

   Its oil was spring, the holy gift was autumn; summer was the wood.

7. They balmed as victim on the grass Purusa born in earliest time.

   With him the Deities and all Sadhyas and Rish sacrificed.

8. From that great general sacrifice the dripping fat was gathered up.

   He formed the creatures of the air, and animals both wild and tame.

9. From that great general sacrifice Richas and Sama-hymns were born:

   Therefrom were spells and charms produced; the Yajus had its birth from it.

10. From it were horses born, from it all cattle with two rows of teeth:

    From it were generated kine, from it the goats and sheep were born.

11. When they divided Purusa how many portions did they make?

    What do they call his mouth, his arms? What do they call his thighs and feet?

12. The Brahmin was his mouth, of both his arms was the Rajanya made.

    His thighs became the Vaishya, from his feet the Shudra was produced.

13. The Moon was gendered from his mind, and from
    his eye the Sun had birth;

    Indra and Agni from his mouth were born, and
    Vayu from his breath.

14. Forth from his navel came mid-air; the sky was
    fashioned from his head;

    Earth from his feet, and from his ear the regions.
    Thus they formed the worlds.

15. Seven fencing-sticks had he, thrice seven layers of
    fuel were prepared,

    When the Gods, offering sacrifice, bound, as their
    victim, Purusa.

16. Gods, sacrificing, sacrificed the victim: these were
    the earliest holy ordinances.

    The Mighty Ones attained the height of heaven,
    there were the Sadhyas, Gods of old, are dwelling.

    (X/90)

Mayabheda: Illusion

-.-

Prajapati

The subject is Mayabheda, 'the discernment of *maya*, or illusion,
the cause of material creation.

पतङ्ग॒मक्तमसुरस्य मायया हृदा पश्यन्ति मनसा विपश्चितः।
समुद्रे अन्तः कवयो वि चक्षते मरीचीनां पदमिच्छन्ति वेधसः॥
पतंङ्गो वाचं मनसा बिभर्ति तां गन्धर्वोऽवद्दगर्भे अन्तः।
तां द्योतमानां स्वर्यं मनीषामृतस्य पदे कवयो नि पान्ति॥
अपश्यं गोपामनिपद्यमानमा च परा च पथिभिश्चरन्तम्।
स सध्रीचीः स विषूचीर्वसान आ वरीवर्ति भुवनेष्वन्तः॥

1. The sapient with their spirit and their mind behold the Bird adorned with all an Asura's magic might.

Sages observe him in the ocean's inmost depth: the wise disposers seek the station of his rays.

2. The flying Bird bears Speech within his spirit: erst the Gandharva in the womb pronounced it:

And at the seat of sacrifice the sages cherish this radiant, heavenly-bright invention.

3. I saw the Herdsman, him who never resteth, approaching and departing on his pathways.

He, clothed in gathered and diffusive splendour, within the worlds continually travels.

(X/177)

Dyava-Prithivi: Heaven and Earth

-·-

Auchathya

ते हि द्यावापृथिवी विश्वशंभुव ऋतावरी रजसो धारयत्कवी।
सुजन्मनी धिषणे अन्तरीयते देवो देवी धर्मणा सूर्य: शुचि:॥
उरुव्यचसा महिनी असश्चता पिता माता च भुवनानि रक्षत:।
सुधृष्टमे वपुष्ये३ न रोदसी पिता यत् सीमभि रूपैरवासयत्॥
स वह्नि: पुत्र: पित्रो: पवित्रवान् पुनाति धीरो भुवनानि मायया।
धेनुं च पृश्निं वृषभं सुरेतसं विश्वाहा शुक्रं पयो अस्य दुक्षत॥
अयं देवानामपसामपस्तमो यो जजान रोदसी विश्वशंभुवा।
वि यो ममे रजसी सुक्रतूयया ऽजरेभि: स्कम्भनेभि: समानृचे॥
ते नो गृणाने महिनी महि श्रव: क्षत्रं द्यावापृथिवी धासथो बृहत्।
येनाभि कृष्टीस्ततनाम विश्वहा पनाय्यमोजो अस्मे समिन्वतम्॥

1. These, Heaven and Earth, bestow prosperity on all, sustainers of the region, Holy Ones and wise,

   Two Bowls of noble kind: between these Goddesses the God, the fulgent Sun, travels by fixed decree.

2. Widely-capacious Pair, mighty, that never fail, the Father and the Mother keep all creatures safe:

   The two world-halves, the spirited, the beautiful, because the Father hath clothed them in goodly forms.

3. Son of these Parents, he the Priest with power to cleanse, Sage, sanctifies the worlds with his surpassing power.

   Thereto for his bright milk he milked through all the days the party-coloured Cow and the prolific Bull.

4. Among the skilful Gods most skilled is he, who made the two world-halves which bring prosperity to all;

   Who with great wisdom measured both the regions out, and established them with pillars that shall ne'er decay.

5. Extolled in song, O Heaven and Earth, bestow on us, ye mighty Pair, great glory and high lordly sway,

   Whereby we may extend ourselves ever over the folk; and send us strength that shall deserve the praise of men.

                                                      (I/160)

●

Agastya

कतरा पूर्वा कतरापरायो: कथा जाते कवय: को वि वेद।
वि श्वं त्मना विभूतो यद्ध नाम वि वर्तेते अहनी चक्रियेव॥
भूरिं द्वे अचरन्ती चरन्तं पद्वन्तं गर्भमपदी दधाते।

नित्यं न सूनुं पित्रोरुपस्थे द्यावा रक्षतं पृथिवी नो अभ्वात्॥

अनेहो दात्रमदितेरनर्वं हुवे स्वर्वदवधं नमस्वत्।
तद् रोदसी जनयतं जरित्रे द्यावा रक्षतं पृथिवी नो अभ्वात्॥

अतप्यमाने अवसावन्ती अनु ष्याम रोदसी देवपुत्रे।
उभे देवानामुभयेभिरह्नां द्यावा रक्षतं पृथिवी नो अभ्वात्॥

संगच्छमाने युवती समन्ते स्वसारा जामी पित्रोरुपस्थे।
अभिजिघ्रन्ती भुवनस्य नाभिं द्यावा रक्षतं पृथिवी नो अभ्वात्॥

उर्वीं सद्मनी बृहती ऋतेन हुवे देवानामवसा जनित्री।
दधाते ये अमृतं सुप्रतीके द्यावा रक्षतं पृथिवी नो अभ्वात्॥

उर्वीं पृथ्वी बहुले दूरेअन्ते उप ब्रुवे नमसा यज्ञे अस्मिन्।
दधाते ये सुभगे सुप्रतूर्ती द्यावा रक्षतं पृथिवी नो अभ्वात्॥

देवान् वा यच्चकृमा कच्चिदागः सखायं वा सदमिज्जास्पतिं वा।
इयं धीर्भूया अवयानमेषां द्यावा रक्षतं पृथिवी नो अभ्वात्॥

उभा शंसा नर्या मामविष्टामुभे मामूती अवसा सचेताम्।
भूरि चिदर्यः सुदास्तरायेषा मदन्त इषयेम देवाः॥

ऋतं दिवे तदवोचं पृथिव्या अभिश्रावाय प्रथमं सुमेधाः।
पातामवद्याद् दुरितादभीके पिता माता च रक्षतामवोभिः॥

इदं द्यावापृथिवी सत्यमस्तु पितर्मातर्यदिहोपब्रुवे वाम्।
भूतं देवानामवमे अवोभिर्विद्यामेषं वृजनं जीरदानुम्॥

1. Whether of these is elder, whether later? How were they born? Who knoweth it, ye sages?

    These of themselves support all things existing: as on a car the Day and Night roll onward.

2. The Twain uphold, though motionless and footless, a widespread offspring having feet and moving.

    Like your own son upon his parents' bosom, protect us, Heaven and Earth, from fearful danger.

3. I call for Aditi's unrivalled bounty, perfect, celestial, deathless, meet for worship.

    Produce this, ye Twain Worlds, for him who lauds you. Protect us, Heaven and Earth, from fearful danger.

4. May we be close to both the Worlds who suffer no pain, Parents of Gods, who aid with favour,

    Both mid the gods, with Day and Night alternate. Protect us, Heaven and Earth, from fearful danger.

5. Faring together, young, with meeting limits, Twin Sisters lying in their Parents' bosom,

    Kissing the centre of the world together. Protect us, Heaven and Earth, from fearful danger.

6. Duly I call the two wide seats, the mighty, the general Parents, with the God's protection.

    Who, beautiful to look on, make the nectar. Protect us, Heaven and Earth, from fearful danger.

7. Wide, vast, and manifold, whose bounds are distant,—these, reverent, I address at this our worship,

    The blessed Pair, victorious, all-sustaining. Protect us, Heaven and Earth, from fearful danger.

8. What sin we have at any time committed against the Gods, our friend, our house's chieftain,

    Thereof may this our hymn be expiation. Protect us, Heaven and Earth, from fearful danger.

9. May both these Friends of man, who bless, preserve me, may they attend me with their help and favour.

    Enrich the man more liberal than the godless. May we, ye Gods, be strong with food rejoicing.

10. Endowed with understanding, I have uttered this truth, for all to hear, to Earth and Heaven.

Be near us, keep us from reproach and trouble. Father and Mother, with your help preserve us.

11. Be this my prayer fulfilled, O Earth and Heaven, wherewith, Father and Mother, I address you.

Nearest of Gods be ye with your protection. May we find strengthening food in full abundance.

(I/185)

Prithivi: Earth

-.-

Atri

बळित्था पर्वतानां खिद्रं बिभर्षि पृथिवि।
प्र या भूमिं प्रवत्वति मह्ना जिनोषि महिनि।।
स्तोमासस्त्वा विचारिणि प्रति ष्टोभन्त्यक्तुभिः।
प्र या वाजं न हेषन्तं पेरुमस्यस्यर्जुनि।।
दृळ्हा चिद् या वनस्पतीन् क्ष्मया दर्धर्ष्योजसा।
यत ते अभ्रस्य विद्युतो दिवो वर्षन्ति वृष्टयः।।

1. Thou, of a truth, O Prthivi, bearest the tool that rends the hills :

Thou rich in torrents, who with might quickens earth, O Mighty One.

2. To thee, O wanderer at will, ring out the lauds with beams of day,

Who drivest, like a neighing steed, the swelling cloud, O bright of hue.

3. Who graspest with thy might on earth e'en the strong sovrans of the wood,

When from the lightning of thy cloud the rain-floods of the heaven descend.

(V/84)

Aapah: Waters

-.-

Vasishtha

समुद्रज्येष्ठाः सलिलस्य मध्यात् पुनाना यन्त्यनिविशमानाः।
इन्द्रो या वज्री वृषभो रराद ता आपो देवीरिह मामवन्तु॥
या आपो दिव्या उत वा स्रवन्ति खनित्रिमा उत वा याः स्वयंजाः।
समुद्रार्था याः शुचयः पावकास्ता आपो देवीरिह मामवन्तु॥
यासां राजा वरुणो याति मध्ये सत्यानृते अवपश्यञ्जनानाम्।
मधुश्रुतः शुचयो याः पावकास्ता आपो देवीरिह मामवन्तु॥
यासु राजा वरुणो यासु सोमो विश्वे देवा यासूर्जं मदन्ति।
वै श्वानरो यास्वग्निः प्रविष्टस्ता आपो देवीरिह मामवन्तु॥

1. Forth from the middle of the flood the Waters—their chief the Sea—flow cleansing, never sleeping.

   Indra, the Bull, the Thunderer, dug their channels: here let those Waters, Goddesses, protect me.

2. Waters which come from heaven, or those that wander dug from the earth, or flowing free by nature,

   Bright, purifying, speeding to the Ocean, here let those Waters, Goddesses, protect me.

3. Those amid whom goes Varuna the Sovran, he who discriminates men's truth and falsehood—

Distilling meath, the bright, the purifying, here
let those Waters, Goddesses, protect me.

4. They from whom Varuna the King, and Soma, and
all the Deities drink strength and vigour,

They into whom Vaishvanara Agni entered, here
let those Waters, Goddesses, protect me.

(VII/49)

Manas : Spirit

-.-

Bandhu

The Hymn is an address to recall the fleeting spirit of a man
at the point of death.

यत् ते यमं वैवस्वतं मनो जगाम दूरकम्।
तत् त आ वर्तयामसीह क्षयाय जीवसे॥
यत् ते दिवं यत् पृथिवीं मनो जगाम दूरकम्।
तत् त आ वर्तयामसीह क्षयाय जीवसे॥
यत् ते भूमिं चतुर्भृष्टिं मनो जगाम दूरकम्।
तत् त आ वर्तयामसीह क्षयाय जीवसे॥
यत् ते चतस्रः प्रदिशो मनो जगाम दूरकम्।
तत् त आ वर्तयामसीह क्षयाय जीवसे॥
यत् ते समुद्रमर्णवं मनो जगाम दूरकम्।
तत् त आ वर्तयामसीह क्षयाय जीवसे॥
यत् ते मरीचीः प्रवतो मनो जगाम दूरकम्।
तत् त आ वर्तयामसीह क्षयाय जीवसे॥
यत् ते अपो यदोषधीर्मनो जगाम दूरकम्।
तत् त आ वर्तयामसीह क्षयाय जीवसे॥
यत् ते सूर्यं यदुषसं मनो जगाम दूरकम्।

तत् त आ वर्तयामसीह क्षयाय जीवसे॥
यत ते पर्वतान् बृहतो मनो जगाम दूरकम्।
तत् त आ वर्तयामसीह क्षयाय जीवसे॥
यत् ते क्ष्विमिदं जगन्मनो जगाम दूरकम्।
तत् त आ वर्तयामसीह क्षयाय जीवसे॥
यत् ते परा: परावतो मनो जगाम दूरकम्।
तत् त आ वर्तयामसीह क्षयाय जीवसे॥
यत् ते भूतं च भव्यं च मनो जगाम दूरकम्।
तत् त आ वर्तयामसीह क्षयाय जीवसे॥

1. Thy spirit, that went far away to Yama to Vivasvan's
   Son,

   We cause to come to thee again that thou mayst
   live and sojourn here.

2. Thy spirit, that went far away, that passed away to
   earth and heaven,

   We cause to come to thee again that thou Mayst
   live and sojourn here.

3. Thy spirit, that went far away, away to the four-
   cornered earth,

   We cause to come to thee again that thou mayst
   live and sojourn here.

4. Thy spirit, that went far away to the four quarters
   of the world,

   We cause to come to thee again that thou mayst
   live and sojourn here.

5. Thy spirit, that went far away, away unto the billowy
   sea,

   We cause to come to thee again that thou mayst
   live and sojourn here.

6. Thy Spirit, that went far away to beams of light that Flash and Flow,

> We cause to come to thee again that thou mayst live and Sojourn here.

7. Thy spirit, that went far away, went to the waters and the plants,

> We cause to come to thee again that thou mayst live and sojourn here.

8. Thy spirit, that went far away, that visited the Sun and Dawn.

> We cause to come to thee again that thou mayst live and sojourn here.

9. Thy spirit, that went far away, away to lofty mountain heights,

> We cause to come to thee again that thou mayst live and sojourn here.

10. Thy spirit, that went far away into this All that lives and moves,

> We cause to come to thee again that thou mayst live and sojourn here.

11. Thy spirit, that went far away to distant realms beyond our ken,

> We cause to come to thee again that thou mayst live and sojourn here.

12. Thy spirit, that went far away to all that is and is to be,

> We cause to come to thee again that thou mayst live and sojourn here.

(X/58)

Vak: Speech

Vagambhrani

Vak is Speech personified, the Word, the first creation and representative of Spirit, and the means of communication between men and Gods. The hymn shows that the primary application of the name was to the voice of the hymn, the means of communication between heaven and earth at the sacrifice.

अहं रुद्रेभिर्वसुभिश्चराम्यहमादित्यैरुत विश्वदेवे:।
अहं मित्रावरुणोभा बिंभर्म्यहमिन्द्राग्नी अहमश्विनोभा॥
अहं सोममाहनसे बिभर्म्यहं त्वष्टारमुत पूषणं भगम्।
अहं दधामि द्रविणं हविष्मते सुप्राव्ये३ यजमानाय सुन्वते॥
अहं राष्ट्री संगमनी वसूनां चिकितुषी प्रथमा यज्ञियानाम्।
तां मा देवा व्यदधु: पुरुत्रा भूरिस्थात्रां भूर्यावेशयन्तीम्॥
मया सो अन्नमत्ति यो विपश्यति य: प्राणिति य ई शृणोत्युक्तम्।
अमन्तवो मां त उप क्षियन्ति श्रुधि श्रुत श्रद्धिवं ते वदामि॥
अहमेव स्वयमिदं वदामि जुष्टं देवेभिरुत मानुषेभि:।
यं कामये तंतमुग्रं कृणोमि तं ब्रह्माणं तमृषिं तं सुमेधाम्॥
अहं रुद्राय धनुरा तनोमि ब्रह्मद्विषे शरवे हन्तवा उ।
अहं जनाय समदं कृणोम्यहं द्यावापृथिवी आ विवेश॥
अहं सुवे पितरमस्य मूर्धन् मम योनिरप्स्वन्त: समुद्रे।
ततो वि तिष्ठे भुवनानु विश्वोतामूं द्यां वर्ष्मणोप स्पृशामि॥
अहमेव वात इव प्र वाम्या रभमाणा भुवनानि विश्वां।
पुरा दिवा पर एना पृथिव्यैतावती महिना सं बभूव॥

1. I travel with the Rudras and the Vasus, with the Adityas and All-Gods I wander.

   I hold aloft both Varuna and Mitra, Indra and Agni, and the Pair of Asvins.

2. I cherish and sustain high-swelling Soma, and Tvastar I support, Pusan, and Bhaga.

   I load with wealth the zealous sacrificer who pours the juice and offers his oblation.

3. I am the Queen, the gatherer-up of treasures, most thoughtful, first of those who merit worship.

   Thus Gods have established me in many places with many homes to enter and abide in.

4. Through me alone all eat the food that feeds them,— each man who sees, breathes, hears the word outspoken.

   They know it not, but yet they dwell beside me. Hear, one and all, the truth as I declare it.

5. I, verily, myself announce and utter the word that Gods and men alike shall welcome.

   I make the man I love exceeding mighty, make him a sage, a Rishi, and a Brahmin.

6. I bend the bow for Rudra that his arrow may strike and slay the hater of devotion.

   I rouse and order battle for the people, and I have penetrated Earth and Heaven.

7. On the world's summit I bring forth the Father: my home is in the waters, in the ocean.

   Thence I extend o'er all existing creatures, and touch even yonder heaven with my forehead.

8. I breathe a strong breath like the wind and tempest, the while I hold together all existence.

   Beyond this wide earth and beyond the heavens I have become so mighty in my grandeur.

(X/125)

Shraddha: Faith

-.-

Kamayani

श्रद्धयाग्निः समिध्यते श्रद्धया हूयते हविः।
श्रद्धां भगस्य मूर्धनि वचसा वेदयामसि॥
प्रियं श्रद्धे ददतः प्रियं श्रद्धे दिदासतः।
प्रियं भोजेषु यज्वस्विदं म उदितं कृधि॥
यथा देवा असुरेषु श्रद्धामुग्रेषु चक्रिरे।
एवं भोजेषु यज्वस्व स्माकमुदितं कृधि॥
श्रद्धां देवा यजमाना वायुगोपा उपासते।
श्रद्धां हृदय्यंश्याकूत्या श्रद्धया विन्दते वसु॥
श्रद्धां प्रातर्हवामहे श्रद्धां मध्यंदिनं परि।
श्रद्धां सूर्यस्य निम्रुचि श्रद्धे श्रद्धापयेह नः॥

1. By Faith is Agni kindled, through Faith is oblation offered up.

   We celebrate with praises Faith upon the height of happiness.

2. Bless thou the man who gives, O Faith; Faith, bless the man who fain would give.

   Bless thou the liberal worshippers: bless thou the word that I have said.

3. Even as the Deities maintained Faith in the mighty Asuras,

   So make this uttered wish of mine true for the liberal worshippers.

4. Guarded by Vayu, Gods and men who sacrifice draw near to Faith.

Man winneth Faith by yearnings of the heart, and opulence by Faith.

5. Faith in the early morning, Faith at noon-day will we invocate,

   Faith at the setting of the Sun. O Faith, endow us with belief.

(X/151)

Jnana: Knowledge

-.-

Brihaspati

Jnana or Knowledge, the subject of this very difficult hymn, is said by Sayana to mean Parama-brahmajnanam, knowledge of the higher truths of Religion, which teaches man his own nature and how he may be reunited to the Supreme Spirit.

बृहस्पते प्रथमं वाचो अग्रं यत् प्रैरत नामधेयं दधाना:।
यदेषां श्रेष्ठं यदरिप्रमासीत् प्रेणा तदेषां निहितं गुहावि:॥
सक्तुमिव तितउना पुनन्तो यत्र धीरा मनसा वाचमक्रत।
अत्रा सखाय: सख्यानि जानते भद्रैषां लक्ष्मीर्निहिताधि वाचि॥
यज्ञेन वाच: पदवीयमायन् तामन्वविन्दन्नृषिषु प्रविष्टाम्।
तामाभृत्या व्यदधु: पुरुत्रा तां सप्त रेमा अभि सं नवन्ते॥
उत त्व: पश्यन् न ददर्श वाचमुत त्व: शृण्वन् न शृणोत्येनाम्।
उतो त्वस्मै तन्वं१ वि संप्रे जायेव पत्य उशती सुवासा:॥
उत त्वं सख्ये स्थिरपीतमाहुनैनं हिन्वन्त्यपि वाजिनेषु।
अधेन्वा चरति माययैष वाचं शुश्रुवाँ अफलामपुष्पाम्॥
यस्तित्याज सचिविदं सखायं न तस्य वाच्यपि भागो अस्ति।
यदीं शृणोत्यलकं शृणोति नहि प्रवेद सुकृतस्य पन्थाम्॥
अक्षण्वन्त: कर्णवन्त: सखायो मनोजवेष्वसमा बभूवु:।

आदघ्नास उपकक्षास उ त्वे हृदा इव स्रात्वा उ त्वे ददृश्रे॥
हृदा तष्टेषु मनसो जवेषु यद्ब्राह्मणाः संयजन्ते सखायः।
अत्राह त्वं वि जहुर्वेद्यामिरोहब्रह्माणो वि चरन्त्यु त्वे॥
इमे ये नार्वाङ्न परश्चरन्ति न ब्राह्मणासो न सुतेकरासः।
त एते वाचमभिपद्य पापया सिरीस्तन्त्रं तन्वते अप्रजज्ञयः॥
सर्वे नन्दन्ति यशसागतेन समासाहेन सख्या सखायः।
किल्विषस्पृत पितुषणिर्ह्लेषामरै हितो भवति त्राजिनाय॥
ऋचां त्वः पोषमास्ते पुपुष्वान् गायत्रं त्वो गायति शक्वरीषु।
ब्रह्म त्वो वदति जातविद्यां यज्ञस्य मात्रां वि मिमीत उ त्वः॥

1. When men, Brihaspati, giving names to objects, sent
   out Vak's first and earliest utterances,

   All that was excellent and spotless, treasured within
   them, was disclosed through their affection.

2. Where, like men cleansing corn flour in a cribble,
   the wise in spirit have created language,

   Friends see and recognize the marks of friendship:
   their speech retains the blessed sign imprinted.

3. With sacrifice the trace of Vak they followed, and
   found her harbouring within the Rishis.

   They brought her, dealt her forth in many places:
   seven singers make her tones resound in concert.

4. One man hath ne'er seen Vak, and yet he seeth:
   One man hath hearing but hath never heard her.

   But to another hath she shown her beauty as
   a fond well-dressed woman to her husband.

5. One man they call a laggard, dull in friendship: they
   never urge him on to deeds of valour.

   He wanders on in profitless illusion: the Voice
   he heard yields neither fruit nor blossom.

6. No part in Vak hath he who hath abandoned his own dear friend who knows the truth of friendship.

   Even if he hears her still in vain he listens: naught knows he of the path of righteous action.

7. Unequal in the quickness of their spirit are friends endowed alike with eyes and hearing.

   Some look like tanks that reach the mouth or shoulder, others like pools of water fit to bathe in.

8. When friendly Brahmins sacrifice together with mental impulse which the heart hath fashioned,

   They leave one far behind through their attainments, and some who count as Brahmins wander elsewhere.

9. Those men who step not back and move not forward, nor Brahmins nor preparers of libations,

   Having attained to Vak in sinful fashion spin out their thread in ignorance like spinsters.

10. All friends are joyful in the friend who cometh in triumph, having conquered in assembly.

    He is their blame-averter, food-provider: prepared is he and fit for deed of vigour.

11. One plies his constant task reciting verses: one sings the holy psalm in Shakvari measures.

    One more, the Brahmin, tells the lore of being, and one lays down the rules of sacrificing.

                                                        (X/71)

DEITIES

Agni: God of Fire

-.-

Madhucchandas

The first hymn of the Rigveda is ascribed to the Rishi or seer Madhucchandas Vaisvamitra, a son or descendant of the famous Visvamitra. The deity to whom this hymn is addressed is Agni, the God of fire, the most prominent of the deities of the Rigveda. Agni is the messenger and mediator between earth and heaven, announcing to the Gods the hymns, and conveying to them the oblations of their worshippers, inviting them with the sound of his crackling flames and bringing them down to the place of sacrifice.

As concentrating in himself the various sacrificial duties of different classes of human priests, Agni is called the Purohita or chosen priest He is a Ritvij, a priest or minister who sacrifices at the proper seasons, and a Hotar, an invoking priest, a herald who calls the Gods to enjoy the offering. All riches are at his disposal, and he is the most bountiful rewarder, both directly and indirectly, of the pious whose oblations he carries to the Gods.

अग्निमीळे पुरोहितं यज्ञस्य देवमृत्विजम्। होतारं रत्नधातमम्।
अग्निः पूर्वेभिर्ऋषिभि रीडयो नूतनैरुत। स देवाँ एह वक्षति॥
अग्नि रयिमश्नवत् पोषमेव दिवेदिवे। यशसं वीरवत्तमम्।
अग्ने यं यज्ञमध्वरं वि श्वतः परिभूरसि। स इद् देवेषु गच्छति॥

अग्निर्होता कविक्रतुः सत्यश्चित्रश्रवस्तमः। देवो देवेभिरा गमत्।
यदङ्ग दाशुषे त्वमग्ने भद्रं करिष्यसि। तवेत् तत् सत्यमङ्गिरः॥
उप त्वाग्ने दिवेदिवे दोषावस्तर्धिया वयम्। नमो भरन्त एमसि।
राजन्तमध्वराणां गोपामृतस्य दीदिविम्। वर्धमानं स्वे दमे॥
स नः पितेव सूनवे ऽग्ने सूपायनो भव। सचस्वा नः स्वस्तये।
इमम् पु वो अतिथिमुषर्बुधं वि श्वासां विशां पतिमृञ्जसे गिरा॥
वेतीद् दिवो जनुषा कच्चिदाशुचिज्योक् चिदत्ति गर्भो यदच्युतम्।
मित्रं न यं सुधितं भृगवो दधुर्वनस्पतावीड्यमूर्ध्वशोचिषम्॥
स त्वं सुप्रीतो वीतहव्ये अखुत प्रशस्तिभिर्महयसे दिवेदिवे।
स त्वं दक्षस्यावृको वृधो भूर्यः परस्यान्तरस्य तरुषः॥
रायः सूनो सहसो मर्त्येष्वा छर्दियच्छ वीतहव्याय सप्रथो भरद्वाजाय सप्रथः।
द्युतानं वो अतिथिं स्वर्णरमग्निं होतारं मनुषः स्वध्वरम्॥
विप्रं न द्युक्षवचसं सुवृक्तिभिर्हव्यवाहमरतिं देवमृञ्जसे।
पावकया यश्चितयन्त्या कृपा क्षामन् रुरुच उषसो न भानुना॥
तूर्वन् न यामन्नेतशस्य नू रण आ यो घृणे न ततृषाणो अजरः।
अग्निमग्निं वः समिधा दुवस्यत प्रियंप्रियं वो अतिथिं गृणीषणि॥

1. I laud Agni, the chosen Priest, God, minister of sacrifice,

   The hoter, lavishest of wealth.

2. Worthy is Agni to be praised by living as by ancient seers.

   He shall bring hitherward the Gods.

3. Through Agni man obtains wealth, yea, plenty waxing day by day.

   Most rich in heroes, glorious.

4. Agni, the perfect sacrifice which thou encompassest about

   Verity goeth to the Gods.

5. May Agni, sapient-minded Priest, truthful, most gloriously great,

   The God, come hither with the Gods.

6. Whatever blessing, Agni, thou wilt grant unto thy worshipper,

   That, Angiras, is indeed thy truth.

7. To thee, dispeller of the night, O Agni, day by day with prayer

   Bringing thee reverence, we come;

8. Ruler of sacrifices, guard of Law eternal, radiant One,

   Increasing in thine own abode.

9. Be to us easy of approach, even as a father to his son:

   Agni, be with us for our weal.

   (I/1)

●

—Bharadwaja

उप वो गीर्भिरमृतं विवासत देवो देवेषु वर्तते हि वार्यं देवो
देवेषु वर्नते हि नो दुव:।
समिद्धमग्निं समिधा गिरा गृणे शुचि पावकं पुरो अध्वरे ध्रुवम्॥
विप्रं होतारं पुरुवारमद्रुहं कवि सुम्नैरीमहे जातवेदसम्।
त्वां दूतमग्ने अमृतं युगे-युगे हव्यवाहं दधिरे पायुमीडयम्॥
देवासश्च मर्तासश्च जागृविं विभुं विश्पतिं नमसा नि षेदिरे।
विभूषन्नग्न उभयाँ अनु व्रता दूतो देवानां रजसी समीयसे॥
यत् ते धीतिं सुमतिमावृणीमहे ऽध स्मा नस्त्रिवरूथ: शिवो भव।
तं सुप्रतीकं सुदृशं स्वञ्चमविद्वांसो विदुष्टरं सपेम॥

स यक्षद् विश्वा वयुनानि विद्वान् प्र हव्यमग्निरमृतेषु वोचत्।
तमग्ने पास्युत तं पिपर्षि यस्त आनट् कवये शूर धीतिम्॥
यज्ञस्य वा निशितिं वोदितिं वा तमित् पृणक्षि शवसोत राया।
त्वमग्ने वनुष्यतो नि पाहि त्वमु नः सहसावन्नवद्यात्॥
सं त्वा ध्वस्मन्वदभ्येतु पाथः सं रयिः स्पृद्ग्याय्यः सहस्री।
अग्निर्होता गृहपतिः स राजा विश्वा वेद जनिमा जातवेदाः॥
देवानामुत यो मर्त्यानां यजिष्ठः स प्र यजतामृतावा।
अग्ने यद्ग्घ विशो अध्वरस्य होतः पावकशोचे वेष्टवं हि यज्वा॥
ऋता यजासि महिना वि यद् भूर्ळव्या वह यविष्ठ या ते अद्य।
अभि प्रयांसि सुधितानि हि ख्यो नि त्वा दधीत रोदसी यजध्यै॥
अवा नो मघवन् वाजसातावग्ने वि श्वानि दुरिता।
तरेम ता तरेम तवावसा तरेम॥
अग्ने विश्वेभिः स्वनीक देवै रूर्णावन्तं प्रथमः सीद् योनिम्।
कुलायिनं घृतवन्तं सवित्रे यज्ञं नय यजमानाय साधु॥
इममु त्यमथर्ववदग्निं मन्थन्ति वेधसः।
यमङ्कूयन्तमानयन्नमूरं श्याव्याभ्यः॥
जनिष्वा देववीतये सर्वताता स्वस्तये।
आ देवान् वक्ष्यमृताँ ऋतावृधो यज्ञं देवेषु पिस्पृशः॥
वयमु त्वा गृहपते जनानामग्ने अकर्म समिधा बृहन्तम्।
अस्थूरि नो गार्हपत्यानि सन्तु तिग्मेन नस्तेजसा सं शिशाधि॥

1. With this my song I strive to reach this guest of
   yours, who wakes at early morn, the Lord of all
   the tribes.

   Each time he comes from heaven, the Pure One
   from of old: from ancient days the Child eats
   everlasting food.

2. Whom, well-disposed, the Bhrigus established as a
   Friend, whom men must glorify, high-flaming in the
   wood.

As such, most friendly, thou art every day extolled in lauds by Vitahavya, O thou wondrous God.

3. Be thou the foeless helper of the skilful man, subduer of the enemy near or far away.

    Bestow a wealthy home on men, O Son of Strength. Give Vitahavya riches spreading far and wide, give Bharadwaja widespread wealth.

4. Him, your refulgent guest, Agni who comes from heaven, the Herald of mankind, well-skilled in sacred rites,

    Who, like a holy singer, utters heavenly words, oblation-bearer, envoy, God, I seek with hymns.

5. Who with his purifying, eye-attracting form hath shone upon the earth as with the light of Dawn;

    Who speeding on, as in the fight of Etasa, cometh, untouched by age, as one athirst in heat.

6. Worship ye Agni, Agni, with your log of wood; praise your beloved, your beloved guest with songs.

    Invite ye the Immortal hither with your hymns. A God among the Gods, he loveth what is choice, loveth our service, God mid Gods.

7. Agni inflamed with fuel in my song I sing, pure, Cleanser, steadfast, set in front at sacrifice.

    Wise Jatavedas we implore with prayers for bliss the Priest, the holy Singer, bounteous, void of guile.

8. Men, Agni, in each age have made thee, Deathless One, their envoy, offering-bearer, guard adorable.

    With reverence Gods and mortals have established thee, the ever-watchful, omnipresent Household Lord.

9. Thou, Agni, ordering the works and ways of both, as envoy of the Gods traverse both the worlds.

When we lay claim to thy regard and gracious care, be thou to us a thrice protecting friendly guard.

10. Him fair of face, rapid, and fair to look on, him very wise may we who know not follow.

    Let him who knows all rules invite for worship, Agni announce our offering to the Immortals.

11. Him, Agni, thou delivers and saves who brings him prayer to thee the Wise, O Hero,

    The end of sacrifice or its inception; yea, thou endowest him with power and riches.

12. Guard us From him who would assail us. Agni; preserve us, O thou Victor, from dishonour.

    Here let the place of darkening come upon thee: may wealth be ours, desirable in thousands.

13. Agni, the Priest, is King, Lord of the homestead, he, Jatavedas, knows all generations.

    Most skilful worshipper mid Gods and mortals, may he begin the sacrifice, the Holy.

14. Whate'er to-day thou, bright-flamed Priest, enjoyest from the man's rite— for thou art sacrificr—

    Worship, for duly dost thou spread in greatness: bear off thine offerings of today, Most Youthful.

15. Look thou upon the viands duly laid for thee. Fain would he set thee here to worship Heaven and Earth.

    Help us, O liberal Agni, in the strife for spoil, so that we may o'ercome all things that trouble, o'ercome them with thy help.

16. Together with all Gods, O fair-faced Agni, be seated first upon the wool-lined altar,

    Nest-like, bedewed with oil. Bear this our worship to Savitar who sacrifices rightly.

17. Here the arranging priests, as did Atharvan, rub this Agni forth,

    Whom, not bewildered, as he moved in winding ways, they brought from gloom.

18. For the Gods' banquet be thou born, for full perfection and for weal,

    Bring the Immortal Gods who strengthen holy Law: so let our sacrifice reach the Gods.

19. O Agni, Lord and Master of men's homesteads, with kindled fuel we have made thee mighty.

    Let not our household gear be found defective. Sharpen us with thy penetrating splendour.

(VI/15)

Indra: Warrior God

-.-

Madhuchchhaudas

Indra was the favourite national deity of the Aryan Indians in the Vedic Age, and more hymns are dedicated to his honour than to the praise of any other divinity. He is the God who reigns over the intermediate region or atmosphere; he fights against and conquers with his thunderbolt the demons of draughts and darkness, and is in general the type of noble heroism.

सुरूपकृत्नुमूतये सुदुघामिव गोदुहे। जुहूमसि द्यविद्यवि।
उप न: सवना गहि सोमस्य सोमपा: पिब। गोदा इद रेवतो मद:॥
अथा ते अन्तमानां विद्याम सुमतीनाम्। मा नो अतिख्य आ गहि।
परेहि विग्रमस्तृतमिन्द्रं पृच्छा विपश्चितम्। यस्ते सखिभ्य आ वरम्॥
उत ब्रुवन्तु नो निदो निरन्यतश्चिदारत। दधाना इन्द्र इद दुव:।
उत न: सुभगाँ अरिर्वचियुर्दस्म कृष्टय:। स्यामेदिन्द्रस्य शर्माणि॥

एमाशुमाशवे भर यज्ञश्रियं नृमादनम्। पतयन् मन्दयत्सखम्।
अस्य पीत्वा शतक्रतो घनो वृत्राणामभव:। प्रावो वाजेषु वाजिनम्॥
त्वं त्वा वाजेषु वाजिनं वाजयाम: शतक्रतो। धनानामिन्द्र सातये।
यो रायो३वनिर्मिहान्त् सुपार: सुन्वत: सखा। तस्मा इन्द्राय गायत॥

1. As a good cow to him who milks, we call the doer of fair deeds,

   To our assistance day by day.

2. Come thou to our libations, drink of Soma, Soma-drinker thou!

   The rich One's rapture giveth kine.

3. So may we be acquanted with thine innermost benevolence:

   Neglect us not, come hitherward.

4. Go to the wise unconquered One, ask thou of Indra, skilled in song,

   Him who is better than thy friends.

5. Whether the men who mock us say, Depart unto another place,

   Ye who serve Indra and none else;

6. Or whether, God of wondrous deeds, all our true people call us blest,

   Still may we dwell in Indra's care.

7. Unto the swift One bring the swift, man-cheering, grace of sacrifice,

   That to the Friend gives wings and joy.

8. Thou, Shatakratu, drankest this and wast the Vritras' slayer; thou

   Helpest the warrior in the fray.

9. We strengthen, Shatakratu, thee, yea, thee the powerful in fight,

That, Indra, we may win us wealth.

10. To him the mighty stream of wealth, prompt friend of him who pours the juice,

Yea, to this Indra sing your song.

(I/4)

•

Bharadwaj

इन्द्रस्य नु वीर्याणि प्र वोचं यानि चकार प्रथमानि वज्री।
अहन्नहिमन्वस्ततर्द प्र वक्षणा अभिनत् पर्वतानाम्।।
अहन्नहिं पर्वते शिश्रियाणं त्वष्टास्मै वज्रं स्वर्यं ततक्ष।
वाश्रा इव धेनवः स्यन्दमाना अञ्जः समुद्रमव जग्मुराप:।।
वृषायमाणो ऽवृणीत सोमं त्रिकद्रुकेष्वपिबत् सुतस्य।
आ सायकं मघवादत्त वज्रमहन्नेनं प्रथमजामहीनाम्।।
यदिन्द्राहन् प्रथमजामहीनामान्मायिनामिनाः प्रोत माया:।
आत् सूर्यं जनयन् द्यामुपासं तादीत्ना शत्रुं न किला विवित्से।।
अहन् वृत्रं वृत्रतरं व्यंसमिन्द्रो वज्रेण महता वधेन।
स्कन्धांसीव कुलिशेना विवृक्णाऽहिः शयत उपपृक् पृथिव्या:।।
अयोद्धेव दुर्मद आहि जुह्वे महावीरं तुविबाधमृजीषम्।
नातारीदस्य समृतिं वधानां सं रुजाना: पिपिष इन्द्रशत्रु:।
अपादहस्तो अपृतन्यदिन्द्रमास्य वज्रमधि सानौ जघान।।
वृष्णो वधिः: प्रतिमानं बुभूषन् पुरुत्रा वृत्रो अशयद् व्यस्त:।
नदं न भिन्नममुया शयानं मनो रुहाणा अति यन्त्याप:।।
याश्चिद् वृत्रो महिना पर्यतिष्ठत् तासामहि: पत्सुतःशीर्बभूव।
नीचावया अभवद् वृत्रपुत्रेन्द्रो अस्या अव वधर्जभार।।
उत्तरा सूरधरः: पुत्र आसीद् दानुः: शये सहवत्सा न धेनु:।
अतिष्ठन्तीनामनिवेशनानां काष्ठानां मध्ये निहितं शरीरम्।।

वृत्रस्य निण्यं वि चरन्त्यापो दीर्घं तम आशयदिन्द्रशत्रुः।
दासपत्नीरहिगोपा अतिष्ठन् निरुद्धा आपः पणिनेव गावः॥
अपां बिलमपिहितं यदासीद् वृत्रं जघन्वाँ अप तद् ववार।
अश्व्यो वारो अभवस्तदिन्द्र सृके यत् त्वा प्रत्यहन् देव एकः॥
अजयो गा अजयः शूर सोम मवासृजः सतवे सप्त सिन्धून्।
नास्मै विद्युन्न तन्यतुः सिषेध न यां मिहमकिरद् ध्रादुनिं च॥
इन्द्रश्च यद् युयुधाते अहिश्चो तापरीभ्यो मघवा वि जिग्ये।
अहेर्यातारं कर्मपश्च इन्द्र हृदि यत ते जघ्नपो भीरगच्छत॥
नव च यन् नवति च सवन्तीः श्येनो न भीतो अतगेग्जीसि।
इन्द्रो यातोऽवसितस्य राजा शमस्य च शृङ्गिणो वज्रबाहुः॥
सेदु राजा क्षयति चर्षणीना मरान् न नेमिः परि ता बभूव।

1. Glorify him whose might is all-surpassing, Indra the
   much-invoked who fights uninjured.

   Magnify with these songs the never-vanquished,
   the Strong, the Bull of men, the Mighty Victor.

2. He, Champion, Hero, Warrior, Lord of battles,
   impetuous, loudly roaring, great destroyer,

   Who whirls the dust on high, alone, o'erthrower,
   hath made all races of mankind his subjects.

3. Thou, thou alone, hast tamed the Dasyus; singly
   thou hast subdued the people for the Arya.

   In this, or is it not, thine hero exploit, Indra?
   Declare it at the proper season.

4. For true, I deem, thy strength is, thine the Mighty,
   thine, O Most Potent, thine the Conquering Victor;

   Strong, of the strong, Most Mighty, of the mighty,
   thine, driver of the churl to acts of bounty.

5. Be this our ancient bond of friendship with you and
   with Angirases here who speak of Vala.

Thou, Wondrous, Shaker of things firm, didst smite him in his fresh strength, and force his doors and castles.

6. With holy thoughts must he be called, the Mighty, showing his power in the great fight with Vritra.

   He must be called to give us seed and offspring, the Thunderer must be moved and sped to battle.

7. He in his might, with name that lives for ever, hath far surpassed all human generations.

   He, most heroic, hath his home with splendour, with glory and with riches and with valour.

8. Stranger to guile, who ne'er was false or faithless, bearing a name that may be well remembered,

   Indra crushed Cumuri, Dhuni, Sambara, Pipru, and Susna, that their castles fell in ruin.

9. With saving might that must be praised and lauded, Indra, ascend thy car to smite down Vritra.

   In thy right hand hold fast thy bolt of thunder, and weaken, Bounteous Lord, his art and magic.

10. As Agni, as the dart burns the dry forest, like the dread shaft burn down the fiends, O Indra;

    Thou who with high deep-reaching spear hast broken, hast covered over mischief and destroyed it.

11. With wealth, by thousand paths come hither, Agni, paths that bring ample strength, O thou Most Splendid.

    Come, Son of Strength, o'er whom, Invoked of many! the godless hath no power to keep thee distant.

12. From heaven, from earth is bruited forth the greatness of him the firm, the fiery, the resplendent.

    No foe hath he, no counterpart, no refuge is there from him the Conqueror full of wisdom.

13. This day the deed that thou hast done is famous, when thou, for him, with many thousand others

Laidest low Kutsa, Ayu, Atithigva, and boldly didst deliver Turvayana.

14. In thee, O God, the wisest of the Sages, all Gods were joyful when thou slewest Ahi.

When, lauded for thyself, thou gavest freedom to sore-afflicted Heaven and to the people.

15. This power of thine both heaven and earth acknowledge, the deathless Gods acknowledge it, O Indra.

Do what thou ne'er hast done, O Mighty Worker: beget a new hymn at thy sacrifices.

(VI/18)

●

Hiranyastupa

तमु ष्टुहि यो अभिभूत्योजा वन्वन्नवातः पुरुहूत इन्द्रः॥
अषाळ्हमुग्रं सहमानमाभिर्गीर्भिर्वर्ध वृषभं चर्षणीनाम्।
स युध्मः सत्वा खजकृत् समद्धा तुविम्रक्षो नदनुमाँ ऋजीषी॥
बृहद्रेणुश्चवनो मानुषीणामेकः कृष्टीनामभवत् सहावा।
त्वं ह नु त्यददमायो दस्यूँरैकः कृष्टीरवनोरार्याय॥
अस्ति स्विन्नु वीर्यं तत् त इन्द्र न स्विदस्ति तदृतुथा वि वोचः।
सदिद्धि ते तुविजातस्य मन्ये सहः सहिष्ठ तुरतस्तुरस्य॥
उग्रमुग्रस्य तवसस्तवीयो ऽरध्रस्य रध्रतुरो बभूव।
तम्रः प्रजं सख्यमस्तु युष्मे इत्था वदखिर्वलमङ्गिरोभिः॥
हन्नच्युतच्युद् दस्मेषयन्तमृणः पुरो वि दुरो अस्य वि श्वाः।
स हि धीभिर्हव्यो अस्त्युग्र ईशानकृन्महति वृत्रतूर्ये॥
स तोकसाता तनये स वज्री वितन्तसाय्यो अभवत् समत्सु।
स मज्मना जनिम मानुषाणाममर्त्येन नाम्नाति प्र सर्ग्रे॥
स द्युम्नेन स शवसोत राया स वीर्येण नृतमः सभोकाः।
स यो न मुहे न मिथ जनो भूत् सुमन्तुनामा चुमुरिं धुनिं च॥

वृणक् पिप्रुं शम्बरं शुष्णमिन्द्रः पुरां च्यौत्नाय शयथाय नू चित्।
उदावता त्वक्षसा पन्यसा च वृत्रहत्याय रथमिन्द्र तिष्ठ॥
धिष्व वज्रं हस्त आ दक्षिणत्रा ऽभि प्र मन्द पुरुदत्र मायाः।
अग्निं शुष्कं वनमिन्द्र हेती रक्षो नि धक्ष्यशर्निन भीमा॥
गम्भीरय ऋष्वया यो रुरोजा ध्वानयद् दुरिता दम्भयच्च।
आ सहस्रं पथिभिरिन्द्र राया तुविद्युम्न तुविवाजेभिरर्वाक्॥
याहि सूनो सहसो यस्य नू चिद्देव ईशे पुरुहूत योतोः।
प्र तुविद्युम्नस्य स्थविरस्य घृष्वेर्दिवो ररप्शे महिमा पृथिव्याः॥
नास्य शत्रुर्न प्रतिमानमस्ति न प्रतिष्ठिः पुरुमायस्य सह्योः।
प्र तत् ते अद्या करणं कृतं भूत् कुत्सं यदायुमतिथिग्वमस्मै॥
पुरू सहस्रा नि शिशा अभि क्षामुत् तूर्वयाणं धृषता निनेथ।
अनु त्वाहिघ्ने अध देव देवा मदन् विश्वे कवितमं कवीनाम्॥
करो यत्र वरिवो बाधिताय दिवे जनाय तन्वे गृणानः।
अनु द्यावापृथिवी तत् त ओजो ऽमर्त्या जिहत इन्द्र देवाः॥
कृष्वा कृत्नो अकृतं यत् ते अस्त्युक्थं नवीयो जनयस्व यज्ञैः॥

1. I will declare the manly deeds of Indra, the first
   that he achieved, the Thunder-wielder.

   He slew the Dragon, then disclosed the waters, and
   cleft the channels of the mountain torrents.

2. He slew the Dragon lying on the mountain: his
   heavenly bolt of thunder Tvastar fashioned.

   Like lowing kine in rapid flow descending the waters
   glided downward to the ocean.

3. Impetuous as a bull, he chose the Soma, and in
   three sacred beakers drank the juices.

   Maghavan grasped the thunder for his weapon, and
   smote to death this first born of the dragons.

4. When, Indra, thou hadst slain the dragon's firstborn,
   and overcome the charms of the enchanters,

Then, giving life to Sun and Dawn and Heaven, thou foundest not one foe to stand against thee.

5. Indra with his own great and deadly thunder smote into pieces Vritra, worst of Vritras.

   As trunks of trees, what time the axe hath felled them, low on the earth so lies the prostrate Dragon.

6. He, like a mad weak warrior, challenged Indra, the great impetuous many-slaying Hero.

   He, brooking not the clashing of the weapons, crushed—Indra's foe—the shattered forts in falling.

7. Footless and handless still he challenged Indra, who smote him with his bolt between the shoulders.

   Emasculate yet claiming manly vigour, thus Vritra lay with scattered limbs dissevered.

8. There as he lies like a bank-bursting river, the waters taking courage flow above him.

   The Dragon lies beneath the feet of torrents which Vritra with his greatness had encompassed.

9. Then humbled was the strength of Vritra's mothor: Indra hath cast his deadly bolt against her.

   The mother was above, the son was under, and like a cow beside her calf lay Danu.

10. Rolled in the midst of never-ceasing currents flowing without a rest for ever onward.

    The waters bear off Vritra's nameless body: the foe of Indra sank to during darkness.

11. Guarded by Ahi stood the thralls of Dasas, the waters stayed like kine held by the robber.

    But he, when he had smitten Vritra, opened the cave wherein the floods had been imprisoned.

12. A horse's tail wast thou when he, O Indra, smote on thy bolt; thou, God without a second,

Thou hast won back the kine, hast won the Soma; thou hast let loose to flow the Seven Rivers.

13. Nothing availed him lightning, nothing thunder, hailstorm or mist which had spread around him:

When Indra and the Dragon strove in battle, Maghavan gained the victory for ever.

14. Whom sawest thou to avenge the Dragon, Indra, that fear possessed thy heart when thou hadst slain him;

That, like a hawk affrighted through the regions, thou crossedst nine-and-ninety flowing rivers?

15. Indra is King of all that moves and moves not, of creatures tame and horned, the Thunder-wielder.

Over all living men he rules as Sovran, containing all as spokes within the felly.

(I/32)

Soma: Energy Drink

-.-

Vishwamitra

Soma is the God who represents and animates the juice of the Soma plant. He was in former times the Indian Dionysus or Bacchus. 'The simple minded Aryan people,' says Professor Whitney, 'whose whole religion was a worship of the wonderful powers and phenomena of nature, had no sooner perceived that Soma juice had power to elevate the spirits, and produce a temporary frenzy, under the influence of which the individual was prompted to and capable of, deeds beyond his natural powers, than they found in it something divine: it was to their apprehension a God, endouring those into whom it entered with godlike powers; the plant which afforded it became to them the king of plants; the process of preparing it became a holy sacrifice.

स्वादिष्ठया मदिष्ठया पवस्व सोम धारया। इन्द्राय पातवे सुतः।
रक्षोहा वि श्वचर्षणिरभि योनिमयोहतम्। द्रुणा सधस्थमासदत्॥
वरिवोधातमो भव महिष्ठो वृत्रहन्तम्। पर्षि राधो मघोनाम्।
अभ्यर्ष महानां देवानां वीतिमन्धसा। अभि वाजमुत श्रवः॥
त्वामच्छा चरामसि तदिदर्थं दिवेदिवे। इन्दो त्वे न आशसः।
पुनाति ते परिस्रुतं सोमं सूर्यस्य दुहिता। वारेण श श्वता तना॥
तमीमण्वीः समर्य आ गृभ्णन्ति योषणो दश। स्वसारः पार्ये दिवि।
तर्मी हिन्वन्त्यग्रुवो धमन्ति बाकुरं दृतिम्। त्रिधातु वारणं मधु॥
अमी३ममघ्न्या उत श्रीणन्ति धेनवः शिशुम्। सोममिन्द्राय पातवे।
अस्येदिन्द्रो मदेष्वा विश्वा वृत्राणि जिघ्नते। शूरो मघा च मंहते॥

1. In sweetest and most gladdening stream flow pure, O Soma, on thy way,

   Pressed out for Indra, for his drink.

2. Fiend-queller, Friend of all men, he hath with the wood attained unto

   His place, his iron-fashioned home.

3. Be thou best Vritra-slayer, best granter of bliss, most liberal:

   Promote our wealthy princes' gifts.

4. Flow onward with thy juice unto the banquet of the Mighty Gods:

   Flow hither for our strength and fame.

5. O Indu, we draw nigh to thee, with this one object day by day:

   To thee alone our prayers are said.

6. By means of this eternal fleece may Surya's Daughter purify

   Thy Soma that is foaming forth.

7. Ten sister maids of slender form seize him within the press and hold

   Him firmly on the final day.

8. The virgins send him forth: they blow the skin musician-like and fuse

   The triple foe-repelling meath.

9. Inviolable milch-kine round about him blend for Indra's drink,

   The fresh young Soma with their milk.

10. In the wild raptures of this draught, Indra slays all the Vritras: he,

    The Hero, pours his wealth on us.

(IX/1)

•

Asit Deval

प्र ते सोतार ओण्यो३ रसं मदाय घृष्वये। सर्गो न तक्त्येतश:।
क्रत्वा दक्षस्य रथ्यमपो वसानमन्धसा। गोषामण्वेषु सश्चिमम।।
अनप्तमप्सु दुष्टरं सोमं पवित्र आ सृज। पुनीहीन्द्राय पातवे।
प्र पुनानस्य चेतसा सोम: पवित्रे अर्षति। क्रत्वा सधस्थमासदत्।।
प्र त्वा नमोभिरिन्दव इन्द्र सोमा असृक्षत। महे भराय कारिण:।
पुनानो रूपे अव्यये विश्वा अर्षन्नभि श्रिय:। शूरो न गोपु तिष्ठति।।
दिवो न सानु पिप्युषी धारा सुतस्य वेधस:। वृथा पवित्रे अर्षति।
त्वं सोम विपश्चितं तना पुनान आयुषु। अव्यो वारं वि धावसि।।

1. The pressers from the Soma-press send forth thy juice for rapturous joy:

   The speckled sap runs like a flood.

2. With strength we follow through the sieve him who brings might and wins the kine,

   Enrobed in water with his juice.

3. Pour on the sieve the Soma, ne'er subdued in waters, waterless,

   And make it pure for Indra's drink.

4. Moved by the purifier's thought, the Soma flows into the sieve:

   By wisdom it hath gained its home.

5. With humble homage, Indra, have the Soma-drops flowed forth to thee,

   Contending for the glorious prize.

6. Purified in his fleecy garb, attaining every beauty, he

   Stands, hero-like, amid the kine.

7. Swelling, as, twere, to heights of heaven, the stream of the creative juice

   Falls lightly on the cleansing sieve.

8. Thus, Soma, purifying him who knoweth song mid living men,

   Thou wanderest through the cloth of wool.

(IX/16)

—Kavi Bhargava

अभि प्रियाणि पवते चनोहितो नामानि यह्वो अधि येषु वर्धते।
आ सूर्यस्य बृहतो बृहन्नधि रथं विष्वञ्चमरुहद्विचक्षण:।।

ऋतस्य जिह्वा पवते मधु प्रियं वक्ता पतिर्धियो अस्या अदाभ्य:।
दधाति पुत्र: पित्रोरपीच्यं१ नाम तृतीयमधि रोचने दिव:।।

अव द्युतान: कलशाँ अचिक्रदन्नृभिर्येमान: कोश आ हिरण्यये।
अभीमृतस्य दोहना अनूषताऽधि त्रिपृष्ठ उषसो वि राजति।।

अद्रिभि: सुतो मतिभिश्चनोहित: प्ररोचयन् रोदसी मातरा शुचि:।
रोमाण्यव्या समया वि धावति मधोर्धारा पिन्वमाना दिवेदिवे।।

परि सोम प्र धन्वा स्वस्तये नृभि: पुनानो अभि वासयाशिरम्।
ये ते मदा आहनसो विहायसस्तेभिरिन्द्रं चोदय दातवे मघम्।।

1. Graciously-minded he is flowing on his way to win
   dear names o'er which the Youthful One grows great.

   The Mighty and Far-seeing One hath mounted now
   the mighty Surya's car which moves to every side.

2. The Speaker, unassailable Master of this hymn, the
   Tongue of sacrifice pours forth the pleasant meath.

   Within the lustrous region of the heavens the
   Son makes the third secret name of Mother and
   of Sire.

3. Sending forth flashes he hath bellowed to the jars,
   led by the men into the golden reservoir.

   The milky streams of sacrifice have sung to him:
   he of the triple height shines brightly through the
   morns.

4. Pressed by the stones, with hymns, and graciously inclined, illuminating both the Parents, Heaven and Earth,

He flows in ordered season onward through the fleece, a current of sweet juice still swelling day by day.

5. Flow onward, Soma, flow to bring prosperity: cleansed by the men, invest thee with the milky draught.

What gladdening drinks thou hast, foaming, exceeding strong, even with these incite Indra to give us wealth.

(IX/75)

Mitra: Light-God

-.--.--.--.--.--.--.--.--.--.--.--.--.--.--.--.--.--.--.-

Vishwamitra

मित्रो जनान् यातयति ब्रुवाणो मित्रो दाधार पृथिवीमुत द्याम्।
मित्र: कृष्टीरनिमिषाभि चष्टे मित्राय हव्यं घृतवज्जुहोत
प्र स मित्र मर्तो अस्तु प्रयस्वान् यस्तं आदित्य शिक्षति व्रतेन।
न हन्यते न जीयते त्वोतो नैनर्महो अश्नोत्यन्तितो न दूरात्
अनमीवास इळया मदन्तो मितज्ञवो वरिमन्ना पृथिव्या:।
आदित्यस्य व्रतमुपक्षियन्तो वयं मित्रस्य सुमतौ स्याम
अयं मित्रो नमस्य: सुशेवो राजा सुक्षत्रो अजनिष्ट वेधा:।
तस्य वयं सुमतौ यज्ञियस्याऽपि भद्रे सौमनसे स्याम
महाँ आदित्यो नमसोपसद्यो यातयज्जनो गृणते सुशेव:।
तस्मा एतत् पन्यतमाय जुष्टमग्नौ मित्राय हविरा जुहोत
मित्रस्य चर्षणीधृतो ऽवो देवस्य सानसि। द्युम्नं चित्रश्रवस्तमम्।
अभि यो महिना दिवं मित्रो बभूव सप्रथा:। अभि श्रवोभि: पृथिवीम्

मित्राय पञ्च येमिरे जना अभिष्टिशवसे। स देवान् विश्वान् विभर्ति।
मित्रो देवेष्वायुषु जनाय वृक्तबर्हिषे। हर्ष इष्टव्रता अक:

1. Mitra, when speaking, stirreth men to labour: Mitra
   sustaineth both the earth and heaven.

   Mitra beholdeth men with eyes that close not.
   To Mitra bring, with holy oil, oblation.

2. Foremost be he who brings thee food, O Mitra, who
   strives to keep thy sacred Law, Aditya.

   He whom thou helpest ne'er is slain or conquered,
   on him, from near or far, falls no affliction.

3. Joying in sacred food and freed from sickness, with
   knees bent lowly on the earth's broad surface,

   Following closely the Aditya's statute, may we
   remain in Mitra's gracious favour.

4. Auspicious and adorable, this Mitra was born with
   fair dominion, King, Disposer.

   May we enjoy the grace of him the Holy, yea,
   rest in his propitious loving-kindness.

5. The great Aditya, to be served with worship, who
   stirreth men, is gracious to the singer.

   To Mitra, him most highly to be lauded, offer
   in fire oblation that he loveth.

6. The gainful grace of Mitra, God, supporter of the
   race of man,

   Gives splendour of most glorious fame.

7. Mitra whose glory spreads afar, he who in might
   surpasses heaven,

   Surpasses earth in his renown.

8. All the Five Races have repaired to Mitra, ever strong to aid.

   For he sustaineth all the Gods.

9. Mitra to Gods, to living men, to him who strews the holy grass,

   Gives food fulfilling sacred Law.

                                                    (III/59)

Varuna: God of Moral Order

-.-

Ajigarta

Varuna is the chief of the lords of natural order. His activity displays itself pre-eminently in the control of the most regular phenomena of nature. Varuna is King of the air and of the sea, the latter being often regarded as identical with the former.

यच्चिद्धि ते विशो यथा प्र देव वरुण व्रतम्। मिनीमसि द्यविद्यवि।
मा नो वधाय हत्नवे जिहीळानस्य रीरधः। मा हृणानस्य मन्यवे॥
वि मृळीकाय ते मनो रथीरश्वं न संदितम्। गीर्भिर्वरुण सीमहि।
परा हि मे विमन्यवः पतन्ति वस्यइष्टये। वयो न वसतीरुप॥
कदा क्षत्रश्रियं नर मा वरुणं करामहे। मृळीकायोरुचक्षसम्।
तदित् समानमाशाते वेनन्ता न प्र युच्छतः। धृतव्रताय दाशुषे॥
वेदा यो वीनां पदमन्तरिक्षेण पतताम्। वेद नावः समुद्रियः।
वेद मासो धृतव्रतो द्वादश प्रजावतः। वेद य उपजायते॥
वेद वातस्य वर्तनिमुरोर्ऋष्वस्य बृहतः। वेदा ये अध्यासते।

नि पसाद धृतव्रतो वरुणः पस्त्या३स्वा। साम्राज्याय सुक्रतुः॥
अतो विश्वान्यखुता चिकित्वाँ अमि पश्यति। कृतानि या च कर्त्वा।
स नो विश्वाहा सुक्रतुरादित्यः सुप्रथा करत्। प्र ण आयूषि तारिषत्॥
बिभ्रद् द्रापि हिरण्ययं वरुणो वस्त निर्णिजम्। परि स्पशो नि पेदिरे।
न यं दिप्सन्ति दिप्सवो न द्रुह्राणो जनानाम्। न देवमभिमातयः॥
उत यो मानुषेष्वा यशश्चक्रे असाम्या। अस्माकमुदरेष्वा।
परा में यन्ति धीतयो गावो न गव्यूतीरनु। इच्छन्तीरुरुचक्षसम्॥
सं नु वोचावहै पुनर्यतो मे मध्वाभृतम्। होतेव क्षदसे प्रियम्।
दर्शनु वि श्वदर्शतं दर्श रथमधि क्षमि। एता जुषत मे गिरः॥
इमं में वरुण श्रुधी हवमद्या च मृळय। त्वामवस्युरा चके।
त्वं विश्वस्य मेधिर दिवश्च मश्च राजसि। स यामनि प्रति श्रुधि॥
उदुत्तमं मुमुग्धि नो वि पाशं मध्यमं चृत। अवाधमानि जीवसे।

1. Whatever law of thine, O God, O Varuna, as we are men,

   Day after day we violate.

2. Give us not as a prey to death, to be destroyed by thee in wrath,

   To thy fierce anger when displeased.

3. To gain thy mercy, Varuna, with hymns we bind thy heart, as binds

   The charioteer his tethered horse.

4. They flee from me dispirited, bent only on obtaining wealth,

   As to their nests the birds of air.

5. When shall we bring, to be appeased, the Hero, Lord of warrior might,

   Him, the far-seeing Varuna?

6. This, this with joy the both accept in common: never do they fail

    The ever-faithful worshipper.

7. He knows the path of birds that fly through heaven, and, Sovran of the sea,

    He knows the ships that are thereon.

8. True to his holy law, he knows the twelve moons with their progeny:

    He knows the moon of later birth.

9. He knows the pathway of the wind, the spreading, high, and mighty wind:

    He knows the Gods who dwell above.

10. Varuna, true to holy law, sits down among his people; he,

    Most wise, sits there to govern all.

11. From thence perceiving he beholds all wondrous things, both what hath been,

    And what hereafter will be done.

12. May that Aditya, very wise, make fair paths for us all our days:

    May he prolong our lives for us.

13. Varuna, wearing golden mail, hath clad him in a shining robe:

    His spies are seated round about.

14. The God whom enemies threaten not, nor those who tyrannize o'er men,

    Nor those whose minds are bent on wrong.

15. He who gives glory to mankind, not glory that is incomplete,

    To our own bodies giving it.

16. Yearning for the wide-seeing One, my thoughts move onward unto him,

As kine unto their pastures move.

17. Once more together let us speak, because my meath is brought: priest-like

Thou eastest what is dear to thee.

18. Now saw I him whom all may see, I saw his car above the earth:

He hath accepted these my songs.

19. Varuna, hear this call of mine : be gracious unto us this day

Longing for help I cried to thee.

20. Thou, O wise God, art Lord of all, thou art the King of earth and heaven:

Hear, as thou goest on thy way.

21. Release us from the upper bond, untie the bond between, and loose

The bonds below, that I may live.

(I/25)

Ashvins: Two Horsemen

-.-

Praskanva

The Ashvins seem to have been a puzzle even to the oldest Indian commentators. Yaska asks: 'Who are these Ashvins?' 'Heaven and Earth', say some. Day and Night, Sun and Moon, or Two kings, say others. Roth says, 'The two Ashvins hold a distinct position in the entire body of the deities of light. They are the earliest bringers of light in the morning sky, who in their chariots hasten onward before the dawn, and prepare the way for.

एषो उषा अपूर्व्या व्युच्छति प्रिया दिवः। स्तुषे वामश्विना बृहत्।
या दस्रा सिन्धुमातरा मनोतरा रयीणाम्। धिया देवा वसुविदा॥
वच्यन्ते वां ककुहासो जूर्णायामधि विष्टपि। यद् वां रथो विभिष्पतात्।
हविषा जारो अपां पिपर्ति पपुरिर्नरा। पिता कुटस्य चर्षणिः॥
आदारो वां मतीनां नासत्या मतवचसा। पातं सोमस्य धृष्णुया।
या नः पीपरदश्विना ज्योतिष्मती तमस्तिरः। तामस्मे रासाथामिषम्॥
आ नो नावा मतीनां यातं पाराय गन्तवे। युञ्जाथामश्विना रथम्।
अरित्रं वां दिवस्पृथु तीर्थे सिन्धूनां रथः। धिया युयुज्र इन्दवः॥
दिवस्कण्वास इन्दवो वसु सिन्धूनां पदे। स्वं वव्रिं कुह धित्सथः।
अभूदु भा उ अंशवे हिरण्यं प्रति सूर्यः। व्यख्यज्जिह्वयासितः॥
अभूदु पारमेतवे पन्था ऋतस्य साधुया। अदर्शि वि स्रुतिर्दिवः।
तत्तदिदश्विनोरवो जरिता प्रति भूषति। मदे सोमस्य पिप्रतोः॥
वावसाना विवस्वति सोमस्य पीत्या गिरा। मनुष्वच्छंभू आ गतम्।
युवोरुषा अनु श्रियं परिज्मनोरुपाचरत्। ऋता वनथो अक्तुभिः॥
उभा पिबतमश्विनोभा नः शर्म यच्छतम्। अविद्रियाभिरूतिभिः।

1. Now Morning with her earliest light shines forth, dear Daughter of the Sky:

   High, Ashvins, I extol your praise,

2. Sons of the Sea, mighty to save discoverers of riches, ye

   Gods with deep thought who find out wealth.

3. Your giant coursers hasten on over the region all in flames,

     When your car flies with winged steeds.

4. He, liberal, lover of the flood, Lord of the House, the vigilant,

     Chiefs! with oblations feeds you full.

5. Ye have regard unto our hymns, Nasatyas, thinking of our words:

     Drink boldly of the Soma juice.

6. Vouchsafe to us, O Ashvin Pair, such strength as, with attendant light,

     May through the darkness carry us.

7. Come in the ship of these our hymns to bear you to the hither shore:

     O Ashvins, harness ye the car.

8. The heaven's wide vessel is your own: on the flood's shore your chariot waits:

     Drops, with the hymn, have been prepared.

9. Kanvas, the drops are in the heaven; the wealth is at the waters' place:

     Where will ye manifest your form?

10. Light came to lighten up the branch, the Sun appeared as it were gold:

     And with its tongue shone forth the dark.

11. The path of sacrifice was made to travel to the farther goal:

     The road of heaven was manifest.

12. The singer of their praise awaits whatever grace the Ashvins give,

Who save when Soma gladdens them.

13. Ye dwellers with Vivasvan come, auspicious, as to Manu erst;

Come to the Soma and our praise.

14. O circumambient Ashvins, Dawn follows the brightness of your way:

Approve with beams our solemn rites.

15. Drink ye of our libations, grant protection, O ye Ashvins Twain,

With aids which none may interrupt.

(I/46)

Vayu: God of Wind

-.-

Vamadeva

विहि होत्रा अवीता विपो न रायो अर्यः।
वायवा चन्द्रेण रथेन याहि सुतस्य पीतये॥
निर्युवाणो अशस्ती निंयुत्वाँ इन्द्रसारथिः।
वायवा चन्द्रेण रथेन याहि सुतस्य पीतये॥
अनु कृष्णे वसुधिती येमाते विश्वपेशसा।
वायवा चन्द्रेण रथेन याहि सुतस्य पीतये॥

वहन्तु त्वा मनोयुजो युक्तासो नवतिर्नव।
वायवा चन्द्रेण रथेन याहि सुतस्य पीतये॥
वायो शतं हरीणां युवस्व पोष्याणाम्।
उत वा ते सहस्रिणो रथ आ यातु पाजसा॥

1. Taste offerings never tasted yet, as bards enjoy the foeman's wealth.

   O Vayu, on refulgent car come to the drinking of the juice.

2. Removing curses, drawn by teams, with Indra seated by thy side,

   O Vayu, on refulgent car come to the drinking of the juice.

3. The two dark treasuries of wealth that wear all beauties wait on thee,

   O Vayu, on refulgent car come to the drinking of the juice.

4. May nine-and-ninety harnessed steeds who yoke them at thy will bring thee.

   O Vayu, on refulgent car come to the drinking of the juice.

5. Harness, O Vayu, to thy car a hundred well-fed tawny steeds,

   Yea, or a thousand steeds, and let thy chariot come to us with might.

                                                    (IV/48)

Rudra: Tempest God

- . -

Kutsa

Rudra: generally explained as the Roarer, from the sound is stormy winds, the God of tempests and father of the Maruts. He is called Kapardin as wearing hair braided and knotted like a cowry shell (*kaparda*) derives Rudra (the Red, the Brilliant) from a lost root *rud*, to be red.

इमा रुद्राय तवसे कपर्दिने क्षयद्वीराय प्र भरामहे मती:।
यथा शमसद् द्विपदे चतुष्पदे विश्वं पुष्टं ग्रामे अस्मिन्ननातुरम्॥

मृळा नो रुद्रोत नो मयस्कृधि क्षयद्वीराय नमसा विधेम ते।
यच्छं च योश्च मनुरायेजे पिता तदश्याम तव रुद्र प्रणीतिषु॥

अश्याम ते सुमतिं देवयज्ज्यया क्षयद्वीरस्य तव रुद्र मीढ्व:।
सुम्नायन्निद् विशो अस्माकमा चरारिष्टवीरा जुहवाम ते हवि:॥

त्वेषं वयं रुद्रं यज्ञसाधं वङ्कुं कविमवसे नि ह्वयामहे।
आरे अस्मद् दैव्यं हेळो अस्यतु सुमतिमिद् वयमस्या वृणीमहे॥

दिवो वराहमरुषं कपर्दिनं त्वेषं रूपं नमसा नि ह्वयामहे।
हस्ते बिभ्रद् भेषजा वार्याणि शर्म वर्मच्छर्दिरस्मभ्ये यंसत्॥

इदं पित्रे मरुतामुच्यते वच: स्वादो: स्वादीयो रुद्राय वर्धनम्।
रास्वा च नो अमृत मर्तभोजनं त्मने तोकाय तनयाय मृळ॥

मा नो महान्तमुत मा नो अर्भकं मा न उक्षन्तमुत मा न उक्षितम्।
मा नो वधी: पितरं मोत मातरं मा न: प्रियास्तन्वो रुद्र रीरिष:॥

मा नस्तोके तनये मा न आयौ मा नो गोषु मा नो अश्वेषु रीरिष:।
वीरान् मा नो रुद्र भामितो वधीर्हविष्मन्त: सद्मित् त्वा हवामहे॥

उप ते स्तोमान् पशुपा इवाकरं रास्वा पितर्मरुतां सुम्नमस्मे।
भद्रा हि ते सुमतिर्मृळयत्तमाथा वयमव इत् ते वृणीमहे॥

आरे ते गोघ्नमुत पूरुषघ्नं क्षयद्वीर सुम्नमस्मे ते अस्तु।
मृळा च नो अधि च ब्रूहि देवाधा च न: शर्म यच्छ द्विबर्हा:॥
अवोचाम नमो अस्मा अवस्यव: शृणोतु नो हवं रुद्रो मरुत्वान्।
तन्नो मित्रो वरुणो मामहन्ता अदिति: सिन्धु: पृथिवी उत द्यौ:॥

1. To the strong Rudra bring we these our songs of praise, to him the Lord of Heroes, with the braided hair,

   That it be well with all our cattle and our men, that in this village all be healthy and well-fed.

2. Be gracious unto us, O Rudra, bring us joy: thee, Lord of Heroes, thee with reverence will we serve.

   Whatever health and strength our father Manu won by sacrifice may we, under thy guidance, gain.

3. By worship of the Gods may we, O Bounteous One, O Rudra, gain thy grace, Ruler of valiant men.

   Come to our families, bringing them bliss: may we, whose heroes are uninjured, bring thee sacred gifts,

4. Hither we call for aid the wise, the wanderer, impetuous Rudra, perfecter of sacrifice.

   May he repel from us the anger of the Gods: verily, we desire his favourable grace.

5. Him with the braided hair we call with reverence down, the wild-boar of the sky, the red, the dazzling shape.

   May he, his hand filled full of sovran medicines, grant us protection, shelter, and a home secure.

6. To him the Maruts' Father is this hymn addressed, to strengthen Rudra's might, a song more sweet than sweet.

Grant us, Immortal One, the food which mortals eat: be gracious unto me, my seed, my progeny.

7. O Rudra, harm not either great or small of us, harm not the growing boy, harm not the full-grown man.

Slay not a sire among us, slay no mother here, and to our own dear bodies, Rudra, do not harm.

8. Harm us not, Rudra, in our seed and progeny, harm us not in the living, nor in cows or steeds,

Slay not our heroes in the fury of thy wrath. Bringing oblations evermore we call to thee.

9. Even as a herdsman I have brought thee hymns of praise: O Father of the Maruts, give us happiness.

Blessed is thy most favouring benevolence, so, verily, do we desire thy saving help.

10. Far be thy dart that killeth men or cattle: thy bliss be with us, O thou Lord of Heroes.

Be gracious unto us, O God, and bless us, and then vouchsafe us doubly-strong protection.

11. We, seeking help, have spoken and adored him: may Rudra, girt by Maruts, hear our calling.

This prayer of ours may Varuna grant, and Mitra, and Aditi and Sindhu, Earth and Heaven.

(I/114)

Maruts: Storm Gods

-.-

Kanva

The Maruts are the Gods of the winds and storms, the companions and friends of Indra. They are said in the Veda to be the sons of Rudra and Prisni, the latter being explained by Sayana as 'the many-coloured earth,' but regarded by Professor Roth as a personification of the speckled clouds.

क्रीळं व: शर्धो मारुतमनर्वाणं रथेशुभम्। कण्वा अभि प्र गायत।
ये पृषतीभिर्ऋष्टिभि: साकं वाशीभिरञ्जिभि:। अजायन्त स्वभानव:॥
इहेव शृण्व एषां कशा हस्तेषु यद् वदान्। नि यामञ्चित्रमृञ्जते।
प्र व: शर्धाय घृष्वये त्वेषद्युम्नाय शुष्मिणे। देवत्तं ब्रह्म गायत॥
प्र शंसा गोष्वघ्न्यं क्रीळं यच्छर्धो मारुतम्। जम्भे रसस्य वावृधे।
को वो वर्षिष्ठ आ नरो दिवश्च ग्मश्च धूतय:। यत सीमन्तं न धूनुथ॥
नि वो यामाय मानुषो दध उग्राय मन्यवे। जिहीत पर्वतो गिरि:।
येषामज्मेषु पृथिवी जुजुर्वा इव विश्पति:। भिया यामेषु रेजते॥
स्थिरं हि जानमेषां वयो मातुर्निरेतवे। यत सीमनु द्विता शव:।
उदु त्ये सूनवो गिर: काष्ठा अज्मेष्वत्नत। वाश्रा अभिज्ञु यातवे॥
त्यं चिद् घा दीर्घं पृथुं मिहो नपातममृधम्। प्र च्यावयन्ति यामभि:।
मरुतो यद्ध वो बलं जनाँ अचुच्यवीतन। गिरीरचुच्यवीतन॥
यद्ध यान्ति मरुत: सं ह ब्रुवतेऽध्वन्ना। शृणोति कश्चिदेपाम्।
प्र यात शीभमाशुभि: सन्ति कण्वेषु वो दुव:। तत्रो पु मादयाध्वै॥
अस्ति हि प्मा मदाय व: स्मसि प्मा वयमेषाम्। विश्वे चिदायुर्जीवसे।

1. Sing forth, O Kanvas, to your band of Maruts unassailable,

    Sporting, resplendent on their car:

2. They who, self-luminous, were born together, with the spotted deer,

    Spears, swords, and glittering ornaments.

3. One hears, as though 'twere close at hand, the cracking of the whips they hold;

    They gather glory on their way.

4. Now sing ye forth the God-given hymn to your exultant Marut host,

    The fiercely-vigorous, the strong.

5. Praise ye the Bull among the cows; for 'tis the Maruts' sportive band:

    It strengthened as it drank the rain.

6. Who is your mightiest, Heroes, when, O shakers of the earth and heaven,

    Ye shake them like a garment's hem?

7. At your approach man holds him down before the fury of your wrath:

    The rugged-jointed mountain yields.

8. They at whose racings forth the earth, like an age-weakened lord of men,

    Trembles in terror on their ways.

9. Strong is their birth: vigour have they to issue from their Mother; strength,

   Yea, even twice enough, is theirs.

10. And these, the Sons, the Singers, in their racings have enlarged the bounds,

    So that the kine must walk knee-deep.

11. Before them, on the ways they go, they drop this offspring of the cloud,

    Long, broad, and inexhaustible.

12. O Maruts, as your strength is great, so have ye cast men down on earth,

    So have ye made the mountains fall.

13. The while the Maruts pass along, they talk together on the way:

    Doth any hear them as they speak?

14. Come quick with swift steeds, for ye have worshippers among Kanva's sons:

    May you rejoice among them well.

15. All is prepared for your delight. We are their servants evermore,

    To live as long as life may last.

(I/37)

Pusan: Giver of Prosperity

-.-

Bharadwaj

Pusan is a God who protects and multiplies cattle and human possessions generally. In character he is a solar deity, beholds the entire universe, and is a guide on roads and journeys.

वयमु त्वा पथस्पते रथं न वाजसातये। धिये पूषन्नयुज्महि।
अभि नो नर्यं वसु वीरं प्रयतदक्षिणम्। वामं गृहपतिं नय।।
अदित्सन्तं चिदाघृणे पूषन् दानाय चोदय। पणेश्चिद् वि म्रदा मनः।
वि पथो वाजसातये चिनुहि विमृधो जहि। साधन्तामुग्र नो धियः।।
परि तृन्धि पणीना मारया हृदया कवे। अथेमस्मभ्यं रन्धय।
वि पूषन्नारया तुद पणेरिच्छ हृदि प्रियम्। अथेमस्मभ्यं रन्धय।।
आ रिख किकिर कृणु पणीनां हृदया कवे। अथेमस्मभ्यं रन्धय।
यां पूषन् ब्रह्मचोदनी मारां बिभर्ष्याघृणे। तया समस्य हृदयमा रिख किकिर कृणु।।
या ते अष्ट्रा गोओपशा ऽऽघृणे पशुसाधनी। तस्यास्ते सुम्नमीमहे।।
उत नो गोषणि धियेम्श्वसां वाजसामुत। नृवत कृणुहि वीतये।

1. Lord of the path, O Pusan, we have yoked and bound thee to our hymn,

   Even as a car, to win the prize.

2. Bring us the wealth that men require, a manly master of a house,

   Free-handed with the liberal meed.

3. Even him who would not give, do thou, O glowing Pusan, urge to give,

   And make the niggard's soul grow soft.

4. Clear paths that we may win the prize; scatter our enemies afar.

   Strong God, be all our thoughts fulfilled.

5. Penetrate with an awl, O Sage, the hearts of avaricious churls,

   And make them subject to our will.

6. Thrust with thine awl,, O Pusan: seek that which the niggard's heart holds dear,

   And make him subject to our will.

7. Tear up and rend in pieces, Sage, the hearts of avaricious churls,

   And make them subject to our will.

8. Thou, glowing Pusan, carriest an awl that urges men to prayer;

   Therewith do thou tear up and rend to shreds the heart of every one.

9. Thou bearest, glowing Lord! a goad with horny point that guides the cows:

   Thence do we seek thy gift of bliss.

10. And make this hymn of ours produce kine, horses, and a store of wealth

    For our delight and use as men.

(VI/53)

Savitar: Stimulating Sun

Gritsamad

Savitar, the generator or vivifier, is a name of the Sun, in the Veda sometimes identified with and sometimes distinguished from Surya.

उदु ष्य देव: सविता सवाय शश्वत्तमं तदपा वह्निरस्थात्।
नूनं देवेभ्यो वि हि धाति रत्नमथामजद् वीतिहोत्रं स्वस्तौ।।
क्रिश्वस्य हि श्रुष्टये देव ऊर्ध्व: प्र बाहवा पृथुपाणि: सिसर्ति।
आपश्चिदस्य व्रत आ निमृग्रा अयं चिद् व्रातो रमते परिज्मन्।।
आशुभिश्चिद्यान् वि मुचाति नूनमरीरमदतमानं चिदेतो:।
अह्यर्षूणां चिन्नययाँ अविष्यामनु व्रतं सवितुर्मोक्यागात्।।
पुन: समव्यद् विततं वयन्ती मध्या कर्तोर्न्यधाच्छक्म धीर:।
उत् संहायास्थाद् वयृ१तूँरदर्धररमति: सविता देव आगात्।।
नानौकांसि दुर्यो क्रिश्वमायुर्वि तिष्ठते प्रभव: शोको अग्ने:।
ज्येष्ठं माता सूनवे भागमाधादन्वस्य केतमिषितं सवित्रा।।
समाववर्ति विष्ठितो जिगीषुर्विश्वेषां कामश्चरताममाभूत्।
शश्वाँ अपो विकृतं हित्व्यागादनु व्रतं सवितुर्दैव्यस्य।।
त्वया हितमप्यमस्सु भागं धन्वान्वा मृगयसो वि तस्थु:।
वनानि विभ्यो नकिरस्य तानि व्रता देवस्य सवितुर्मिनन्ति।।
याद्राध्यं१ वरुणो योनिमप्यमनिशितं निमिषि जर्भुराण:।
विश्वो मार्ताण्डो ब्रजमा पशुर्गात् स्थशो जन्मानि सविता व्याक:।।
न यस्येन्द्रो वरुणो न मित्रो व्रतमर्यमा न मिनन्ति रुद्र:।
नारातयस्तमिदं स्वस्ति हुवे देवं सवितारं नमोभि:।।

भगं धियं वाजयन्तः पुरंधि नराशंसो ग्नास्पतिर्नो अव्याः।
आये वामस्य संगथे रयीणां प्रिया देवस्य सवितुः स्याम॥
असमभ्यं तद् दिवो अद्रयः पृथिव्यास्त्वया दत्तं काम्यं राध आ गात्।
शं यत् स्तोतृभ्य आपये भवात्युरुशंसाय सवितर्जरित्रे॥

1. Uprisen is Savitar, this God, to quicken, Priest who
   neglects not this most constant duty.

   To the Gods, verily, he gives rich treasure, and
   blesses him who calls them to the banquet.

2. Having gone up on high, the God broad-handed
   spreads his arms widely forth that all may mark
   him.

   Even the waters bend them to his service: even
   this wind rests in the circling region.

3. Though borne by swift steeds he will yet unyoke
   them: e'en the fleet chariot hath he stayed from
   going.

   He hath checked e'en their haste who glide like
   serpents. Night closely followed Savitar's dominion.

4. What was spread out she weaves afresh, re-weaving:
   the skilful leaves his labour half-completed.

   He hath arisen from rest, and parted seasons:
   Savitar hath approached, God, holy-minded.

5. Through various dwellings, through entire existence,
   spreads, manifest, the house hold light of Agni.

   The Mother gives her Son the goodliest portion,
   and Savitar hath sped to meet his summons.

6. He comes again, unfolded, fain for conquest: at home was he, the love all things moving.

   Each man hath come leaving his evil doings, after the Godlike Savitar's commandment.

7. The wild beasts spread through desert places seeking their watery share which thou hast set in waters.

   The woods are given to the birds. These statutes of the God Savitar none disobeyeth.

8. With utmost speed, in restless haste at sunset Varuna seeks his watery habitation.

   Then seeks each bird his nest, each beast his lodging. In due place Savitar hath set each creature.

9. Him whose high law not Varuna nor Indra, not Mitra, Aryaman, nor Rudra breaketh,

   Nor evil-hearted fiends, here for my welfare him I invoke, God Savitar, with worship.

10. May they who strengthen bliss, and thought and wisdom, and the Dames' Lord and Narasamsa aid us.

    That good may come to us and wealth be gathered, may we be Savitar the God's beloved.

11. So came to us our heart's desire, the bounty bestowed by thee, From heaven end earth and waters,

    That it be well with Friends and those who praise thee, and, Savitar, with the loud-lawding singer.

(II/38)

Adityas: Sons of Aditi

-.-

Gritsamad

In the highest heaven dwell and reign those Gods who bear in common the name of Adityas. They are the inviolable, imperishable, eternal beings. Aditi, eternity or the eternal, is the element which sustains them and is sustained by them. The eternal and inviolable element in which the Adityas dwell, and which forms their essence, is the celestial light.

इम गिरं आदित्येभ्यो घृतम्नूः सनाद् राजभ्यो जुह्वा जुहोमि।
सुगोतु मित्रो अर्यमा भर्गो नस्तुविजातो वरुणो दक्षो अंशः॥

नमं स्तानं सक्रनवो में अद्य मित्रो अर्यमा वरुणो जुषन्त।
आदित्यासःशुचयो धारपूता अवृजिना अनवद्या अरिष्टाः॥

न अमदत्यास उरवो गभीरा अदब्धासो दिप्सन्तो भूर्यक्षाः।
अन्तः पश्यन्ति वृजिनोत साधु सर्वं राजभ्यः परमा चिदन्ति॥

धारयन्त आदित्यासो जगत् स्था देवा विश्वस्य भुवनस्य गोपाः।
दीर्घाधियो रक्षमाणा असुर्यमृतावान्श्रयमाना ऋणानि॥

विद्यामादित्या अवसो वो अस्य यदर्यमन् भय आ चिन्मयोभु।
युष्माकं मित्रावरुणा प्रणीतौ परि श्वभ्रेव दुरितानि वृज्याम्॥

सुगो हि वो अर्यमन् मित्र पन्था अनृक्षरो वरुण साधुरस्ति।
तेनादित्या अधि वोचता नो यच्छता नो दुष्परिहन्तु शर्म॥

पिपर्तु नो अदिती राजपुत्रा अति द्वेषांस्यर्यमा सुगेभिः।
बृहन्मित्रस्य वरुणस्य शर्मोप स्याम पुरुवीत अरिष्टाः॥

तिस्रो भूमीधारयन् त्रीरुत द्यून् त्रीणि व्रता विदथे अन्तरेषाम्।
ऋतेनादित्या महि वो महित्वं तदर्यमन् वरुण मित्र चारु॥

त्री रोचना दिव्या धारयन्त हिरण्यया: शुचयो धारपूता:।
अस्वप्नजो अनिमिषा अदब्धा उरुशंसा ऋजवे मर्त्याय।।

त्वं वि श्वेषां वरुणासि राजा ये च देवा असुर ये च मर्ता:।
शतं नो रास्व शरदो विचक्षे ऽश्यामायूंषि सुधितानि पूर्वा।।

न दक्षिणा वि चिकिते न सव्या न प्राचीनभादिव्या नोत पश्चा।
पाक्या चिद् वसवो धीर्या चिद् युष्मानीतो अभयं ज्योतिरश्याम्।।

यो राजभ्य ऋतनिभ्यो ददाश यं वर्धयन्ति पुष्टश्च नित्या:।
स ग्वान याति प्रथमो रथेन वसुदावा विदथेषु प्रशस्त:।।

शुचिग्प: सूयवसा अदब्ध उप क्षेति वृद्धवया: सुवीर:।
नकिष्टं घ्नन्त्यन्तितो न दूराद् र आदित्यानां भवति प्रणीतौ।।

अदिते मित्र वरुणोत मृळ यद वो वयं चकृमा कच्चिदाभ:।
उर्वश्यामभयं ज्योतिरिन्द्र मा नो दीर्घा अभि नशन्तमिस्रा:।।

उभे अस्मै पीपयत: समीची दिवोदशष्टिं सुभगो नाम पुष्यन।
उभा क्षयावाजयन् याति पृत्सूभावर्धौ भवत: साधू अस्मै।।

या वो माया अभिद्वहे यजत्रा: पाशा आदित्या रिपवे विचृत्ता:।
अ श्वीव ताँ अति येशं रथेनारिष्टा उरावा शर्मन् त्स्याम।।

माहं मघोनो वरुण प्रियस्य भूरिदान्न आ विदं शूनमापे:।
मा रायो राजन् त्सुयमादव स्थां बृहद् वदेम विदथे सुवीर:।।

1. These hymns that drop down fatness, with the ladle
   I ever offer to the Kings Adityas.

   May Mitra, Aryaman, and Bhaga hear us, the mighty
   Varuna, Daksa, and Amsa.

2. With one accord may Aryaman and Mitra and Varuna
   this day accept this praise song—

   Adityas bright and pure as streams of water, free
   from all guile and falsehood, blameless, perfect.

3. These Gods, Adityas, vast, profound, and faithful, with many eyes, fain to deceive the wicked,

   Looking within behold the good and evil: near to the Kings is even the thing most distant.

4. Upholding that which moves and that which moves not, Adityas, Gods, protectors of all being,

   Provident, guarding well the world of spirits, true to eternal Law, the debt-exactors.

5. May I, Adityas, share in this your favour which, Aryaman, brings profit e'en in danger.

   Under your guidance, Varuna and Mitra, round troubles may I pass, like rugged places.

6. Smooth is your path, O Aryaman and Mitra; excellent is it, Varuna, and thornless.

   Thereon, Adityas, send us down your blessing: grant us a shelter hard to be demolished.

7. Mother of Kings, may Aditi transport us, by fair paths Aryaman, beyond all hatred.

   May we uninjured, girt by many heroes, win Varuna's and Mitra's high protection.

8. With their support they stay three earths, three heavens; three are their functions in the Gods' assembly.

   Mighty through Law, Adityas, is your greatness; fair is it, Aryaman, Varuna, and Mitra.

9. Golden and splendid, pure like streams of water, they hold aloft the three bright heavenly regions.

   Ne'er do they slumber, never close their eyelids, faithful, far-ruling for the righteous mortal.

10. Thou over all, O Varuna, art Sovran, be they Gods, Asura! or be they mortals.

    Grant unto us to see a hundred autumns: ours be the blest long lives of our forefathers.

11. Neither the right nor left do I distinguish, neither the east nor yet the west, Adityas.

    Simple and guided by your wisdom, Vasus! may I attain the light that brings no danger.

12. He who bears gifts unto the Kings, true Leaders, he whom their everlasting blessings prosper,

    Moves with his chariot first in rank and wealthy, munificent and lauded in assemblies.

13. Pure, faithful, very strong, with heroes round him, he dwells beside the waters rich with pasture.

    None slays, from near at hand or from a distance, him who is under the Adityas' guidance.

14. Aditi, Mitra, Varuna, forgive us however we have erred and sinned against you.

    May I obtain the broad light free from peril: O Indra, let not during darkness seize us.

15. For him the Twain united pour their fulness, the rain from heaven: he thrives most highly favoured.

    He goes to war mastering both the mansions: to him both portions of the world are gracious.

16. Your guiles, ye Holy Ones, to quell oppressors, your snares spread out against the foe, Adityas,

May I car-borne pass like a skilful horseman: uninjured may we dwell in spacious shelter.

17. May I not live, O Varuna, to witness my wealthy, liberal, dear friend's destitution.

King, may I never lack well-ordered riches. Loud may we speak, with heroes, in assembly.

(II/27)

Ribhus: Deities of Midair

-.-

Vamadeva

The divine class or race of the Ribhus, the three sons of Sudhanvan who is said to have been a descendant of Angiras.Through their assiduous performance of good works they obtained divinity and became entitled to receive praise and adoration.

इहोप यात शवसो नपातः सौधन्वना ऋभवो माप भूत।
अस्मिन् हि वः सवने रत्नेधयं गमन्त्विन्द्रमनु वो मदासः॥
आगन्नृभूणामिह रत्नधेयमभूत् सोमस्य सुषुतस्य पीतिः।
सुकृत्यया यत् स्वपस्यया चँ एकं विचक्र चमसं चतुर्धा॥
व्यकृणोत चमसं चतुर्धा सखे वि शिक्षेत्यब्रवीत।
अथैत वाजा अमृतस्य पन्थां गणं देवानामृभवः सुहस्ताः॥
किंमयः स्विच्चमस एष आस यं काव्येन चतुरो विचक्र।
अथा सुनुब्वं सवनं मदाय पात ऋभवो मधुनः सोम्यस्य॥

शच्याकर्त पितरा युवाना शच्याकर्त चमसं देवपानम्।
शच्या हरी धनुतरावतष्ठेन्द्रवाहावृभवो वाजरत्ना:॥
यो व: सुनोत्यभिपित्वे अह्नना तीव्रं वाजास: सवनं मदाय।
तस्मै रयिमृभव: सर्ववीरमा तक्षत वृषणो मन्दसाना:॥
प्रात: सुतमपिबो हर्यश्व माध्यंदिनं सवनं केवलं ते।
सममुभि: पिबस्व रत्नधेमि: सखीर्या इन्द्र चकृषे सुकृत्या॥
ये देवासो अमवता सुकृत्या श्येना इवेदधि दिवि निषेद।
ते रत्नं धात शवसो नपात: सौधन्वना अभवतामृतास:॥
यत् तृतीयं सवनं रत्नधेयमकृणुध्वं स्वपस्या सुहस्ता:।
तदूभव: परिषिक्तं व एतत् सं मदेभिरिन्द्रियेभि: पिबध्वम्॥

1. Come hither, O ye Sons of Strength, ye Ribhus; stay not afar, ye Children of Sudhanvan.

   At this libation is your gift of treasure. Let gladdening draughts approach you after Indra's.

2. Hither is come the Ribhus' gift of riches; here was the drinking of the well-pressed Soma,

   Since by dexterity and skill as craftsmen ye made the single chalice to be fourfold.

3. Ye made fourfold the chalice that was single: ye spake these words and said, O Friend, assist us;

   Then, Vajas! gained the path of life eternal, deft-handed Ribhus, to the Gods' assembly.

4. Out of what substance was that chalice fashioned which ye made fourfold by your art and wisdom?

   Now for the gladdening draught press out the liquor, and drink, O Ribhus, of the meath of Soma.

5. Ye with your cunning made your Parents youthful; the cup, for Gods to drink, ye formed with cunning;

With cunning, Ribhus, rich in treasure, fashioned the two swift Tawny Steeds who carry Indra.

6. Whoso pours out for you, when days are closing, the sharp libation for your joy, O Vajas,

   For him, O mighty Ribhus, ye, rejoicing, have fashioned wealth with plenteous store of heroes.

7. Lord of Bay Steeds, at dawn the juice thou drankest: thine, only thine, is the noon day libation.

   Now drink thou with the wealth-bestowing Ribhus, whom for their skill thou madest friends, O Indra.

8. Ye, whom your artist skill hath raised to Godhead have set you down above in heaven like falcons.

   So give us riches, Children of Sudhanvan, O Sons of Strength; ye have become immortal.

9. The third libation, that bestoweth treasure, which ye have won by skill, ye dexterous-handed,—

   This drink hath been effused for you, O Ribhus: drink it with high delight, with joy like Indra's.

(IV/35)

Aapris: Propitiatory Hymns

-.-

Vasushruta

Aapris is the collective name of the Gods and deified objects addressed in the hymn.

सुसमिद्धाय शोचिषे घृतं तीव्रं जुहोतन। अग्नये जातवेदसे।
नराशंस: सुषूदतीमं यज्ञमदाभ्य:। कविर्हि मधुहस्त्य:॥

इळितो अग्र आ वहेन्द्रं चित्रमिह प्रियम्। सुखै रथेभिरूतये।
ऊर्णम्रदा वि प्रथस्वाऽभ्याऽर्का अनूषत। भवा नः शुभ्र सातये॥
देवीद्वारो वि श्रयध्वं सुप्रायणा न ऊतये। प्रप्र यज्ञं पृणीतन।
सुप्रतीके वयोवृधा यह्वी ऋतस्य मातरा। दोषामुषासमीमहे॥
वातस्य पत्मन्रीळिता दैव्या होतारा मनुषः। इमं नो यज्ञमा गतम्।
इळा सरस्वती मही तिस्रो देवीर्मयोभुवः। बर्हिः सीदन्त्वस्रिधः॥
शिवस्त्वष्टरिहा गहि विभुः पोष उतत्मना। यज्ञेयज्ञे न उदव।
यत्र वेत्थ वनस्पते देवानां गुह्या नामानि। तत्र हव्यानि गामय॥
स्वाहाग्नये वरुणाय स्वाहेन्द्राय मरुद्भयः। स्वाहा देवेभ्यो हविः।

1. To Agni, Jatavedas, to the flame, the well-enkindled
   God,

   Offer thick sacrificial oil.

2. He, Narasamsa, ne'er beguiled, inspireth this
   sacrifice:

   For sage is he, with sweets in hand.

3. Adored, O Agni, hither bring Indra the Wonderful,
   the Friend,

   On lightly-rolling car to aid.

4. Spread thyself out, thou soft as wool! The holy
   hymns have sung to thee.

   Bring gain to us, O beautiful!

5. Open yourselves, ye Doors Divine, easy of access
   for our aid:

   Fill, more and more, the sacrifice.

6. Fair strengtheners of vital power, young Mothers of
   eternal Law,

   Morning and Night we supplicate.

7. On the wind's flight come, glorified, ye two celestial Priests of man:

Come ye to this our sacrifice.

8. Ila, Sarasvati, Mahi, three Goddesses who bring us weal,

Be seated harmless on the grass.

9. Rich in all plenty, Tvastar, come auspicious of thine own accord:

Help us in every sacrifice.

10. Vanaspati, wherever thou knowest the Gods' mysterious names,

Send our oblations thitherward.

11. To Agni and to Varuna, Indra, the Maruts, and the Gods,

With Svaha be oblation brought.

(V/5)

Visnu: The Pervader of All

-.-

Auchathya

This God, 'the all-pervading or encompassing,' is not placed in the Veda in the foremost rank of deities, and, though frequently invoked with Indra, Varuna, the Maruts, Rudra, Vayu and the Adityas, his superiority to them is never stated, and he is even described in one place as celebrating the praise of Indra and deriving his power from that God. The point which distinguishes him from the other Vedic deities is chiefly his striding over the heavens, which he is said to do in three paces.

विष्णोर्नु कं वीर्याणि प्र वोचं यः पार्थिवानि विममे रजांसि।
यो अस्कभायदुत्तरं सधस्थं विचक्रमाणस्त्रे धोरुगायः॥
प्र तद् विष्णुः स्तवते वीर्येण मृगो न भीमः कुचरो गिरिष्ठाः।
यस्योरुषु त्रिषु विक्रमणेष्वधिक्षियन्ति भुवनानि विश्वा॥
प्र विष्णवे शूषमेतु मन्म गिरिक्षित उरुगायाय वृष्णे।
य इदं दीर्घं प्रयतं सधस्थमेको विममे त्रिभिरित् पदेभिः॥
यस्य त्री पूर्णा मधुना पदा न्यक्षीयमाणा स्वधया मदन्ति।
य उ त्रिधातु पृथिवीमुत द्यामेको दाधार भुवनानि क्विश्वा॥
तदस्य प्रियमभि पाथो अश्यां नरो यत्र गावो देवयवो मदन्ति।
उरु क्रमस्य स हि बन्धुरित्था विष्णोः पदे परमे मध्व उत्सव।
ता वां वास्तून्युश्मसि गमध्यै यत्र गावो भूरिश्रृंगा अवासः॥
अत्राह तदुरुगायस्य वृष्णः परमं पदमव भाति भूरि॥

1. I will declare the mighty deeds of Visnu, of him
   who measured out the earthly regions,

   Who propped the highest place of congregation,
   thrice setting down his footstep, widely striding.

2. For this his mighty deed is Visnu lauded, like some
   wild beast, dread, prowling, mountain-roaming;

   He within whose three wide-extended paces all
   living creatures have their habitation.

3. Let the hymn lift itself as strength to Visnu, the
   Bull far -striding, dwelling on the mountains,

   Him who alone with triple step hath measured
   this common dwelling-place, long, far extended.

4. Him whose three paces that are filled with sweetness,
   imperishable, joy as it may list them,

   Who, verily, alone upholds the threefold, the earth,
   the heaven, and all living creatures.

5. May I attain to that his well-loved mansion where men devoted to the Gods are happy.

    For there springs, close akin to the Wide-Strider, the well of meath in Visnu's highest footstep.

6. Fain would we go unto your dwelling places where there are many-horned and nimble oxen,

    For mightily, there, shineth down upon us the widely-striding Bull's sublimest mansion.

(I/154)

●

—Vasishtha

परो मात्रया तन्वा वृधान न ते महित्वमन्वश्नुवन्ति।
उभे ते विद्म रजसी पृथिव्या विष्णो देव त्वं परमस्य वित्से॥
न ते विष्णो जायमानो न जाते देव महिम्न: परमन्तमाप।
उदस्तभ्ना नाकमृष्वं बृहन्तं दाधर्थ प्राचीं ककुभं पृथिव्या:॥
इरावती धेनुमती हि भूतं सूयवसिनी मनुषे दशस्या।
व्यस्तभ्ना रोदसी विष्णवेते दाधर्थ पृथिवीमभितो मयखै:॥
उरुं यज्ञाय चक्रथुरु लोकं जनयन्ता सूर्यमुषासमग्निम्।
दासस्य चिद् वृषशिप्रस्य माया जघ्नथुर्नरा पृतनाज्येषु॥
इन्द्राविष्णू दृंहिता: शम्बरस्य नव पुरो नवति च श्नथिष्टम्।
शतं वर्चिन: सहस्रं च साकं हथो अप्रत्यसुरस्य वीरान्॥
इयं मनीषा बृहती बृहन्तोरुक्रमा तवसा वर्धयन्ती।
ररे वां स्तोम विदथेषु विष्णो पिन्वतमिषो वृजनेष्विन्द्र॥
वषट् ते विष्णवास आ कृणोमि तन्मे जुषस्व शिपिविष्ट हव्यम्।
वर्धन्तु त्वा सुष्टुतयो गिरो मे यूयं पात स्वस्तिभि: सदा न:॥

1. Men come not nigh thy majesty who growest beyond

all bound and measure with thy body.

Both thy two regions of the earth, O Visnu, we know: thou God, knowest the highest also.

2. None who is born or being born, God Visnu, hath reached the utmost limit of thy grandeur.

    The vast high vault of heaven hast thou supported, and fixed earth's eastern pinnacle securely.

3. Rich in sweet food be ye, and rich in milch-kine, with fertile pastures, fain to do men service.

    Both these worlds, Visnu, hast thou stayed asunder, and firmly fixed the earth with pegs around it.

4. Ye have made spacious room for sacrificing by generating Surya, Dawn, and Agni.

    O Heroes, ye have conquered in your battles even the bull-jawed Dasa's wiles and magic.

5. Ye have destroyed, thou, Indra, and thou, Visnu, Sambara's nine-and-ninety fenced castles.

    Ye Twain smote down a hundred times a thousand resistless heroes of the royal Varcin.

6. This is the lofty hymn of praise, exalting the Lords of Mighty Stride, the strong and lofty.

    I laud you in the solemn synods, Visnu: pour ye food on us in our camps, O Indra.

7. O Visnu, unto thee my lips cry Vasat! Let this mine offering, Sipivista, please thee.

    May these my songs of eulogy exalt thee. Preserve us evermore, ye Gods, with blessings.

(VII/99)

Surya: The Sun

Praskanva

उद् त्यं जातवेदसं देवं वहन्ति केतव:। दृशे वि श्वाय सूर्यम्।
अप त्ये तायवो यथा नक्षत्रा यन्त्यक्तुभि:। सूराय वि श्वचक्षसे॥
अदृश्रमस्य केतवो वि रश्मयो जनाँ अनु। भ्राजन्तो अग्नयो यथा।
तरणिर्वि श्वदर्शतो ज्योतिष्कृदसि सूर्य। वि श्वमा भासि रोचनम्॥
प्रत्यङ् देवानां विश: प्रत्यङ्देषि मानुषान्। प्रत्यङ् विश्वं स्वदृशे।
येना पावक चक्षसा भुरण्यन्तं जनाँ अनु। त्वं वरुण पश्यसि॥
वि द्यामेषि रजस्पृथ्वहा मिमानो अक्तुभि:। पश्यञ्जन्मानि सूर्य।
सप्त त्वा हरितो रथे वहन्ति देव सूर्य। शोचिष्केशं विचक्षण॥
अयुक्त सप्त शुन्ध्युव: सूरो रथस्य नप्त्य:। ताभिर्याति स्वयुक्तिभि:॥
उद् वयं तमसस्परि ज्योतिष्पश्यन्त उत्तरम्। देवं देवत्रा सूर्यमगन्म ज्योतिरुत्तमम्॥
उद्यन्नद्य मित्रमह आरोहन्नुत्तरां दिवम्। हृद्रोगं मम सूर्य हरिमाणं च नाशय॥
शुकेषु मे हरिमाणं रोपणाकासु धद्मसि। अथो हारिद्रवेषु मे हरिमाणं नि दध्मसि॥
उद्गादयमादित्यो विश्वेन सहसा सह। द्विषन्तं मह्यं रन्धयन् मो अहं द्विषते रधम्॥

1. His bright rays bear him up aloft, the God who knoweth all that lives,

   Surya, that all may look on him.

2. The constellations pass away, like thieves, together with their beams,

   Before the all-beholding Sun.

3. His herald rays are seen afar refulgent o'er the word of men,

   Like flames of fire that burn and blaze.

4. Swift and all beautiful art thou, O Surya, maker of the light,

   Illumine all the radiant realm.

5. Thou goest to the hosts of Gods, thou comest hither to mankind,

   Hither all light to be beheld.

6. With that same eye of thine wherewith thou lookest, brilliant Varuna,

   Upon the busy race of men,

7. Traversing sky and wide mid-air, thou metest with thy beams our days,

   Sun, seeing all things that have birth.

8. Seven Bay Steeds harnessed to thy car bear thee, O thou farseeing One,

   God, Surya, with the radiant hair.

9. Surya hath yoked the pure bright Seven, the daughters of the car; with these,

   His own dear team, he goeth forth.

10. Looking upon the loftier light above the darkness we have come

    To Surya, God among the Gods, the light that is most excellent.

11. Rising this day, O rich in friends, ascending to the loftier heaven,

    Surya, remove my heart's disease, take from me this my yellow hue.

12. To parrots and to starlings let us give away my yellowness,

    Or this my yellowness let us transfer to Haritala trees.

13. With all his conquering vigour this Aditya hath gone up on high,

    Giving my foe into mine hand: let me not be my foeman's prey.

(I/50)

Parjanya: God of Rain-clouds

-.-

Atri

Parjanya is the God of thunder-storms and rain, the generator and nourisher of plants and living creatures.

अच्छा वद तवसं गीर्भिराभिः स्तुहि पर्जन्यं नमसा विवास।
कनिक्रदद् वृषभो जीरदानू रेतो दधात्योषधीषु गर्भम्॥

वि वृक्षान् हन्त्युत हन्ति रक्षसो विश्वं बिभाय भुवनं महावधात्।
उतानागा ईषते वृष्ण्यावतो यत् पर्जन्यः स्तनयन् हन्ति दुष्कृतः॥

रथीव कशया श्वाँ अभिक्षिपन्नाविर्दूतान् कृणुते वर्ष्याँ३ अह।
दूरात् सिंहस्य स्तनथा उदीरते यत् पर्जन्यः कृणुते वर्ष्यं१नभः॥

प्र वाता वान्ति पतयन्ति विद्युत उदोषधीर्जिहते पिन्वते स्वः।
इरा विश्वस्मै भुवनाय जायते यत् पर्जन्यः पृथिवीं रेतसावति॥

यस्य व्रते पृथिवी नंनमीति यस्य व्रते शफवज्जर्भुरीति।
यस्य व्रत ओषधीर्विश्वरूपाः स नः पर्जन्य महि शर्म यच्छ॥

दिवो नो वृष्टिं मरुतो ररीध्वं प्र पिन्वत वृष्णो अश्वस्य धाराः।
अर्वांडे.तेन स्तनयित्नुनेह्यपो निषिञ्चन्नसुरः पिता नः॥

अभि क्रन्द स्तनय गर्भमा धा उदन्वता परि दीया रथेन।
दृति सु कर्ष विषितं न्यञ्चं समा भवन्तूद्वतो निपादाः॥

महान्तं कोशमुदचा निषिञ्च स्यन्दन्तां कुल्या विषिताः पुरस्तात्।
घृतेन द्यावापृथिवी व्युन्धि सुप्रपाणं भवत्वघ्न्याभ्यः॥

यत् पर्जन्य कनिक्रदत् स्तनयन् हंसि दुष्कृतः।
प्रतीदं विश्वं मोदते यत् किं च पृथिव्यामधि॥

अवर्षीर्वर्षमुदु षू गृभायाऽकर्धन्वान्यत्येतवा उ।
अजीजन ओषधीर्भोजनाय कमुत प्रजाभ्योऽविदो मनीषां॥

1. Sing with these songs thy welcome to the Mighty, with adoration praise and call Parjanya.

The Bull, loud roaring, swift to send his bounty,
lays in the plants the seed for germination.

2. He smites the trees apart, he slays the demons:
all life fears him who wields the mighty weapon.

From him exceeding strong flees e'en the guiltless,
when thundering Parjanya smites the wicked.

3. Like a car-driver whipping on his horses, he makes
the messengers of rain spring forward.

Far off resounds the roaring of the lion, what
time Parjanya fills the sky with rain-cloud.

4. Forth burst the winds, down come the lightning-
flashes: the plants shoot up, the realm of light is
streaming.

Food springs abundant for all living creatures,
what time Parjanya quickens earth with moisture.

5. Thou at whose bidding earth bows low before thee,
at whose command hoofed cattle fly in terror,

At whose behest the plants assume all colours,
even thou Parjanya, yield us great protection.

6. Send down for us the rain of heaven, ye Maruts,
and let the Stallion's flood descend in torrents.

Come hither with this thunder while thou pourest
the waters down, our heavenly Lord and Father.

7. Thunder and roar: the germ of life deposit. Fly round
us on thy chariot water laden.

Thine opened water-skin draw with thee downward,
and let the hollows and the heights be level.

8. Lift up the mighty vessel, pour down water, and
let the liberated streams rush forward.

Saturate both the earth and heaven with fatness,
and for the cows let there be drink abundant.

9. When thou, with thunder and with roar, Parjanya, smitest sinners down,

This universe exults thereat, yea, all that is upon the earth.

10. Thou hast poured down the rain-flood: now withhold it. Thou hast made desert places fit for trave.

Thou hast made herbs to grow for our enjoyment: yea, thou hast won thee praise from living creatures.

(V/83)

Brihaspati: Lord of Prayer

-.-

Agastya

Brihaspati is the name of a deity in whom the action of the worshipper upon the Gods is personified. He is the suppliant, the priest who intercedes with the Gods for men, and protects them against the wicked. Hence he appears as the prototype of the priests and the priestly order, and is also designated as the Purohita of the divine community.

अनर्वाणं वृषभं मन्द्रजिह्वं बृहस्पतिं वर्धया नव्यमर्कैः।
गाथान्यः सुरुचो यस्य देवा आशृण्वन्ति नवमानस्य मर्ताः॥
तमृत्विया उप वाचः सचन्ते सर्गो न यो देवयतामसर्जि।
बृहस्पतिः स ह्यञ्जो वरांसि विभ्वाभवत् समृते मातरिश्वा॥
उपस्तुतिं नमस उद्यतिं च श्लोकं यंसत् सवितेव प्र बाहू।
अस्य क्रत्वाहन्योऽ३ यो अस्ति मृगो न भीमो अरक्षसस्तुविष्मान्॥
अस्य श्लोको दिवीयते पृथिव्यामत्यो न यंसद् यक्षभृद् विचेताः।
मृगाणां न हेतयो यन्ति चेमा बृहस्पतेरहिमायाँ अभि द्यून्॥

ये त्वा देवोस्मिकं मन्यमानाः पापा भद्रमुपजीवन्ति पज्ञाः।
न दूढ्ये३ अनु ददासि वामं बृहस्पते चयस इत् पियारुम्॥
सुप्रैतुः सूयवसो न पन्था दुर्नियन्तुः परिप्रीतो न मित्रः।
अनर्वाणो अभि ये चक्षते नो ऽपीवृता अपोर्णुवन्तो अस्थुः॥
सं यं स्तुभोऽवनयो न यन्ति समुद्रं न स्रवतो रोधचक्राः।
स विद्वाँ उभयं चष्टे अन्तर्बृहस्पतिस्तर आपश्च गृध्रः॥
एवा महस्तुविजातस्तुविष्मान् बृहस्पतिर्वृषभो धायि देवः।
स नः स्तुतो वीरवद् धातु गोमद् विद्यामेषं वृजनं जीरदानुम् ॥

1. Glorify thou Brihaspati, the scathless, who must be
   praised with hymns, sweet. tongued and mighty,

   To whom as leader of the song, resplendent,
   worthy of lauds, both Gods and mortals listen.

2. On him wait songs according to the season even
   as a stream of pious men set moving.

   Brihaspati—for he laid out the expanses—was, at
   the sacrifice, vast Matarisvan.

3. The praise, the verse that offers adoration, may he
   bring forth, as the Sun sends his arms out,

   He who gives daily light through this God's wisdom,
   strong as a dread wild beast, and inoffensive.

4. His song of praise pervades the earth and heaven:
   let the wise worshipper draw it, like a courser.

   These of Brihaspati, like hunters' arrows, go to
   the skies that change their hue like serpents.

5. Those, God, who count thee as a worthless bullock,
   and, wealthy sinners, live on thee the Bounteous,—

   On fools like these no blessing thou bestowest:
   Brihaspati, thou punishest the spiteful.

6. Like a fair path is he, where grass is pleasant, though

hard to win, a Friend beloved most dearly.

Those who unharmed by enemies behold us,
while they would make them bare, stood closely
compassed.

7. He to whom songs of praise go forth like torrents,
as rivers eddying under banks flow sea-ward—

Brihaspati the wise, the eager, closely looks upon
both, the waters and the vessel.

8. So hath Brihaspati, great, strong and mighty, the
God exceeding powerful, been brought hither.

May he thus lauded give us kine and horses.
May we find strengthening food in full abundance.

(I/190)

Vishvakarman: Creator of the Universe

-.-

Vishvakarman

Visvakarman, the Omnific, is represented in this hymn as
the universal Father and Generator, the Creator of all things
and Architect of the worlds.

य इमा विश्वा भुवनानि जुह्वदृषिर्होता न्यसीदत्पिता न:।
स आशिषा द्रविणमिच्छमान: प्रथमच्छदवराँ आ विवेश॥
किं स्विदासीदधिष्ठानमारम्भणं कतमत् स्वित् कथासीत्।
यतो भूमि जनयन् विश्व कर्मा वि घामौर्णोन्माहिना विश्वचक्षा:॥
विश्वतश्चक्षुरुत विश्वतोमुखो विश्वतोबाहुरुत विश्वतस्पात्।
सं बाहुभ्यां धमति सं पतत्रैर्द्यावाभूमी जनयन् देव एक:॥
किं स्विद्वनं क उ स वृक्ष आस यतो द्यावापृथिवी निष्टतक्षु:।

मनीषिणो मनसा पृच्छतेदु तद् यद्ध्यतिष्ठद्भुवनानि धारयन्॥
या ते धामानि परमाणि यावमा या मध्यमा क्विश्वकर्मन्नुतेमा।
शिक्षा सखिभ्यो हविषा स्वधाव: स्वयं यजस्व तन्वं वृद्यान:॥
विश्वकर्मन हविषा वावृधान: स्वयं यजस्व पृथिवी मुतद्याम्।
मुह्यन्त्वन्ये अभितो जनास इहास्माकं मघवा सूरिस्तु।
वाचस्पतिं क्विश्वकर्माणमूतये मनोजुवं वाजे अद्या हुवेम॥
स नो क्विश्वानि हवनानि जोषद् क्विश्वशम्भूरवसे साधुकर्मा।

1. He who sat down as Hotar-priest, the Rishi, our
   Father, offering up all things existing,—

   He, seeking through his wish a great possession,
   came among men on earth as archetypal.

2. What was the place whereon he took his station?
   What was it that supported him? How was it?

   Whence Visvakarman, seeing all, producing the
   earth, with mighty power disclosed the heavens.

3. He who hath eyes on all sides round about him,
   a mouth on all sides, arms and feet on all sides,

   He, the Sole God, producing earth and heaven,
   weldeth them, with his arms as wings, together.

4. What was the tree, what wood in sooth produced
   it, from which they fashioned out the earth and
   heaven?

   Ye thoughtful men inquire within your spirit
   whereon he stood when he established all things.

5. Thine highest, lowest, sacrificial natures, and these
   thy mid-most here, O Visvakarman,

   Teach thou thy friends at sacrifice, O Blessed,
   and come thyself, exalted, to our worship.

6. Bring thou thyself, exalted with oblation, O
   Visvakarman, Earth and Heaven to worship.

Let other men around us live in folly: here let us have a rich and liberal patron.

7. Let us invoke today, to aid our labour, the Lord of Speech, the thought-swift Visvakarman.

May he hear kindly all our invocations who gives all bliss for aid, whose works are righteous.

(X/81)

Sarasvati: The River

-.-

Vasishtha

Sarasvati is a goddess not of very great importance in the Rgveda. She is celebrated both as a river and as a deity. She was, no doubt, primarily a river deity, as her name, "the watery", clearly denotes, and in this capacity she is celebrated in a few separate passages. Allusion is made in the Hymns, as well as in the Brahmanas...to sacrifices being performed on the banks of this river and of the adjoining Drsadvati; and the Sarasvati in particular seems to have been associated with the reputation for sanctity, which was ascribed to the whole region, called Brahmavarta, lying between these two small streams, and situated immediately to the westward of the Jumna. The Sarasvati thus appears to have been to the early Indians what the Ganges became to their descendants.

बृहद् गायिषे वचो ऽसुर्या नदीनाम्।
सरस्वतीमिन्महया सुवृक्तिभिः स्तोमैर्वसिष्ठ रोदसी।।
उभे यत् ते महिना शुभ्रे अन्धसी अधिक्षियन्ति पूरव:।
सा नो बोध्यवित्री म्.रुत्सखा चोद राधो मघोनाम्।।

भद्रमिद् भद्रा कृणवत् सरस्वत्यकवारी चेतति वाजिनीवती।
गृणाना जमदग्निवत् स्तुवाना च वसिष्ठवत्॥
जनीयन्तो न्वग्रवः पुत्रीयन्तः सुदानवः। सरस्वन्तं हवामहे।
ये ते सरस्व ऊर्मयो मधुमन्तो घृतश्चुतः। तेभिर्नोऽविता भव॥
पीपिवांसं सरस्वतः स्तनं यो विश्वदर्शतः। भक्षीमहि प्रजामिषम्।

1. I sing a lofty song, for she is mightiest, most divine of Streams.

   Sarasvati will I exalt with hymns and lauds, and, O Vasistha, Heaven and Earth.

2. When in the fulness of their strength the Purus dwell, Beauteous One, on thy two grassy banks,

   Favour us thou who hast the Maruts for thy friends: stir up the bounty of our chiefs.

3. So may Sarasvati auspicious send good luck; she, rich in spoil, is never niggardly in thought,

   When praised in Jamadagni's way and lauded as Vasistha lauds.

4. We call upon Sarasvan, as unmarried men who long for wives,

   As liberal men who yearn for sons.

5. Be thou our kind protector, O Sarasvan, with those waves of thine

   Laden with sweets and dropping oil.

6. May we enjoy Sarasvan's breast, all-Beautiful, that swells with streams,

   May we gain food and progeny.

(VII/96)

Vishvedevas: Gods of the Universe

-·-

Gotama

Visvedevas may have originally denoted 'all the Gods collectively,' though the introduction of the Vishvas under the name *vishvedevah* as a separate troop of deities seems to have taken place at an early period.

आ नो भद्रा: क्रतवो यन्तु विश्वतो ऽदब्धासो अपरीतास उद्भिद:।
देवा नो यथा सद्मिद् वृधे असन्नप्रायुवो रक्षितारो दिवेदिवे॥
देवानां भद्रा सुमतिर्ऋजूयतां देवानां रातिरभि नो नि वर्तताम्।
देवानां सख्यमुप सेदिमा वयं देवा न आयु: प्र तिरन्तु जीव से॥
तान् पूर्वया निविदा हूमहे वयं भंगे मित्रमदितिं दक्षमस्त्रिधम्।
अर्यमणं वरुणं सोममश्विना सरस्वती न: सुभगा मयस्करत्॥
तन्नो वातो मयोभु बातु भेषजं तन्माता पृथिवी तत् पिता द्यौ:।
तद् ग्रावाण: सोमसुतो मयोभुवस्तदश्विना शृणुतं धिष्ण्या युवम्॥
तमीशानं जगतस्तस्थुषस्पतिं धियंजिन्वमवसे हूमहे वयम्।
पूषा नो यथा वेदसामसद् वृधे रक्षिता पायुरदब्ध: स्वस्तये॥
स्वस्ति न इन्द्रो वृद्धश्रवा: स्वस्ति न: पूषा विश्ववेदा:।
स्वस्ति नस्ताक्ष्र्यो अरिष्टनेमि: स्वस्ति नो बृहस्पतिर्दधातु॥
पृषदश्वा मरुत: पृश्निमातर: शुभंयावानो विदथेषु जग्मय:।
अग्निजिह्वा मनव: सूरचक्षसो विश्वे नो देवा अवसा गमन्निह॥
भद्रं कर्णेभि: शृणुयाम देवा भद्रं पश्येमाक्षभिर्यजत्रा:।
स्थिरैरङ्गैस्तुष्टुवांसस्तनूभिर्व्यशेम देवहितं यदायु:॥
शतमिन्नु शरदो अन्ति देवा यत्रा नश्चक्रा जरसं तनूनाम्।
पुत्रासो यत्र पितरो भवन्ति मा नो मध्या रीरिषतायुर्गन्तो:॥
अदितिर्द्यौरदितिरन्तरिक्षमदितिर्माता स पिता स पुत्र:।
विश्वे देवा अदिति: पञ्ज जना अदितिर्जातमदितिर्जनित्वम्॥

1. May powers auspicious come to us from every side, never deceived, unhindered, and victorious,

   That the Gods ever may be with us for our gain, our guardians day by day unceasing in their care.

2. May the auspicious favour of the Gods be ours, on us descend the bounty of the righteous Gods.

   The friendship of the Gods have we devoutly sought: so may the Gods extend our life that we may live.

3. We call them hither with a hymn of olden time, Bhaga, the friendly Daksa, Mitra, Aditi,

   Aryaman, Varuna, Soma, the Asvins. May Sarasvati, auspicious, grant felicity.

4. May the Wind waft to us that pleasant medicine, may Earth our Mother give it, and our Father Heaven,

   And the joy-giving stones that press the Soma's juice. Asvins, may ye, for whom our spirits long, hear this.

5. Him we invoke for aid who reigns supreme the Lord of all that stands or moves, inspirer of the soul,

   That Pusan may promote the increase of our wealth, our keeper and our guard infallible for our good.

6. Illustrious far and wide, may Indra prosper us: may Pusan prosper us, the Master of all wealth.

   May Tarksya with uninjured fellies prosper us; Brihaspati vouchsafe to us prosperity.

7. The Maruts, Sons of Prsni, borne by spotted steeds, moving in glory, oft visiting holy rites,

   Sages whose tongue is Agni, brilliant as the Sun,— hither let all the Gods for our protection come.

8. Gods, may we with our ears listen to what is good, and with our eyes see what is good, ye Holy Ones.

   With limbs and bodies firm may we extolling you attain the term of life appointed by the Gods.

9. A hundred autumns stand before us, O ye Gods, within whose space ye bring our bodies to decay;

   Within whose space our sons become fathers in turn. Break ye not in the midst our course of fleeting life.

10. Aditi is the heaven, Aditi is mid-air, Aditi is the mother and the sire and Son.

    Aditi is all Gods, Aditi five-classed men, Aditi all that hath been born and shall be born.

    (I/89)

Bhaga: God of Fortune

-.-

Vasishtha

Bhaga, the gracious lord and protector is regarded as the bestower of wealth. The hymn is addressed chiefly to Bhaga the bountiful, whose name, slightly corrupted, survives in the Slavonic languages as a general name for God; but the Gods mentioned in the first stanza, and Usas, Dawn or Morning, are also regarded as the deities of the verses in which their names occur.

प्रातरग्नि प्रातरिन्द्रं हवामहे प्रातर्मित्रावरुणा प्रातरश्विना।
प्रातर्भगं पूषणं ब्रह्मणस्पतिं प्रातः सोममुत रुद्रं हुवेम॥
प्रातर्जितं भगमुग्रं हुवेम वयं पुत्रमदितेर्यो विधर्ता।

आध्रश्चिचवद् यं मन्यमानस्तुरश्चिद् राजा चिद् यं भगं भक्षीत्याह॥

भग प्रणेतर्भग सत्यराधो भगेमां धियमुदवा ददन्न:।
भग प्र णो जनय गोभिरश्वैर्भग प्र नृभिर्नृवन्त: स्याम॥

उतेदानीं भगवन्त: स्यामोत प्रपित्व उत मध्ये अह्नाम्।
उतोदिता मघवन् त्सूर्यस्य वयं देवानां सुमतौ स्याम॥

भग एव भगवाँ अस्तु देवास्तेन वयं भगवन्त: स्याम।
तं त्वा भग सर्व इज्जोहवीति स नो भग पुरएता भवेह॥

समध्वरायोषसो नमन्त दधिक्रावेव शुचये पदाय।
अर्वाचीनं वसुविदं भगं नो रथमिवाश्वा वाजिन आ वहन्तु॥

अश्वावतीर्गोमतीर्न उषासो वीरवती: सदमुच्छन्तु भद्रा:।
घृतं दुहाना विश्वत: प्रपीता यूयं पात स्वस्तिभि: सदा न:॥

1. Agni at dawn, and Indra we invoke at dawn, and
   Varuna and Mitra, and the Asvins twain:

   Bhaga at dawn, Pusan, and Brahmanaspati, Soma
   at dawn, Rudra we will invoke at dawn.

2. We will invoke strong, early-conquering Bhaga, the
   Son of Aditi, the great supporter:

   Thinking of whom, the poor, yea, even the mighty,
   even the King himself says, Give me Bhaga.

3. Bhaga our guide, Bhaga whose gifts are faithful, favour this song, and give us wealth, O Bhaga.

   Bhaga, augment our store of kine and horses, Bhaga,
   may we be rich in men and heroes.

4. So may felicity be ours at present, and when the
   day approaches, and at noontide;

   And may we still, O Bounteous One, at sunset
   be happy in the Deities' loving kindness.

5. May Bhaga, verily, be bliss-bestower, and through
   him, Gods! may happiness attend us.

As such, O Bhaga, all with might invoke thee:
as such be thou our Champion here, O Bhaga.

6. To this our worship may all Dawns incline them,
and come to the pure place like Dadhikravan.

As strong steeds draw a chariot may they bring
us hitherward Bhaga who discovers treasure.

7. May blessed Mornings dawn on us for ever, with
wealth of kine, of horses, and of heroes,

Streaming with all abundance, pouring fatness.
Preserve us evermore, ye Gods, with blessings.

(VII/41)

Vena: A King

-.-

Bhargava

Vena, the loving Sun, is the God of the middle region. He
is, apparently, the Sun as he rises in the mist and dew of
the morning.

अयं वेनश्चोदयत् पृश्निगर्भा ज्योतिर्जरायू रजसो विमाने।
इममपां संगमे सूर्यस्य शिशुं न विप्रा मतिभी रिहन्ति।।
समुद्रादूर्मिमुदियर्ति वेनो नभोजाः पृष्ठं हर्यतस्य दर्शि।
ऋतस्य सानावधि विष्टपि भ्राटू समानं योनिमभ्यनूषत व्राः।।
समानं पूर्वीरभि वावशानास्तिष्ठन् वत्सस्य मातरः सनीळाः।
ऋतस्य सानावधि चक्रमाणा रिहन्ति मध्वो अमृतस्य वाणीः।।
जानन्तो रूपमकृपन्त विप्रा मृगस्य घोषं महिषस्य हि ग्मन्।
ऋतेन यन्तो अधि सिन्धुमस्थुर्विदद्गन्धर्वो अमृतानि नाम।।
अप्सरा जारमुपसिष्मियाणा योषा बिभर्ति परमे व्योमन्।

चरत् प्रियस्य योनिषु प्रिय: सन् त्सीदत् पक्षे हिरण्यये स वेन:॥
नाके सुपर्णमुप यत् पतन्तं हृदा वेनन्तो अभ्यचक्षत त्वा।
हिरण्यपक्षं वरुणस्य दूतं यमस्य योनौ शकुनं भुरण्युम्॥
ऊर्ध्वो गन्धर्वो अधि नाके अस्थात् प्रत्यङ् चित्रा बिभ्रदस्यायुधानि।
वसानो अत्कं सुरभिं दृशे कं स्वर्णं नाम जनत प्रियाणि॥
द्रप्स: समुद्रमभि यज्जिगाति पश्यन् गृध्रस्य चक्षसा विधर्मन्।
भानु: शुक्रेण शोचिषा चकानस्तृतीये चक्रे रजसि प्रियाणि॥

1. See, Vena, born in light, hath driven hither, on chariot of the air, the Calves of Prsni.

   Singers with hymns caress him as an infant there where the waters and the sunlight mingle.

2. Vena draws up his wave from out of the ocean: mist-born, the fair one's back is made apparent,

   Brightly he shone aloft on Order's summit: the hosts sang glory to their common birthplace.

3. Full many, lowing to their joint-possession, dwelling together stood the Darling's Mothers.

   Ascending to the lofty height of Order, the bands of singers sip the sweets of Amrta.

4. Knowing his form the sages yearned to meet him: they have come nigh to hear the wild Bull's bellow.

   Performing sacrifice they reached the river: for the Gandharva found the immortal waters.

5. The Apsaras, the Lady, sweetly smiling, supports her Lover in sublimest heaven.

   In his Friend's dwelling as a Friend he wanders: he, Vena, rests him on his golden pinion.

6. They gaze on thee with longing in their spirit, as on a strong-winged bird that mounteth skyward;

On thee with wings of gold, Varuna's envoy, the
Bird that hasteneth to the home of Yama.

7. Erect, to heaven hath the Gandharva mounted,
pointing at us his many-coloured weapons;

Clad in sweet raiment beautiful to look on, for
he, as light, produceth forms that please us.

8. When as a spark he cometh near the ocean, still
looking with a vulture's eye to heaven,

His lustre, joying in its own bright splendour,
maketh dear glories in the lowest region.

(X/123)

Manyu: Wrath

-.-

Manyustapasa

Manyu means Anger, Passion, personified.

त्वया मन्यो सरथमारुजन्तो हर्षमाणासो धृषिता मरुत्व:।
तिग्मेषव आयुधा संशिशाना अभि प्र यन्तु नरो अग्निरूपा:॥
अग्निरिव मन्यो त्विषित: सहस्व सेनानीर्न: सहुरे हूत एधि।
हत्वाय शत्रून् वि भजस्व वेद ओजो मिमानो वि मृधो नुदस्व॥
सहस्व मन्यो अभिमातिमस्मे रुजन् मृणन् प्रमृणन् प्रेहि शत्रून्।
उग्रं ते पाजो नन्वा रुरुध्रे वशी वश नयस एकज त्वम्॥
एको बहूनामसि मन्यवीळितो विशंविशं युधये सं शिशाधि।
अकृत्तरुक् त्वया युजा वयं द्युमन्तं घोषं विजयाय कृण्महे॥
विजेषकृदिन्द्र इवानवब्रवो३ऽस्माकं मन्यो अधिपा भवेह।
प्रियं ते नाम सहुरे गृणीमसि विद्मा तमुत्सं यत आबभूथ॥
आभूत्या सहजा वज्र सायक सहो बिभर्ष्यभिभूत उत्तरम्।

क्रत्वा नो मन्यो सह मे॒द्योधि महाधनस्य पुरुहूत संसृजि॥
संसृष्टं धनमुभयं समाकृतमस्मभ्यं दत्तां वरुणश्च मन्युः।
भियं दधाना हृदयेषु शत्रवः पराजितासो अप नि लयन्ताम्॥

1. He who hath reverenced thee, Manyu, destructive bolt, breeds for himself forthwith all conquering energy.

   Arya and Dasa will we conquer with thine aid, with thee the Conqueror, with conquest conquest-sped.

2. Manyu was Indra, yea, the God was Manyu, Manyu was Hotar, Varuna, Jatavedas.

   The tribes of human lineage worship Manyu, Accordaint with thy Fervour, Manyu guard us.

3. Come hither, Manyu, mightier than the mighty; chase, with thy fervour for ally, our foemen.

   Slayer of foes, of Vritra, and of Dasyu, bring thou to us all kinds of wealth and treasure.

4. For thou art, Manyu, of surpassing vigour, fierce, queller of the foe, and self-existent,

   Shared by all men, victorious, subduer: vouchsafe to us superior strength in battles.

5. I have departed, still without a portion, wise God! according to thy will, the Mighty.

   I, feeble man, was wroth thee, O Manyu! I am myself; come thou to give me vigour.

6. Come hither, I am all thine own; advancing turn thou to me, Victorious, All supporter!

   Come to me, Manyu, Wielder of the Thunder: bethink thee of thy friend, and slay the Dasyus.

7. Approach, and on my right hand hold thy station: so shall we slay a multitude of foemen.

The best of meath I offer to support thee: may
we be first to drink thereof in quiet.

(X/83)

Apamnapat: Offspring of Waters

-.-

Gritsamad

Apamnapat, the Flood's Child, or Son of Waters, a name
of Agni as born in the form of lightning from the waters
of the aerial ocean or firmament.

उपेमसृक्षि वाजयुर्वचस्यां चनो दधीत नाद्यो गिरो मे।
अपां नपादाशुहेमा कुवित् स सुपेशसस्करति जोषिषद्धि॥
इमं स्वस्मै हृद आ सुतष्टं मन्त्रं वोचेम कुविदस्य वेदत्।
अपां नपादसुर्यस्य मह्ना विश्वान्यर्यो भुवना जजान॥
समन्या यन्त्युप यन्त्यन्या: समानमूर्वं नद्य: पृणन्ति।
तमू शुचिं शुचयो दीदिवांसमपां नपातं परि तस्थराप:॥
तमस्मेरा युगतयो युवानं मर्मृज्यमाना: परियन्त्याप:।
स शुक्रेभि: शिक्वभी रेवदस्मे दीदायानिध्मो घृतनिर्णिगप्सु॥
अस्मै तिस्रो अव्यथ्याय नारीर्देवाय देवीर्दिधिषन्त्यन्नम्।
कृता इवोप हि प्रसर्स्रे अप्सु स पीयूषं धयति पूर्वसूनाम्॥
अश्वस्यात्र जनिमास्य च स्वर्दुहो रिष: संपृच: पाहि सूरीन्।
आमासु पूर्षु परो अप्रमृष्यं नारातयो वि नशन्नानृतानि॥
स्व आ दमे सुदुघा यस्य धेनु: स्वधां पीपाय सुभ्वन्नमत्ति।
सो अपां नपादूर्जयन्नप्स्वन्तर्वसुदेयाय विधते वि भाति॥
यो अप्स्वा शुचिना दैव्येन ऋतावाजस्र उर्विया विभाति।

वया इदन्या भुवनान्यस्य प्र जायन्ते वीरुधश्चव प्रजाभिः॥

अपां नपादा ह्यस्थादुपस्थं जिह्वानामूर्ध्वो विद्युतं वसानः।

तस्य ज्येष्ठं महिमानं वहन्तीर्हिरण्यवर्णाः परि यन्ति यीह्वः॥

हिरण्यरूपः स हिरण्यसंदृगपां नपात् सेदु हिरण्यवर्णः।

हिरण्ययात् परि योनेर्निषद्या हिरण्यदा ददत्यन्नमस्मै॥

तदस्यानीकमुत चारु नाना पीच्यं वर्धते नप्तुरपाम्।

यमिन्धते युवतयः समित्था हिरण्यवर्णं घृतमन्नमस्य॥

अस्मै बहूनामवमाय सख्ये यज्ञौर्विधेम नमसा हविर्भिः।

सं सानु मार्ज्मि दिधिषामि बिल्मैर्दधाम्यन्नै: परि वन्द ऋग्भिः॥

स ई वृषाजनयत् तासु गर्भं स ई शिशुर्धयति तं रिहन्ति।

सो अपां नपादनभिम्लातवर्णो ऽन्यस्येवेह तन्वा विवेष॥

अस्मिन् पदे परमे तस्थिवांसमध्वस्मभिर्विश्वहा दीदिवांसम्।

आपो नप्त्रे घृतमन्नं वहन्ती: स्वयमत्कैः परि दीयन्ति यह्वीः॥

अयांसमग्न सुक्षितिं जनायायांसमु मघवद्भयः सुवृक्तिम्।

विश्वं तद् भद्रं यदवन्ति देवा बृहद् वदेम विदथे सुवीराः॥

1. Eager for spoil my flow of speech I utter: may the Floods' Child accept my songs with favour.

   Will not the rapid Son of Waters make them lovely, for he it is who shall enjoy them?

2. To him let us address the song well fashioned, forth from the heart. Shall he not understand it?

   The friendly Son of Waters by the greatness of Godhead hath produced all things existing.

3. Some floods unite themselves and others join them: the sounding rivers fill one common storehouse.

   On every side the bright Floods have encompassed the bright resplendent Offspring of Waters.

4. The never-sullen waters, youthful Maidens, carefully decking, wait on him the youthful.

He with bright rays shines forth in splendid beauty, unfed with wood. in waters, oil-enveloped.

5. To him three Dames are offering food to feed him, Goddesses to the God whom none may injure.

Within the waters hath he pressed, as hollows, and drinks their milk who now are first made mothers.

6. Here was the horse's birth; his was the sunlight. Save thou our princes from the oppressor's onslaught.

Him, indestructible, dwelling at a distance in forts unwrought lies and ill spirits reach not.

7. He, in whose mansion is the teeming Milch-cow, swells the Gods' nectar and eats noble viands.

The Son of Waters, gathering strength in waters, shines for his worshipper to give him treasures.

8. He who in waters with his own pure Godhead shines widely, law-abiding, everlasting—

The other worlds are verily his branches, and plants are born of him with all their offspring.

9. The Waters' Son hath risen, and clothed in lightning ascended up unto the curled cloud's bosom;

And bearing with them his supremest glory the Youthful Ones, gold-coloured, move around him.

10. Golden in form is he, like gold to look on, his colour is like gold, the Son of Waters.

When he is seated fresh from golden birthplace those who present their gold give food to feed him.

11. This the fair name and this the lovely aspect of him the Water's Son increase in secret.

Whom here the youthful Maids together kindle,
his food is sacred oil of golden colour.

12. Him, nearest Friend of many, will we worship with
sacrifice and reverence and oblation.

I make his back to shine, with chips provide him;
I offer food and with my songs exalt him.

13. The Bull hath laid his own life-germ within them.
He sucks them as an infant, and they kiss him.

He, Son of Waters, of unfading colour, hath entered
here as in another's body.

14. While here he dwelleth in sublimest station,
resplendent with the rays that never perish,

The Waters, bearing oil to feed their offspring,
flow, Youthful Ones, in wanderings about him.

15. Agni, I gave good shelter to the people, and to the
princes goodly preparation.

Blessed is all that Gods regard with favour. Loud
may we speak, with heroes, in assembly.

(II/35)

Kapinjala: Bird of Good Omen

-.-
Gritsmad

This Hymn is said to be addressed to Indra in the form of
a Kapinjala, the bird of good omen.

कनिक्रदज्जनुषं प्रब्रुवाण इयर्ति वाचमरितेव नावम्।
सुमङ्गलश्च शकुने भवासि मा त्वा का चिदभिभा विश्व्या विदत्॥

मा त्वा श्येन उद् वधीन्मा सुपर्णो मा त्वा विददिपुमान् वीरो अस्ता।
पित्र्यामनु प्रदिशं कनिक्रदत् सुमङ्गलो भद्रवादी वदेह॥
अव क्रन्द दक्षिणतो गृहाणां सुमङ्गलो भद्रवादी शकुन्ते॥
मा नः स्तेन ईशत माघशंसो बृहद् वदेम विदथे सुवीराः।

1. Telling his race aloud with cries repeated, he sends his voice out as his boat a steersman.

   O Bird, be ominous of happy fortune: from no side may calamity befall thee.

2. Let not the falcon kill thee, nor the eagle: let not the arrow-bearing archer reach thee.

   Still crying in the region of the Fathers, speak here auspicious, bearing joyful tidings.

3. Bringing good tidings, Bird of happy omen, call thou out loudly southward of our dwellings,

   So that no thief, no sinner may oppress us. Loud may we speak, with heroes, in assembly.

   (II/42)

Dadhikra: Morning Sun

-.-

Vamadeva

Dadhikra is the name of a mythical being. He is described as a kind of divine horse and probably personification of the morning sun and is invoked in the morning together with Agni, Usas, and the Asvins. The name is probably derived from *dadhi*, thickened milk, and *kri*, to scatter, in allusion to the rising sun spreading dew and hoar-frost like milk.

उतो हि वां दात्रा सन्ति पूर्वा या पृरुभ्यस्त्रसदस्युर्निंतोशे।
क्षेत्रासां ददथुरुर्वरासां घनं दस्युभ्यो अभिभूतिमुग्रम्॥

उत वाजिनं पुरुनिष्षिध्वानं दधिक्रामु ददथुर्विश्वकृष्टिम्।
ऋजिप्यं श्येनं प्रुषितप्सुमाशुं चर्कृत्यमर्यो नृपतिं न शूरम्॥

यं सीमनु प्रवतेव द्रवन्तं विश्वः पूरुर्मदति हर्षमाणः।
पदिभर्गृध्यन्तं मेधयुं न शूरं रथतुरं वातमिव ध्रजन्तम्॥

यः स्मारुन्धानो गध्या समत्सु सनुतरश्चरति गोपु गच्छन्।
आवित्र्ऋजीको विदथा निचिक्यत् तिरो अरति पर्याप आयोः॥

उत स्मैनं वस्त्रमथिं न तायुनमु क्रोशन्ति क्षितयो भरेषु।
नीचायमानं जसुरिं न श्येनं श्रवश्चाच्छा पशुमच्च यूथम्॥

उत स्मासु प्रथमः सरिष्यन् नि वेवेति श्रेणिभी रथानाम्।
स्रजं कृण्वानो जन्यो न शुभ्वा रेणुं रेरिहत् किरणं ददश्वान्॥

उत स्य वाजी सहुरिर्ऋतावा शुश्रूषमाणस्तन्वा समर्ये।
तुरं यतीषु तुरयन्नृजिप्यो ऽधि भ्रुवोः किरते रेणुमृञ्जन्॥

उत स्मास्य तन्यतोरिव घ्रोर्ऋघायतो अभियुजो भयन्ते।
यदा सहस्रमभिषीमयोधीद् दुर्वर्तुः स्मा भवति भीम ऋञ्जन्॥

उत स्मास्य पनयन्ति जना जूतिं कृष्टिप्रो अभिभूतिमाशोः।
उतैनमाहुः समिथे वियन्तः परा दधिक्रा असरत् सहस्रैः॥

आ दधिक्राः शवसा पञ्च कृष्टीः सूर्य इव ज्योतिषापस्ततान।
सहस्रसाः शतसा वाज्यर्वा पृणक्तु मध्वा समिमा वचांसि॥

1. From you two came the gifts in days aforetime which
   Trasadasyu granted to the Purus.

   Ye gave the winner of our fields and plough-lands,
   and the strong smiter who subdued the Dasyus.

2. And ye gave mighty Dadhikras, the giver of many
   gifts, who visiteth all people,

   Impetuous hawk, swift and of varied colour, like
   a brave King whom each true man must honour.

3. Whom, as 'twere down a precipice, swift rushing,
   each Pure praises and his heart rejoices,—

   Springing forth like a hero fain for battle, whirling
   the car and flying like the tempest.

4. Who gaineth precious booty in the combats and
   moveth, winning spoil, among the cattle;

   Shown in bright colour, looking on the assemblies,
   beyond the churl, to worship of the living.

5. Loudly the folk cry after him in battles, as 'twere
   a thief who steals away a garment;

   Speeding to glory, or a herd of cattle, even as
   a hungry falcon swooping downward.

6. And, fain to come forth first amid these armies,
   this way and that with rows of cars he rushes,

   Gay like a bridesman, making him a garland,
   tossing the dust, champing the rein that holds him.

7. And that strong Steed, victorious and faithful,
   obedient with his body in the combat,

   Speeding straight on amid the swiftly pressing,
   casts o'er his brows the dust he tosses upward.

8. And at his thunder, like the roar of heaven, those
   who attack tremble and are affrighted;

   For when he fights against embattled thousands,
   dread is he in his striving; none may stay him.

9. The people praise the overpowering swiftness of
   this fleet Steed who giveth men abundance.

   Of him they say when drawing back from battle.
   Dadhikras hath sped forward with his thousands.

10. Dadhikras hath o'erspread the Fivefold People with
    vigour, as the Sun lightens the waters.

May the strong Steed who winneth hundreds, thousands, requite with sweetness these my words and praises.

(IV/38)

Gavah: Cows

-.-

Bharadwaj

आ गावो अग्मन्नुत भद्रमक्रन् त्सीदन्तु गोष्ठे रणयन्त्वस्मे।
प्रजावती: पुरुरूपा इह स्युरिन्द्राय पूर्वीरुषसो दुहाना:॥
इन्द्रो यज्वने पृणते च शिक्षत्युपेद् ददाति न स्वं मुषायति।
भूयोभूयो रयिमिदस्य वर्धयन्नभिन्ने खिल्ये नि दधाति देवयुम्॥
न ता नशन्ति न दभाति तस्करो नासामामित्रो व्यथिरा दधर्षति।
देवाँश्च याभिर्यजते ददाति च ज्योगित् ताभि: सचते गोपति: सह॥
न ता अर्वा रेणुककाटो अश्नुते न संस्कृतत्रमुप यन्ति ता अभि।
उरुगामयभयं तस्य ता अनु गावो मर्तस्य क्विरन्ति यज्वन:॥
गावो भगो गाव इन्द्रो में अच्छान् गाव: सोमस्य प्रथमस्य भक्ष:।
इमा या गाव: स जनास इन्द्र इच्छामीद्धृदा मनसा चिदिन्द्रम्॥
यूयं गावो मेदयथा कृशं चिदश्रीरं चित् कृणुथा सुप्रतीकम्।
भद्रं गृहं कृणुथ भद्रवाचो बृहद् वो वय उच्यते सभासु॥
प्रजावती: सूर्यवसं रिशन्ती: शुद्ध अप: सुप्रपाणे पिबन्ती:।
मा व: स्तेन ईशत माघशंस: परि वो हेती रुद्रस्य वृज्या:॥
उपेदमुपपर्चनमासु गोषूप पृच्यताम्।
उप ऋषभस्य रेतस्युपेन्द्र तव वीर्ये॥

1. The Kine have come and brought good fortune: let them rest in the cow-pen and be happy near us.

   Here let them stay prolific, many-coloured, and yield through many morns their milk for Indra.

2. Indra aids him who offers sacrifice and gifts: he takes not what is his, and gives him more thereto.

   Increasing ever more and ever more his wealth, he makes the pious dwell within unbroken bounds.

3. These are ne'er lost, no robber ever injures them: no evil-minded foe attempts to harass them.

   The master of the Kine lives many a year with these, the cows whereby he pours his gifts and serves the Gods.

4. The charger with his dusty brow o'ertakes them not, and never to the shambles do they take their way.

   These Cows, the cattle of the pious worshipper, roam over widespread pasture where no danger is.

5. To me the Cows seem Bhaga, they seem Indra, they seem a portion of the first poured Soma,

   These present Cows, they, O ye men, are Indra. I long for Indra with my heart and spirit.

6. O Cows, ye fatten e'en the worn and wasted, and make the unlovely beautiful to look on.

   Prosper my house, ye with auspicious voices. Your power is glorified in our assemblies.

7. Crop goodly pasturage and be prolific: drink pure sweet water at good drinking places.

   Never be thief or sinful man your master, and may the dart of Rudra still avoid you.

8. Now let this close admixture be close intermigled with these Cows,

Mixt with the Steer's prolific flow, and, Indra, with thy hero might.

(VI/28)

Mandukah: Frogs

Vasishtha

संवत्सरं शशयाना ब्राह्मणा व्रतचारिण:।
वाचं पर्जन्यजिन्वितां प्र मण्डूका अवादिषु:॥

दिव्या आपो अभि यदेनमायन् दृतिं न शुष्कं सरसी शयानम्।
गवामह न मायुर्वत्सिनीनां मण्डूकानां वग्नुरत्रा समेति॥

यदीमेनाँ उशतो अभ्यवर्षीत् तृष्यावत: प्रावृष्यागतायाम्।
अक्खलीकृत्या पितरं न पुत्रो अन्यो अन्यमुप वदन्तमेति॥

अन्यो अन्यमनु गृभ्णात्येनोरपां प्रसर्गे यदमन्दिपाताम्।
मण्डूको यद्भिवृष्ट: कनिष्कन् पृश्नि: संपृङ्क हरितेन वाचम्॥

यदेषामन्यो अन्यस्य वाचं शाक्तस्येव वदति शिक्षमाण:।
सर्वं तदेषां समृधेव पर्व यत् सुवाचो वदथनाध्यप्सु॥

गोमायुरेको अजमायुरेक: पृश्निरेको हरित एक एषाम्।
समानं नाम बिभ्रतो विरूपा: पुरुत्रा वाचं पिपिशुर्वदन्त:॥

ब्राह्मणासो अतिरात्रे न सोमे सगे न पूर्णमभितो वदन्त:।
संवत्सरस्य तदह: परिष्ठ यन्मण्डूका: प्रावृषीणं बभूव॥

ब्राह्मणास: सोमिनो वाचमक्रत ब्रह्म कृण्वन्त: परिवत्सरीणम्॥
अध्वर्यवो घर्मिण: सिष्विदाना आविर्भवन्ति गुह्या न के चित्।
देवहितिं जुगुपुर्द्वादशस्य ऋतुं नगे न प्र मिनन्त्येते॥

संवत्सरे प्रावृष्यागतायां तप्ता घर्मा अश्नुवते विसर्गम्।

गोमायुरदादजमायुरदात् पृश्निरदाद्धरितो नो वसूनि॥
गवां मण्डूका ददत: शतानि सहस्रसावे प्र तिरन्त आयु:।

1. They who lay quiet for a year, the Brahmans who fulfil their vows,

   The Frogs have lifted up their voice, the voice Parjanya hath inspired.

2. What time on these, as on a dry skin lying in the pool's bed, the floods of heaven descended,

   The music of the Frogs comes forth in concert like the cows lowing with their calves beside them.

3. When at the coming of the Rains the water has poured upon them as they yearned and thirsted,

   One seeks another as he talks and greets him with cries of pleasure as a son his father.

4. Each of these twain receives the other kindly, while they are revelling in the flow of waters,

   When the Frog moistened by the rain springs forward, and Green and Spotty both combine their voices.

5. When one of these repeats the other's language, as he who learns the lesson of the teacher,

   Your every limb seems to be growing larger as ye converse with eloquence on the waters.

6. One is Cow-bellow and Goat-bleat the other, one Frog is Green and one of them is Spotty.

   They bear one common name, and yet they vary, and, talking, modulate the voice diversely.

7. As Brahmins, sitting round the brimful vessel, talk at the Soma-rite of Atiratra,

So, Frogs, ye gather round the pool to honour this day of all the year, the first of Rain-time.

8. These Brahmins with the Soma juice, performing their year-long rite, have lifted up their voices;

   And these Adhvaryus, sweating with their kettles, come forth and show themselves, and none are hidden.

9. They keep the twelve month's God appointed order, and never do the men neglect the season.

   Soon as the Rain-time in the year returneth, these who were heated kettles gain their freedom.

10. Cow-bellow and Goat-bleat have granted riches, and Green and Spotty have vouchsafed us treasure.

   The Frogs who give us cows in hundreds lengthen our lives in this most fertilizing season.

   (VII/103)

Aayudha: Weapons of War

-.-

Payu

जीमूतस्येव भवति प्रतीकं यद् वर्मी याति समदामुपस्थे।
अनाविद्धया तन्वा जय त्वं स त्वा वर्मणो महिमा पिपर्तु॥
धन्वना गा धन्वनाजिं जयेम धन्वना तीव्रा: समदो जयेम।
धनु: शत्रोरपकामं कृणोति धन्वना सर्वा: प्रदिशो जयेम॥
वक्ष्यन्तीवेदा गनीगन्ति कर्ण प्रियं सखायं परिषस्वजाना।
योषेव शिङ्क्ते वितताधि धन्वज्ज्या इयं समने पारयन्ती॥
ते आचरन्ती समनेव योषा मातेव पुत्रं बिभृतामुपस्थे।

अप शत्रून् विध्यतां संविदाने आर्ती इमे विष्फुरन्ती अमित्रान्॥

बह्वीनां पिता बहुरस्य पुत्रश्चिच्चा कृणोति समनावगत्य।

इषुधिः सङ्काः पृतनाश्च सर्वाः पृष्ठे निनद्धो जयति प्रसूतः॥

रथे तिष्ठन् नयति वाजिनः पुरो यत्रयत्र कामयते सुषारथिः।

अभीशूनां महिमानं पनायत मनः पश्चादनु यच्छन्ति रश्मयः॥

तीव्रान् घोषान् कृण्वते वृषपाणयो ऽश्वा रथेभिः सह वाजयन्तः।

अवक्रामन्तः प्रपदैरमित्रान् क्षिणन्ति शत्रूँरनपव्ययन्तः॥

रथवाहनं हविरस्य नाम यत्रायुधं निहितमस्य वर्म।

तत्रा रथमुप शग्मं सदेम क्ष्वाहा वयं सुमनस्यमानाः॥

स्वादुर्षसदः पितरो वयोधाः कृच्छ्रेश्रितः शक्तीवन्तो गभीराः।

चित्रसेना इषुबला अमृध्राः सतोवीरा उव्रो व्रातसाहाः॥

ब्राह्मणासः पितरः सोम्यासः शिवे नो द्यावापृथिवी अनेहसा।

पूषा नः पातु दुरितादृतावृधो रक्षा माकिनों अधशंस ईशत॥

सुपर्णं वस्ते मृगो अस्या दन्तो गोभिः संनद्धा पतति प्रसूता।

यत्रा नरः सं च वि च द्रवन्ति तत्रास्मभ्यमिषवः शर्म यंसन्॥

ऋजीते परि वृङ्धि नो ऽस्मा भवतु नस्तनूः।

सोमो अधि ब्रवीतु नो ऽदितिः शर्म यच्छतु॥

आ जङ्घन्ति सान्वेषां जघनाँ उप जिघ्नते।

अश्वाजनि प्रचेतसो ऽश्वान् त्समत्सु चोदय॥

अहिरिव भोगैः पर्येति बाहुं ज्याया हेतिं परिबाधमानः।

हस्तघ्नोविश्वा वयुनानि विद्वान् पुमान् पुमांसं परि पातु विश्वतः॥

आलाक्ता या रुरुशीष्ण्यथो यस्या अयो मुखम्।

इदं पर्जन्यरेतस इष्वै देव्यै बृहन्नमः॥

अवसृष्टा परा पत शरव्ये ब्रह्मसंशिते।

गच्छामित्रान् प्र पद्यस्व प्र पद्यस्व मामीषां कं चनोच्छिषः॥

यत्र बाणाः संपतन्ति कुमारा विशिखा इव।

तत्रा नो ब्रह्मणस्पतिरदितिः शर्म यच्छतु विश्वाहा शर्म यच्छतु॥

मर्माणि ते वर्मणा छादयामि सोमस्त्वा राजामृतेनानु वस्ताम्।

उरोर्वरीयो वरुणस्ते कृणोतु जयन्तं त्वानु देवा मदन्तु॥

यो नः स्वो अरणो य श्वनिष्ट्यो जिघांसति।
देवास्तं सर्वे धूर्वन्तु ब्रह्म वर्म म मान्तरम्॥

1. The warrior's look is like a thunderous rain-cloud's,
   when, armed with mail, he seeks the lap of battle.

   Be thou victorious with unwounded body: so let
   the thickness of thy mail protect thee.

2. With Bow let us win kine, with Bow the battle, with
   Bow be victors in our hot encounters.

   The Bow brings grief and sorrow to the foeman:
   armed with the Bow may we subdue all regions.

3. Close to his ear, as fain to speak, She presses,
   holding her well-loved Friend in her embraces.

   Strained on the Bow, She whispers like a woman—
   this bowstring that preserves us in the combat.

4. These, meeting like a woman and her lover, bear,
   mother-like, their child upon their bosom.

   May the two Bow-ends starting swift asunder, scatter, in unison, the foes who hate us.

5. With many a son, father of many daughters, He
   clangs and clashes as he goes to battle.

   Slung on the back, pouring his brood, the Quiver
   vanquishes all opposing bands and armies.

6. Upstanding in the Car the skilful Charioteer guides
   his strong Horses on whithersoe'er he will.

   See and admire the strength of those controlling
   Reins which from behind declare the will of him
   who drives.

7. Horses whose hoofs rain dust are neighing loudly,
   yoked to the Chariots, showing forth their vigour,

   With their forefeet descending on the foemen,

they, never flinching, trample and destroy them.

8. Car-bearer is the name of his oblation, whereon are laid his Weapons and his Armour.

So let us here, each day that passes, honour the helpful Car with hearts exceeding joyful.

9. In sweet association lived the fathers who gave us life, profound and strong in trouble,

Unwearied, armed with shafts and wondrous weapons, free, real heroes, conquerors of armies.

10. The Brahmins, and the Fathers meet for Soma-draughts, and, graciously inclined, unequalled Heaven and Earth.

Guard us from evil, Pusan, guard us strengtheners of Law: let not the evil-wisher master us.

11. Her tooth a deer, dressed in an eagle's feathers, bound with cow-hide, launched forth, She flieth onward.

There where the heroes speed hither and thither, there may the Arrows shelter and protect us.

12. Avoid us thou whose flight is straight, and let our bodies be as stone.

May Soma kindly speak to us, and Aditi protect us well.

13. He lays his blows upon their backs, he deals his blows upon their thighs.

Thou, Whip, who urgest horses, drive sagacious horses in the fray.

14. It compasses the arm with serpent windings, fending away the friction of the bowstrings,

So may the Brace, well-skilled in all its duties, guard manfully the man from every quarter.

15. Now to the Shaft with venom smeared, tipped with deer-horn, with iron mouth,

    Celestial, of Parjanya's seed, be this great adoration paid.

16. Loosed from the Bowstring fly away, thou Arrow, sharpened by our prayer.

    Go to the foemen, strike them home, and let not one be left alive.

17. There where the flights of Arrows fall like boys whose locks are yet unshorn.

    Even there may Brahmanaspati, and Aditi protect us well, protect us well through all our days.

18. Thy vital parts I cover with thine Armour: with immortality King Soma clothe thee.

    Varuna give thee what is more than ample, and in thy triumph may the Gods be joyful.

19. Whoso would kill us, whether he be a strange foe or one of us,

    May all the Gods discomfit him. My nearest, closest Mail is prayer.

                              (VI/75)

Nirrati: Goddess of Death and Destruction

-.-

Bandhu

प्र तार्यायुः प्रतरं नवीयः स्थातारेव क्रतुमता रथस्य।
अध च्यवान उत् तवीत्यर्थं परातरं सु निर्ऋतिर्जिहीताम्॥
सामन् नु राये निधिमन्नवत्रं करामहे सु पुरुध श्रवांसि।
ता नो विश्वानि जरिता ममत्तु परातरं सु निर्ऋतिर्जिहीताम्॥

अभीष्व१र्यः पौंस्यैर्भवेम द्यौर्न भूमिं गिरयो नाज्रान्।
ता नो विश्वानि जरिता चिकेत परातरं सु निर्ऋतिर्जिहीताम्॥
मोयुणः सोम मृत्यवे परा दाः पश्येम नु सूर्यमुच्चरन्तम्॥
द्युभिर्हितो जरिमा सू नो अस्तु परातरं सु निर्ऋतिर्जिहीताम्।
असुनीते मनो अस्मासु धारय जीवातवे सुप्र तिरा न आयुः॥
रारन्धि नः सूर्यस्य संदृशि घृतेन त्वं तन्वं वर्धयस्व।
असुनीते पुनरस्मासु चक्षुः पुनः प्राणमिह नो धेहि भोगम्॥
ज्योक् पश्येम सूर्यमुच्चरन्तमनुमते मृळया नः स्वस्ति।
पुनर्नो असुं पृथिवी ददातु पुनर्द्यौर्देवी पुनरन्तरिक्षम्॥
पुनर्नः सोमस्तन्वं ददातु पुनः पूषा पथ्यां३ या स्वस्तिः।
शं रोदसी सुबन्धवे यह्वी ऋतस्य मातरा॥
भरतामप यद्रपो द्यौः पृथिवि क्षमा रपो मो पु ते किं चनाममत्।
अव द्वके अव त्रिका दिवश्चरन्ति भेषजा॥
क्षमा चरिष्ण्वेककं भरतामप यद्रपो द्यौः पृथिवि क्षमा रपो
मो पु ते किं चनाममत्।
समिन्द्रेरय गामनड्डाहं य आवहदुशीनराण्या अनः।
भरतामप यद्रपो द्यौः पृथिवि क्षमा रपो मो पु ते किं चनाममत्॥

1. His life hath been renewed and carried forward as
   two men, car-borne, by the skilful driver.

   One falls, then seeks the goal with quickened
   vigour. Let Nirrti depart to distant places.

2. Here is the psalm for wealth, and food, in plenty:
   let us do many deeds to bring us glory.

   All these our doings shall delight the singer. Let
   Nirrti depart to distant places.

3. May we o'ercome our foes with acts of valour, as
   heaven is over earth, hills over lowlands.

   All these our deeds the singer hath considered.
   Let Nirrati depart to distant places.

4. Give us not up as prey to death. O Soma: still let us look upon the Sun arising.

   Let our old age with passing days be kindly. Let Nirrti depart to distant places.

5. O Asuniti, keep the soul within us, and make the days we have to live yet longer.

   Grant that we still may look upon the sunlight: strengthen thy body with the oil we bring thee.

6. Give us our sight again, O Asuniti, give us again our breath and our enjoyment. Long may we look upon the Sun uprising; O Asuniti, favour thou and bless us.

7. May Earth restore to us our vital spirit, may Heaven the Goddess and mid-air restore it.

   May Soma give us once again our body, and Pusan show the Path of peace and comfort.

8. May both Worlds bless Subandhu, young Mothers of everlasting Law.

   May Heaven and Earth uproot and sweep iniquity and shame away: nor sin nor sorrow trouble thee.

9. Health-giving medicines descend sent down from heaven in twos and threes, Or wandering singly on the earth.

   May Heaven and Earth uproot and sweep iniquity and shame away : nor sin nor sorrow trouble thee.

10. Drive forward thou the wagon-ox, O Indra, which brought Usinarani's wagon hither.

    May Heaven and Earth uproot and sweep iniquity and shame away: nor sin nor sorrow trouble thee.

(X/59)

LIFE

Usas: Dawn

Praskanva

सह वामन न उषो व्युच्छा दुहितर्दिव:।
सह द्युम्नेन बृहता विभावरि राया देवि दास्वती॥
अश्वावतीर्गोमतीर्विश्वसुविदो भूरि च्यवन्त वस्तवे।
उदीरय प्रति मा सूनृता उषश् चोद राधो मघोनाम्॥
उवासोषा उच्छाच्च नु देवी जीरा रथानाम्।
ये अस्या आचरणेषु दध्रिरे समुद्रे न श्रवस्यव:॥
उषो ये ते प्र यामेचु युञ्जते मनो दानाय सूरय:।
पत्राह तत् कण्व एषां कण्वतमो नाम गृणाति नृणाम्॥
आ घा योषेव सूनर्युषा याति प्रभुञ्जती।
जरयन्ती वृजनं प्रद्वदीयत् उत्पातयति पक्षिण:॥
वे या सृजति समनं व्यश्र्थिन: पदं न वेत्योदती।
वयो नकिष्टे पप्तिवांस आसते व्युष्टौ वाजिनीवति॥
एषायुक्त परावत: सूर्यस्योदयनादधि।
शतं रथेभि: सुभगोषा इयं वि यात्यभि मानुपान॥
विश्वमस्या नानाम् चक्षसे जगज् ज्योतिष्कृणोति सूनरी।
अप द्वेषो मघोनी दुहिता दिव उषा उच्छदप स्निध:॥
उष आ भाहि भानुना चन्द्रेण दुहितर्दिव:।

आवहन्ती भूर्यस्मभ्यं सौभगं व्युछन्ती दिविष्टिषु॥
विश्वस्य हि प्राणनं जीवनं त्वे वि यदुच्छसि सूनरि।
सा नो रथेनबृहता विभावरि श्रुधि चित्रामघे हवम्॥
उषोवाजं हि वंस्व यश्चिवत्रो मानुषे जने।
तेना वह सुकृतो अध्वरॉँ उप ये त्वा गृणन्ति बाह्यः॥
विश्वान् देवाँ आ वह सोमपीतये ऽन्तरिक्षादुपस्त्वम्।
सास्मासु धा गोमद्श्वावटुकथ्यऽमुषो वाजं सुवीर्यम्॥
यस्या रुषन्तो अर्चयः प्रति भद्रा अदृक्षत।
सा नो रयिं क्विश्ववारं सुपेश समुषा ददातु सुग्म्यम्॥
ये चिद्धि त्वामृयः पूर्व ऊतये जुहूरेऽवसे महि।
सा नः स्तोमाँ अभि गृणीहि राधसोष: शुक्रेण शोचिपा॥
उज्ञो यद्घ भानुना वि द्वारावृणवो दिवः।
प्र नो यच्छताद् वृकं पृथु च्छर्दिः प्र देवि गोमतीरिपः॥
सं नो राया बृहता विश्वपेशसा मिमिक्ष्वा समिळाभिरा।
सं द्युम्नेन क्विश्वतुरोषो महि सं वाजेवाजिनीवति॥

1. Dawn on us with prosperity, O Usas, Daughter of
   the Sky,

   Dawn with great Glory, Goddess, Lady of the Light,
   dawn thou with riches, Bounteous One.

2. They, bringing steeds and kine, boongivers of all
   wealth, have oft spedforth to lighten us.

   O Usas, waken up for me the sounds of joy: send
   us the riches of the great.

3. Usas hath dawned, and now shall dawn,the Goddess,
   driver forth of cars

   Which, as she cometh nigh, have fixed their thought
   on her, like glory-seekers on the flood.

4. Here Kanva, chief of Kanva's race, sings forth aloud
   the glories of the heroes' names,—

The princes who, O Usas, as thou comest near, direct their thoughts to liberal gifts.

5. Like a good matron Usas comes carefully tending everything:

    Rousing all life she stirs all creatures that have feet, and makes the birds of air fly up.

6. She sends the busy forth, each man to his pursuit: delay she knows not as she springs.

    O rich in opulence, after thy dawning birds that have flown forth no longer rest.

7. This Dawn hath yoked her steeds afar, beyond the rising of the Sun:

    Borne on a hundred chariots she, auspicious Dawn, advances on her way to men.

8. To meet her glance all living creatures bend them down: Excellent One, she makes the light.

    Usas, the Daughter of the Sky, the opulent, shines foes and enmities away.

9. Shine on us with thy radiant light, O Usas, Daughter of the Sky,

    Bringing to us great store of high felicity, and beaming on our solemn rites.

10. For in thee is each living creature's breath and life, when, Excellent! thou dawnest forth.

    Borne on thy lofty car, O Lady of the Light, hear, thou of wondrous wealth, our call.

11. O Usas, win thyself the strength which among men is wonderful.

    Bring thou thereby the pious unto holy rites, those who as priests sing praise to thee.

12. Bring from the firmament, O Usas, all the Gods, that they may drink our Soma juice,

And, being what thou art, vouchsafe us kine and steeds, strength meet for praise and hero might.

13. May Usas whose auspicious rays are seen resplendent round about,

Grant us great riches, fair in form, of all good things, wealth which light labour may attain.

14. Mighty One, whom the Rishis of old time invoked for their protection and their help,

O Usas, graciously answer our songs of praise with bounty and with brilliant light.

15. Usas, as thou with light today hast opened the twin doors of heaven,

So grant thou us a dwelling wide and free from foes. O Goddess, give us food with kine.

16. Bring us to wealth abundant, sent in every shape, to plentiful refreshing food,

To all-subduing splendour, Usas, Mighty One, to strength, thou rich in spoil and wealth.

(I/48)

Ratri: Night

-.-

Kushika

रात्री व्यख्यदायती पुरुत्रा देव्यंश्रभिः। विश्वा अधि श्रियोऽधित।
ओर्वप्रा अमर्त्या निवतो देव्युंश्रद्वतः। ज्योतिषा बाधते तमः॥
निरु स्वसारमस्कृतोषसं देव्यायती। अपेदु हासते तमः।

सा नो अद्य यस्या वयं नि ते यामन्नविक्ष्महि। वृक्षे न वसतिं वयः॥
नि ग्रामासो अविक्षत् नि पद्वन्तो नि पक्षिणः। नि श्येनासश्चिदर्थिनः।
यावया वृक्यं१ वृकं यवय स्तेनमूर्म्ये। अथा नः सुतरा भव॥
उप मा पेपशत् तमः कृष्णं व्यक्तमस्थित। उष ऋणेव यातय।
उप ते गा इवाकरं वृणीष्व दुहितर्दिवः। रात्रि स्तोमं न जिग्युषे॥

1. With all her eyes the Goddess Night looks forth approaching many a spot:

   She hath put all her glories on.

2. Immortal she hath filled the waste, the Goddess hath filled height and depth:

   She conquers darkness with her light.

3. The Goddess as she comes hath set the Dawn her Sister in her place:

   And then the darkness vanishes.

4. So favour us this night, O thou whose pathways we have visited

   As birds their nest upon the tree.

5. The villagers have sought their homes, and all that walks and all that flies,

   Even the falcons fain for prey.

6. Keep off the she-wolf and the wolf; O Urmya, keep the thief away;

   Easy be thou for us to pass.

7. Clearly hath she come nigh to me who decks the dark with richest hues:

   O Morning, cancel it like debts.

8. These have I brought to thee like kine. O Night, thou Child of Heaven, accept

   This laud as for a conqueror.

(X/127)

Nadyah: Rivers

‑.‑‑

Sindhukshit

The poet addresses first the most distant rivers. *Ganga:* the Ganges is mentioned, indirectly, in only one other verse of the Rigveda, and even there, the word is said by some to be the name of a woman. *Yamuna:* the Jumna. *Sutudri:* the Sutlej. *Parusni:* the Ravi. *Sarasvati: Asikni:* the ancient Acesines: the Vedic name of the Chandrabhaga, the present Chenab. *Vitasta:* Jhelum, the Hydaspes of the Greeks. *Marudvrdha:* meaning, increased by the Maruts: not identified. *Arjikiya* and *Susoma* are said by Yaska to be the Vipasa and the Sindhu; but this is not possible, and it is uncertain what rivers are meant; *Kubha, Krumu,* and *Gomati.* The other streams whose names occur in this stanza are probably unimportant affluents of the Indus.

प्र सु व आपो महिमानमुत्तमं कारुर्वोचाति सदने विवस्वतः।
प्र सप्तसप्त त्रेधा हि चक्रमुः प्र सृत्वरीणामति सिन्धुरोजसा।।
प्र तेऽरदद्वरुणो यातवे पथः सिन्धो यद्व्राजाँ अभ्यद्रवस्त्वम्।
भूम्या अधि प्रवता यासि सानुना यदेषामग्रं जगतामिरज्यसि।।
दिवि स्वनो यतते भूम्योपर्यनन्तं शुष्ममुदियर्ति भानुना।
अभ्रादिव प्र स्तनयन्ति वृष्टयः सिन्धुर्यदेति वृषभो न रोरुवत्।।
अभि त्वा सिन्धो शिशुमिन्न मातरो वाश्रा अर्षन्ति पयसेव धेनवः।
राजेव युध्वा नयसि त्वमित् सिचौ यदासामग्रं प्रवतामिनक्षसि।।
इमं मे गङ्गे यमुने सरस्वति शुतुद्रि स्तोमं सचता परुष्ण्या।
असिक्न्या मद्वृधे वितस्तया ऽऽर्जीकीये श्टणुह्वा सुषोमया।।
तुष्टामया प्रथमं यातवे सजूः सुसर्त्वा रसया श्वेत्या त्या।
त्वं सिन्धो कुभया गोमती क्रुमुं मेहत्वा सरथं याभिरीयसे।
ऋजीत्येनी रुषती महित्वा परि जयांसि भरते रजांसि।

अदब्धा सिन्धुरपसामपस्तमा ऽश्वा न चित्रा वपुषीव दर्शता॥

स्वश्वा सिन्धुः सुरथा सुवासा हिरण्ययी सुकृता वाजिनीवती।

ऊर्णावती युवतिः सीलमावत्युताधि वस्ते सुभगा मधुवृधम्॥

सुखं रथं युयुजे सिन्धुरश्विनं तेन वाजं सनिषद्स्मिन्नाजौ।

महान् ह्यस्य महिमा पनस्यते ऽदब्धस्य स्वयशसो विरप्शिनः॥

1. The singer, O ye Waters in Vivasvan's place, shall tell your grandeur forth that is beyond compare.

    The Rivers have come forward triply, seven and seven. Sindhu in might surpasses all the streams that flow.

2. Varuna cut the channels for thy forward course, O Sindhu, when thou rannest on to win the race.

    Thou speedest o'er precipitous ridges of the earth, when thou art Lord and Leader of these moving floods.

3. His roar is lifted up to heaven above the earth: he puts forth endless vigour with a flash of light.

    Like floods of rain that fall in thunder from the cloud, so Sindhu rushes on bellowing like a bull.

4. Like mothers to their calves, like milch kine with their milk, so, Sindhu, unto thee the roaring rivers run.

    Thou leadest as a warrior king thine army's wings what time thou comest in the van of these swift streams.

5. Favour ye this my laud, O Ganga, Yamuna, O Sutudri, Parusni and Sarasvati:

    With Asikni, Vitasta, O Marudvridha, O Arjikiya with Susoma hear my call.

6. First with Tristama thou art eager to flow forth, with Rasa, and Susartu, and with Svetya here,

With Kubha; and with these, Sindhu! and Mehatnu,
thou seekest in thy course Krumu and Gomati.

7. Flashing and whitely-gleaming in her mightiness, she
moves along her ample volumes through the realms,

Most active of the active, Sindhu unrestrained, like
a dappled mare, beautiful fair to see.

8. Rich in good steeds is Sindhu, rich in cars and robes,
rich in gold, nobly-fashioned, rich in ample wealth.

Blest Silamavati and young Urnavati invest
themselves with raiment rich in store of sweets.

9. Sindhu hath yoked her car, light-rolling, drawn by
steeds, and with that car shall she win booty in this
fight.

So have I praised its power, mighty and
unrestrained, of independent glory, roaring as it runs.

(X/75)

Aranyani: The Forest Goddess

-.-

Airammada

अरण्यान्यरण्यान्यसौ या प्रेव नश्यसि।
कथा ग्रामं न पृच्छसि न त्वा भीरिव विन्दतीइँ॥
वृषारवाय वदते यदुपावति चिच्चिकः।
आघाटिभिरिव धावयन्नरण्यानिर्महीयते॥
उत गावइवादन्त्युत वेश्मेव दृश्यते।
उतो अरण्यानिः सायं शकटीरिव सर्जति॥
गामङ्गैष आ ह्वयति दार्वङ्गैषो अपावधीत्।

वसन्नरण्यान्यां सायमक्रुक्षदिति मन्यते ॥

न वा अरण्यानिर्हन्त्यन्यश्चेन्नाभिगच्छति।

स्वादो: फलस्य जग्ध्वाय यथाकामं नि पद्यते॥

आञ्जनगन्धिं सुरभिं बह्वन्नामकृषीवलाम्।

प्राहं मृगाणां मातरं मरण्यानिमशंसिषम्॥

1. Goddess of wild and forest who seemest to vanish from the sight.

    How is it that thou seekest not the village? Art thou not afraid?

2. What time the grasshopper replies and swells the shrill cicala's voice,

    Seeming to sound with tinkling bells, the Lady of the Wood exults.

3. And, yonder, cattle seem to graze, what seems a dwelling-place appears:

    Or else at eve the Lady of the Forest seems to free the wains.

4. Here one is calling to his cow, another there hath felled a tree:

    At eve the dweller in the wood fancies that somebody hath screamed.

5. The Goddess never slays, unless some murderous enemy approach.

    Man eats of savoury fruit and then takes, even as he wills, his rest.

6. Now have I praised the Forest Queen, sweet-scented, redolent of balm,

    The Mother of all sylvan things, who tills not but hath stores of food.

(X/146)

Annam: Food

-.-

Atri

पितुं नु स्तोषं महो धर्माणं तविषीम्।
यस्य त्रितो व्योजसा वृत्रं विपर्वमर्दयत्॥
स्वादो पितो मधो पितो वयं त्वा ववृमहे।
अस्माकमविता   भव॥
उप नः पितवा चर शिवः शिवाभिरूतिभिः।
मयोभुरद्विषेण्यः सखा सुशेवो अद्वयाः॥
तव त्ये पितो रसा रजांस्यनु विष्ठिताः।
दिवि   वाता   इव   श्रिताः॥
तव त्ये पितो ददतस्तव स्वादिष्ठ ते पितो।
प्र स्वाद्मानो रसानां तुविग्रीवा इवेरते॥
त्वे पितोमहानां देवानां मनो हितम्।
अकारि चारु केतुना तवाहिमवसावधीत्॥
यद्दो पितो अजगन् विवस्व पर्वतानाम्।
अत्रा चिन्नो मधो पितो ऽरं भक्षाय गम्याः॥
यद्पामोषधीनां   परिंशमारिशामहे।
वातापे   पीव   इद्   भव॥
करम्भ ओषधे भव पीवो वृक्क उदारथिः।
वातापे   पीव   इद्   भव॥
तं त्वा वयं पितो वचोभिर्गावो न हव्या सुषूदिम।
देवेभ्यस्त्वा सधमादमस्मभ्यं त्वा सधमादम्॥

1. Now will I glorify Food that upholds great strength,

   By whose invigorating power Trita rent Vritra limb
   from limb.

2. O pleasant Food, O Food of meath, thee have we chosen for our own,

    So be our kind protector thou.

3. Come hitherward to us, O Food, auspicious with auspicious help,

    Health-bringing, not unkind, a dear and guileless friend.

4. These juices which, O Food, are thine throughout the regions are diffused.

    Like winds they have their place in heaven.

5. These gifts of thine, O Food, O Food most sweet to taste,

    These savours of thy juices work like creatures that have mighty necks.

6. In thee, O Food, is set the spirit of great Gods.

    Under thy flag brave deeds were done: he slew the Dragon with thy help.

7. If thou be gone unto the splendour of the clouds,

    Even from thence, O Food of meath, prepared for our enjoyment, come.

8. Whatever morsel we consume from waters or from plants of earth,

    O Soma, wax thou fat thereby.

9. What, Soma, we enjoy from thee in milky food or barley-brew,

    Vatapi, grow thou fat thereby.

10. O Vegetable, Cake of meal, be wholesome, firm, and strengthening:

    Vatapi, grow thou fat thereby.

11. O Food, from thee as such have we drawn forth
    with lauds, like cows, our sacrificial gifts,

    From thee who banquetest with Gods, from thee
    who banquetest with us.

(I/187)

Aushadhayah: Herbal Medicines

-·-

Atharvan

या ओषधी: पूर्वा जाता देवेभ्यस्त्रियुगं पुरा।
मनै नु बभ्रूणामहं शतं धामानि सप्त च।।
शतं वो अम्ब धामानि सप्त च।
शतं वो अम्ब धामानि सहस्रमुत वो रुह:।।
अधा शतक्रत्वो यूयमिमं मे अगदं कृत।
ओषधी: प्रति मोदध्वं पुष्पवती: प्रसूवरी:।।
अश्वा इव सजित्वरीवीरुध: पारयिष्ण्व:।
ओषधीरिति मातरस्तद्वो देवीरुप ब्रुवे।।
सनेयमश्वं गां वास आत्मानं तव पूरुष।
अश्वत्थे वो निषदनं पर्णे वो वसतिष्कृता।।
गोभाज इत् किलासथ यत् सनवथ पूरुषम्।
यत्रौषधी: समग्मत राजान: समिताविव।।
विप्र: स उच्यते भिषग् रक्षोहामीवचातन:।
अश्वावती सोमावतीमूर्जयन्तीमुदोजसम्।।
आवित्सि सर्वा ओषधीरस्मा अरिष्टतातये।
उच्छुष्मा ओषधीनां गावो गोष्ठादिवेरते।।
धन सनिष्यन्तीनामात्मानं तव पूरुष।
इष्कृतिर्नाम वो माता ऽथो यूयं स्थ निष्कृती:।।

सीरा: पतत्रिणी: स्थन यदामयति निष्कृथ।
अति विश्वा: परिष्ठा: स्तेन इव व्रजमक्रमु:॥
औषधी: प्राचुच्यवुर्यत् किं च तन्वो३ रप:।
यदिमा वाजयन्नहमोषधीर्हस्त आदधे॥
आत्मा यक्ष्मस्य नश्यति पुरा जीवगृभो यथा।
यस्यौषधी: प्रसर्पथाङ्ग मङ्गं परुष्परु:॥
ततो यक्ष्मं वि बाधध्व उग्रो मध्यमशीरिव।
साकं यक्ष्म प्र पत चाषेण किकिदीविना॥
साकं वातस्य ध्राज्या साकं नश्य निहाकया।
अन्या वो अन्यामवत्वन्यान्यस्या उपावत॥
ता: सर्वा: संविदाना इदं मे प्रावता वच:॥
या: फलिनीर्या अफला अपुष्पा याश्चव पुष्पिणी:॥
बृहस्पतिप्रसूतास्ता नो मुञ्चन्त्वंहस:।
मुञ्चन्तु मा शपथ्या३दथो वरुणयादुत॥
अथो यमस्य पड्वीशात् सर्वस्मादेवकिल्बिषात्।
अवपतन्तीरवदन् दिव ओषधयस्परि॥
यं जीवमश्रवामहै न स रिष्याति पूरुष:।
या ओषधी: सोमराज्ञीर्बह्वी: शतविचक्षणा:॥
तासां त्वमस्युत्तमारं कामाय शं हृदे।
या ओषधी: सोमराज्ञीर्विष्ठिता: पृथिवीमनु॥
बृहस्पतिप्रसूता अस्यै सं दत्त वीर्यम्।
मा वो रिषत् खनिता यस्मै चाहं खनाभि व:॥
द्विपच्चतुष्पदस्माकं सर्वमस्त्वनातुरम्।
या श्चेदमुपशृण्वान्ते याश्च दूरं परागता:॥
सर्वा: संगत्य वीरुधो ऽस्यै सं दत्त वीर्यम्।
ओषधय: सं वदन्ते सोमेन सह राज्ञा॥
यस्मै कृणोति ब्राह्मणस्तं राजन् पारयामसि।
त्वमुत्तमास्योषधे तव वृक्षा उपस्तय:॥
उपस्तिरस्तु सो३स्माकं यो अस्माँ अभिदासति।

1. Herbs that sprang up in time of old, three ages earlier than the Gods,—

    Of these, whose hue is brown, will I declare the hundred powers and seven.

2. Ye, Mothers, have a hundred homes, yea, and a thousand are your growths.

    Do ye who have a thousand powers free this my patient from disease.

3. Be glad and joyful in the Plants, both blossoming and bearing fruit,

    Plants that will lead us to success like mares who conquer in the race.

4. Plants, by this name I speak to you, Mothers, to you the Goddesses:

    Steed, cow, and garment may I win, win back thy very self, O man.

5. The Holy Fig tree is your home, your mansion is the Parna tree:

    Winners of cattle shall ye be if ye regain for me this man.

6. He who hath store of Herbs at hand like Kings amid a crowd of men,—

    Physician is that sage's name, fiend-slayer, chaser of disease.

7. Herbs rich in Soma, rich in steeds, in nourishments, in strengthening power,—

    All these have I provided here, that this man may be whole again.

8. The healing virtues of the Plants stream forth like cattle from the stall,—

Plants that shall win me store of wealth, and save thy vital breath, O man.

9. Reliever is your mother's name, and hence Restorers are ye called.

   Rivers are ye with wings that fly: keep far whatever brings disease.

10. Over all fences have they passed, as steals a thief into the fold.

    The Plants have driven from the frame whatever malady was there.

11. When, bringing back the vanished strength, I hold these herbs within my hand,

    The spirit of disease departs ere he can seize upon the life.

12. He through whose frame, O Plants, ye creep member by member, joint by joint,—

    From him ye drive away disease like some strong arbiter of strife.

13. Fly, Spirit of Disease, begone, with the blue jay and kingfisher.

    Fly with the wind's impetuous speed, vanish together with the storm.

14. Help every one the other, lend assistance each of you to each,

    All of you be accordant, give furtherance to this speech of mine.

15. Let fruitful Plants, and fruitless, those that blossom, and the blossomless,

    Urged onward by Brihaspati, release us from our pain and grief;

16. Release me from the curse's plague and woe that comes from Varuna;

Free me from Yama's fetter, from sin and offence against the Gods.

17. What time, descending from the sky, the Plants flew earthward, thus they spake:

No evil shall befall the man whom while he liveth we pervade.

18. Of all the many Plants whose King is Soma, Plants of hundred forms,

Thou art the Plant most excellent, Prompt to the wish, sweet to the heart.

19. O all ye various Herbs whose King is Soma, that o'erspread the earth,

Urged onward by Brihaspati, combine your virtue in this Plant.

20. Unharmed be he who digs you up, unharmed the man for whom I dig:

And let no malady attack biped or quadruped of ours.

21. All Plants that hear this speech, and those that have departed far away,

Come all assembled and confer your healing power upon this Herb.

22. With Soma as their Sovran Lord the Plants hold colloquy and say:

O King, we save from death the man whose cure a Brahmin undertakes.

23. Most excellent of all art thou, O Plant: thy vassals are the trees.

Let him be subject to our power, the man who seeks to injure us.

(X/97)

Shyenah: Falcon

-.

Vamadeva

गर्भे नु सन्नन्वेषामवेदमहं देवानां जनिमानि वि श्वा।
शतं मा पुर आयसीररक्षन्नध श्येनो जवसा निरदीयम्॥
न घा स मामप जोषं जभाराऽभीमासं त्वक्षसा वीर्येण।
ईर्मा पुरंधिरजहादरातीरुत वाताँ अतरच्छूशुवानः॥
अव यच्छ्येनो अस्वनीदध द्योर्वि यद् यदि वात ऊहूः पुरंधिम्।
सृजद् यदस्मा अव ह क्षिपज्ज्यां कृशानुरस्ता मनसा भुरण्यन्॥
ऋजिप्य ईमिन्द्रावतो न भुज्युं श्येनो जभार बृहतो अधि ष्णोः।
अन्तः पतत् पतत्र्यस्य पर्णमध यामनि प्रसित्स्य तद् वेः॥
अध श्वेतं कलशं गोभिरक्तमापिप्यानं मघवा शुक्रमन्थः।
अध्वर्युभिः प्रयतं मध्वो अग्रमिन्द्रो मदाय प्रति धत् पिबध्यै
शूरो मदाय प्रति धत् पिबध्यै॥

1. I, as I lay within the womb, considered all generations of these Gods in order.

   A hundred iron fortresses confined me but forth I flew with rapid speed a Falcon.

2. Not at his own free pleasure did he bear me: he conquered with his strength and manly courage.

   Straightway the Bold One left the fiends behind him and passed the winds as he grew yet more mighty.

3. When with loud cry from heaven down sped the Falcon, thence hasting like the wind he bore the Bold One.

   Then, wildly raging in his mind, the archer Krisanu aimed and loosed the string to strike him.

4. The Falcon bore him from heaven's lofty summit as the swift car of Indra's Friend bore Bhujyu.

   Then downward hither fell a flying feather of the Bird hasting forward in his journey.

5. And now let Maghavan accept the beaker, white, filled with milk, filled with the shining liquid;

   The best of sweet meath which the priests have offered: that Indra to his joy may drink, the Hero, that he may take and drink it to his rapture.

(IV/27)

Dakshina: Priests' Remuneration

Divya

The hymn eulogizes Daksina, the largess, guerdon, or honorarium presented by the institutors of the sacrifices to the priests who perform the ceremonies. The *yajamanas* who give this guerdon liberally are alternatively the deified subjects of the hymn.

आविर्भून्महि माघोनमेषां क्ष्वं जीवं तमसो निरमोचि।
महि ज्योति: पितृभिर्दत्तमागादुरु: पन्था दक्षिणाया अदर्शि॥
उच्चा दिवि दक्षिणावन्तो अस्थुर्ये अश्वदा: सह ते सूर्येण।

हिरण्यदा अमृतत्वं भजन्ते वासोदाः सोम प्र तिरन्त आयुः॥
दैवी पूर्तिर्दक्षिणा देवयज्या न कवारिभ्यो नहि ते पृणन्ति।
अथा नरः प्रयतदक्षिणासो ऽवद्यभिया बहवः पृणन्ति॥
शतधारं वायुमर्कं स्वर्विदं नृचक्षसस्ते अभि चक्षते हविः।
ये पृणन्ति प्र च यच्छन्ति संगमे ते दक्षिणां दुहते सप्तमातरम्॥
दक्षिणावान् प्रथमो हूत एति दक्षिणावान् ग्रामणीरग्रमेति।
तमेव मन्ये नृपतिं जनानां यः प्रथमो दक्षिणामाविवाय॥
तमेव ऋषिं तमु ब्रह्माणमाहुर्यज्ञन्यं सामगामुक्थशासम्।
स शुक्रस्य तन्वो वेद तिस्रो यः प्रथमो दक्षिणया रराध॥
दक्षिणाश्वं दक्षिणा गां ददाति दक्षिणा चन्द्रमुत यद्धिरण्यम्।
दक्षिणान्नं वनुते यो न आत्मा दक्षिणां वर्म कृणुते विजानन्॥
न भोजा ममुर्न न्यर्थमीयुर्न रिष्यन्ति न व्यथन्ते ह भोजाः।
इदं यद्विश्वं भुवनं स्वश्चै तत् सर्वं दक्षिणैभ्यो ददाति॥
भोजा जिग्युः सुरभिं योनिमग्रे भोजा जिग्युर्वध्वंऽ या सुवासाः।
भोजा जिग्युरन्तःपेयं सुराया भोजा जिग्युर्ये अहूताः प्रयन्ति॥
भोजायाश्वं सं मृजन्त्याशुं भोजायास्ते कन्याऽ शुम्भमाना।
भोजस्येदं पुष्करिणीव वेश्म परिष्कृतं देवमानेव चित्रम्॥
भोजमश्वाः सुष्टुवाहो वहन्ति सुवृद्रथो वर्तते दक्षिणायाः।
भोजं देवासोऽवता भरेषु भोजः शत्रून्त्समनीकेषु जेता॥

1. These men's great bounty hath been manifested, and the whole world of life set free from darkness.

   Great light hath come, vouchsafed us by the Fathers: apparent is the spacious path of Guerdon.

2. High up in heaven abide the Guerdon-givers: they who give steeds dwell with the Sun for ever.

   They who give gold are blest with life eternal: they who give robes prolong their lives, O Soma.

3. Not from the niggards—for they give not freely—comes Meed at sacrifice, Gods' satisfaction:

Yea, many men with hands stretched out with Guerdon present their gifts because they dread dishonour.

4. These who observe mankind regard oblation as streamy Vayu and light-finding Arka.

   They satisfy and give their gifts in synod, and pour in streams the seven-mothered Guerdon.

5. He who brings Guerdon comes as first invited: chief of the hamlet comes the Guerdon-bearer.

   Him I account the ruler of the people who was the first to introduce the Guerdon.

6. They call him Rishi, Brahmin, Sama-chanter, reciter of the laud, leader of worship.

   The brightly-shining God's three forms he knoweth who first bestowed the sacrificial Guerdon.

7. Guerdon bestows the horse, bestows the bullock, Guerdon stows, moreover, gold that glistens.

   Guerdon gives food which is our life and spirit. He who is wise takes Guerdon for his armour.

8. The liberal die not, never are they ruined: the liberal suffer neither harm nor trouble.

   The light of heaven, the universe about us,—all this doth sacrificial Guerdon give them.

9. First have the liberal gained a fragrant dwelling, and got themselves a bride in fair apparel.

   The liberal have obtained their draught of liquor, and conquered those who, unprovoked, assailed them.

10. They deck the fleet steed for the bounteous giver: the maid adorns herself and waits to meet him.

    His home is like a lake with lotus blossoms, like the Gods' palaces adorned and splendid.

11. Steeds good at draught convey the liberal giver, and lightly rolling moves the car of Guerdon.

Assist, ye Gods, the liberal man in battles: the liberal giver conquers foes in combat.

(X/107)

Dana: Charity

-.-

Bhikshu

The hymn eulogises Liberality or Bounty in the shape of gifts of wealth and food.

न वा उ देवाः क्षुधामिद्वधं ददुरुताशितमुप गच्छन्ति मृत्यवः।
उतो रयिः पृणतो नोप दस्यत्युतापृणन् मर्डितारं न विन्दते॥
य आध्राय चकमानाय पित्वो ऽन्नवान्त्सन् रफितायोपजग्मुषे।
स्थिरं मनः कृणुते सेवते पुरोतो चित् स मर्डितारं न विन्दते॥
स इद्भोजो यो गृहवे ददात्यन्नकामाय चरते कृशाय।
अरमस्मै भवति यामहूता उतापरीषु कृणुते सखायम्॥
न स सखा यो न ददाति सख्ये सचाभुवे सचमानाय पित्वः।
अपास्मात् प्रेयान्न तदोको अस्ति पृणन्तमन्यमरणं चिदिच्छेत्॥
पृणीयादिन्नाधमानाय तव्यान् द्राघीयांसमनु पश्येत पन्थाम्।
ओ हि वर्तन्ते रथ्येव चक्रा ऽन्यमन्यमुप तिष्ठन्त रायः॥
मोघमन्नं विन्दते अप्रचेताः सत्यं ब्रवीमि वध इत् स तस्य।
नार्यमणं पुष्यति नो सखायं केवलाघो भवति केवलादी॥
कृषन्नित् फाल आशितं कृणोति यन्नध्वानमप वृङ्क्ते चरित्रैः।
वदन् ब्रह्मावदतो वनीयान् पृणन्नापिरपृणन्तमभि ष्यात्॥
एकपाद्भ्यो द्विपदो वि चक्रमे द्विपात् त्रिपादमभ्येति पश्चात्।

चतुष्पादेति द्विपदामभिस्वरे संपश्यन् पङ्क्तीरुपतिष्ठमान:॥
समौ चिद्धस्तौ न समं विविष्ट: संमातरा चित्र समं दुहाते।
यमयौश्रिवन्न समा वीर्याणि ज्ञाती चितसन्तौ न समं पृणीत:॥

1. The Gods have not ordained hunger to be our death:
   even to the well-fed man comes death in varied shape.

   The riches of the liberal never waste away, while
   he who will not give finds none to comfort him.

2. The man with food in store who, when the needy
   comes in miserable case begging for bread to eat,

   Hardens his heart against him—even when of old
   he did him service—finds not one to comfort him.

3. Bounteous is he who gives unto the beggar who comes
   to him in want of food and feeble. .

   Success attends him in the shout of battle. He
   makes a friend of him in future troubles.

4. No friend is he who to his friend and comrade who
   comes imploring food, will offer nothing.

   Let him depart—no home is that to rest in— and
   rather seek a stranger to support him.

5. Let the rich satisfy the poor implorer, and bend his
   eye upon a longer pathway.

   Riches come now to one, now to another, and
   like the wheels of cars are ever rolling.

6. The foolish man wins food with fruitless labour: that
   food—I speak the truth—shall be his ruin.

   He feeds no trusty friend, no man to love him.
   All guilt is he who eats with no partaker.

7. The ploughshare ploughing makes the food that feeds
   us, and with its feet cuts through the path it follows.

   Better the speaking than the silent Brahmin: the
   liberal friend outvalues him who gives not.

8. He with one foot hath far outrun the biped, and the two-footed catches the three-footed.

Four-footed creatures come when bipeds call them, and stand and look where five are met together.

9. The hands are both alike: their labour differs. The yield of sister milch-kine is unequal.

Twins even differ in their strength and vigour: two, even kinsmen, differ in their bounty.

(X/117)

Samjnanam: Unanimity

Samvanana

संसमिद्युवसे वृषन्नग्ने विश्वान्यर्य आ।
इळस्पदे समिध्यसे स नो वसून्या भर॥
सं गच्छध्वं सं वदध्वं सं वो मनांसि जानताम्।
देवा भागं यथा पूर्वे संजानाना उपासते॥
समानो मन्त्र: समिति: समानी समानं मन: सह चित्तमेषाम्।
समानं मन्त्रमभि मन्त्रये व: समानेन वो हविषा जुहोमि॥
समानी व आकूति: समाना हृदयानि व:।
समानमस्तु वो मनो यथा व: सुसहासति॥

1. Thou, mighty Agni, gatherest up all that is precious for thy friend.

   Bring us all treasures as thou art enkindled in libation's place.

2. Assemble, speak together: let your minds be all of one accord,

As ancient Gods unanimous sit down to their appointed share.

3. The place is common, common the assembly, common the mind, so be their thought united.

   A common purpose do I lay before you, and worship with your general oblation.

4. One and the same be your resolve, and be your minds of one accord.

   United be the thoughts of all that all may happily agree.

(X/191)

Vasishtha: The Rishi

-.-

Vasishtha

The hymn is a glorification of Vasishtha and his family, the latter part relating his birth and the earlier verses, referring to his connexion with King Sudas.

श्वित्यञ्चो मा दक्षिणतस्कपर्दा धियंजिन्वासो अभि हि प्रमन्दुः।
उत्तिष्ठन् वोचे परि बर्हिषो नॄन् न मे दूरादवितवे वसिष्ठाः॥
दूरादिन्द्रमनयन्ना सुतेन तिरो वैशन्तमति पान्तमुग्रम्।
पाशद्युम्नस्य वायतस्य सोमात् सुतादिन्द्रोऽवृणीता वसिष्ठान्॥
एवेन्नु कं सिन्धुमेभिस्ततारेवेन्नु कं भेदमेभिर्जघान।
एवेन्नु कं दाशराज्ञे सुदासं प्रावदिन्द्रो ब्रह्मणा वो वसिष्ठाः॥
जुष्टी नरो ब्रह्मणा वः पितृणामक्षमव्ययं न किला रिषाथ।
यच्छक्करीषु बृहता रवेणेन्द्रे शुष्ममदधाता वसिष्ठाः॥
उद् द्यामिवेत् तृष्णजो नाथितासो ऽदीधयुर्दाशराज्ञे वृतासः।

वसिष्ठस्य स्तुवत इन्द्रो अश्रोदुरं तृत्सुभ्यो अकृणोदु लोकम्॥
दण्डा इवेद् गोअजनास आसन् परिच्छिन्ना भरता अर्भकास:।
अभवच्च पुरएता वसिष्ठ आदित् तृत्सूनां विशो अप्रथन्त॥
त्रय: कृण्वन्ति भुवनेषु रेतस्तिस्र: प्रजा आर्या ज्योतिरग्रा:।
त्रयो घर्मास उषसं सचन्ते सर्वा इत् ताँ अनु विदुर्वसिष्ठा:॥
सूर्यस्येव वक्षथो ज्योतिरेषां समुद्रस्येव महिमा गभीर:।
वातस्येव प्रजवो नान्येन स्तोमो वसिष्ठा अन्वेतवे व:॥
त इन्निण्यं हृदयस्य प्रकेतै: सहस्रवल्शमभि सं चरन्ति।
यमेन ततं परिधिं वयन्तो ऽप्सरस उप सेदुर्वसिष्ठा:॥
विद्युतो ज्योति: परि संजिहानं मित्रावरुणा यदपश्यतां त्वा।
तत् ते जन्मोतैकं वसिष्ठाऽगस्त्यो यत् त्वा विश आजभार॥
उतासि मैत्रावरुणो वसिष्ठोर्वश्या ब्रह्मन् मनसोऽधि जात:।
द्रप्सं स्कन्नं ब्रह्मणा दैव्येन विश्वे देवा: पुष्करे त्वाददन्त॥
स प्रकेत उभयस्य प्रविद्वान् त्सहस्रदान उत वा सदान:।
यमेन ततं परिधिं वयिष्यन्नप्सरस: परि जज्ञे वसिष्ठ:॥
सत्रे ह जाताविषिता नमोभि: कुम्भे रेत: सिषिचतु: समानम्।
ततो ह मान उदियाय मध्यात् ततो जातमृषिमाहुर्वसिष्ठम्॥
उक्थभृतं सामभृतं बिभर्ति ग्रावाणं बिभ्रत् प्र वदात्यग्रे।
उपैनमाध्वं सुमनस्यमाना आ वो गच्छाति प्रतृदो वसिष्ठ:॥

1. These who wear hair-knots on the right, the movers of holy thought, white-robed, have won me over.

   I warned the men, when from the grass I raised me, Not from afar can my Vasishthas help you.

2. With Soma they brought Indra from a distance, over Vaisanta, from the strong libation

   Indra preferred Vasishthas to the Soma pressed by the son of Vayata, Pasadyumna.

3. So, verily, with these he crossed the river, in company with these he slaughtered Bheda.

So in the fight with the Ten Kings, Vaisishthas!
did Indra help Sudas through your devotions.

4. I gladly, men! with prayer prayed by our fathers have
fixed your axle: ye shall not be injured:

Since, when ye sang aloud the Sakvari verses,
Vasisthas! ye invigorated Indra.

5. Like thirsty men they looked to heaven, in battle
with the Ten Kings, surrounded and imploring.

Then Indra heard Vasishtha as he praised him,
and gave the Tritsus ample room and freedom.

6. Like sticks and staves wherewith they drive the cattle,
stripped bare, the Bharatas were found defenceless:

Vasishtha then became their chief and leader: then
widely were the Tritsus' clans extended.

7. Three fertilize the worlds with genial moisture: three
noble Creatures cast a light before them.

Three that give warmth to all attend the morning.
All these have they discovered, these Vasishthas.

8. Like the Sun's growing glory is their splendour, and
like the sea's is their unfathomed greatness.

Their course is like the wind's. Your laud,
Vasishthas, can never be attained by any other.

9. They with perceptions of the heart in secret resort
to that which spreads a thousand branches.

The Apsaras brought hither the Vasishthas wearing
the vesture spun for them by Yama.

10. A form of lustre springing from the lightning wast
thou, when Varuna and Mitra saw thee.

Thy one and only birth was then, Vasishtha, when
from thy stock Agastya brought thee hither.

11. Born of their love for Urvashi,Vasishtha thou, priest, art son of Varuna, and Mitra;

And as a fallen drop, in heavenly fervour, all the Gods laid thee on a lotus-blossom.

12. He, thinker, knower both of earth and heaven, endowed with many a gift, bestowing thousands,

Destined to wear the vesture spun by Yama, sprang from the Apsaras to life, Vasishtha.

13. Born at the sacrifice, urged by adoration, both with a common flow bedewed the pitcher.

Then from the midst thereof there rose up Mana, and thence they say was born the sage Vasishtha.

14. He brings the bearer of the laud and Saman: first shall he speak bringing the stone for pressing.

With grateful hearts in reverence approach him: to you, O Pratradas, Vasishtha cometh.

(VII/33)

Pitarah: Fathers

Shankh

उदीरतामवर उत् परास उन्मध्यमा: पितर: सोम्यास:।
असुं य ईयुरवृक: ऋतज्ञास्ते नोऽवन्तु पितरो हवेषु॥
इदं पितृभ्यो नमो अस्त्वद्य ये पूर्वासो य उपरास ईयु:।
ये पार्थिवे रजस्या निषत्ता ये वा नूनं सुवृजनासु विक्षु॥
आहं पितृन् सुविदत्राँ अवित्सि नपातं च विक्रमणं च विष्णो:।
बर्हिषदो ये स्वधया सुतस्य भजन्त पित्वस्त इहागमिष्ठा:॥

बर्हिषद: पितर ऊत्यऽर्वागिमा वो हव्या चकृमा जुषध्वम्।
त आ गतावसा शंतमेनाऽथा न: शं योररपो दधात।।
उपहूता: पितर: सोम्यासो बर्हिष्येषु निधिषु प्रियेषु।
त आ गमन्तु त इह भुवन्त्वधि ब्रुवन्तु तेऽवन्त्वस्मान्।।
आच्या जानु दक्षिणतो निषद्येमं यज्ञमभि गृणीत क्विश्वे।
मा हिंसिष्ट पितर: केन चिन्नो यद्व आग: पुरुषता कराम।।
आसीनासो अरुणीनामुपस्थे रयिं धत्त दाशुषे मर्त्याय।
पुत्रेभ्य: पितरस्तस्य वस्व: प्र यच्छत त इहोर्जं दधात।।
ये न: पूर्वे पितर: सोम्यासो ऽनूहिरे सोमपीथं वसिष्ठा:।
तेभिर्यमं सरराणो हवींष्यु शत्रशाद्धि: प्रतिकाममत्तु।।
ये तातृषुर्देवत्रा जेहमाना होत्राविद: स्तोमतष्टासो अर्कैं:।
आग्ने याहि सुविदत्रेभिरर्वाङ् सत्यै: कव्यै: पितृभिर्घर्मसद्धि:।।
ये सत्यासो हविरदो हविष्पा इन्द्रेण देवै: सरथं दधाना:।
आग्रे याहि सहस्रं देववन्दै: परै: पूर्वै: पितृभिर्घर्मसद्धि:।।
अग्निष्वात्ता: पितर एह गच्छत् सद:सद: सदत सुप्रणीतय:।
अत्ता हवींषि प्रयतानि बर्हिष्यथा रयिं सर्ववीरं दधातन।।
त्वमग्न ईळितो जातवेदो ऽवाड्ढव्यानि सुरभीणि कृत्वी।
प्रादा: पितृभ्य: स्वधया ते अक्षन्नद्धि त्वं देव प्रयता हवींषि।।
ये चेह पितरो ये च नेह याँश्च विद्म याँ उ च न प्रविद्म।
त्वं वेत्थ यति ते जातवेद: स्वाभिर्यज्ञं सुकृतं जुषस्व।।
ये अग्निदग्धा ये अनग्निदग्धा मध्ये दिव: स्वधया मादयन्ते।
तेभि: स्वराळसुनीतिमेतां यथावशं तन्वं कल्पयस्व।।

1. May they ascend, the lowest, highest, midmost, the
   Fathers who deserve a share of Soma.

   May they who have attained the life of spirits, gentle
   and righteous, aid us when we call them.

2. Now let us pay this homage to the Fathers, to those
   who passed of old and those who followed,

   Those who have rested in the earthly region, and

those who dwell among the Mighty Races.

3. I have attained the gracious-minded Fathers, I have gained son and progeny from Visnu.

    They who enjoy pressed juices with oblation seated on sacred grass, come oftenest hither.

4. Fathers who sit on sacred grass, come, help us: these offerings have we made for you; accept them.

    So come to us with most auspicous favour, and give us health and strength without a trouble.

5. May they, the Fathers, worthy of the Soma, invited to their favourite oblations.

    Laid on the sacred grass, come nigh and listen: may they be gracious unto us and bless us.

6. Bowing your bended knees and seated southward, accept this sacrifice of ours with favour.

    Punish us not for any sin, O Fathers, which we through human frailty have committed.

7. Lapped in the bosom of the purple Mornings, give riches to the man who brings oblations.

    Grant to your sons a portion of that treasure, and, present, give them energy, ye Fathers.

8. Our ancient Fathers who deserve the Soma, who came, most noble, to our Soma banquet,—

    With these let Yama, yearning with the yearning, rejoicing eat our offerings at his pleasure.

9. Come to us, Agni, with the gracious Fathers who dwell in glowing light, the very Kavyas,

    Who thirsted mid the Gods, who hasten hither, oblation winners, theme of singers' praises.

10. Come, Agni, come with countless ancient Fathers,

dwellers in light, primeval, God-adorers,

Eaters and drinkers of oblations,truthful, who travel with the Deities and Indra.

11. Fathers whom Agni's flames have tested, come ye nigh: ye kindly leaders, take ye each your proper place.

Eat sacrificial food presented on the grass: grant riches with a multitude of hero sons.

12. Thou, Agni Jatavedas, when entreated, didst bear the offerings which thou madest fragrant,

And give them to the Fathers who did eat them with Svadha. Eat, thou God, the gifts we bring thee.

13. Thou, Jatavedas, knowest well the number of Fathers who are here and who are absent,

Of Fathers whom we know and whom we know not: accept the sacrifice well prepared with portions.

14. They who, consumed by fire or not cremated, joy in their offering in the midst of heaven,—

Grant them, O Sovran Lord, the word, the world of spirits and their own body, as thy pleasure wills it.

(X/15)

Kshetrapati: Lord of the Field

-.--.-

Vamadeva

In this hymn various agricultural personifications are addressed, the deity of the first three stanzas being called Ksetrapati, of the fourth Suna, of the fifth and eighth Sunasira, of the sixth and seventh Sita. Each verse is to be silently repeated, with an oblation to fire, at the commencement of ploughing.

क्षेत्रस्य पतिना वयं हितेनेव जयामसि।
गाम् श्वं पोषयित्वा स नो मृळातीदृशे॥
क्षेत्रस्य पते मधुमन्तमूर्मिं धेनुरिव पयो अस्मासु धुक्ष्व।
मधुश्चुतं घृतमिव सुपूतमृतस्य नः पतयो मृळयन्तु॥
मधुमतीरोषधीर्द्याव आपो मधुमन्नो भवत्वन्तरिक्षम्।
क्षेत्रस्य पतिर्मधुमान् नो अस्त्वरिष्यन्तो अन्वेनं चरेम॥
शुनं वाहाः शुनं नरः शुनं कृषतु लाङ्गलम्।
शुनं वरत्रा बध्यन्तां शुनमष्ट्रामुदिङ्गय॥
शुनासीराविमां वाचं जुषेथां यद् दिवि चक्रथुः पयः।
तेनेमामुप सिञ्चतम्॥
अर्वाचीं सुभगे भव सीते वन्दामहे त्वा।
यथा नः सुभगाससि यथा नः सुफलाससि॥
इन्द्रः सीतां नि गृह्णातु तां पूषानु यच्छतु।
सा नः पयस्वती दुहामुत्तरामुत्तरां समाम्॥
शुनं नः फाला वि कृषन्तु भूमिं शुनं कीनाशा अभि यन्तु वाहैः।
शुनं पर्जन्यो मधुना पयोभिः शुनासीरा शुनमस्मासु धत्तम्॥

1. We through the Master of the Field, even as through a friend, obtain

   What nourisheth our kine and steeds. In such may he be good to us.

2. As the cow yieldeth milk, pour for us freely, Lord of the Field, the wave that beareth sweetness,

   Distilling meath, well-purified like butter, and let the Lords of holy Law be gracious.

3. Sweet be the plants for us, the heavens, the waters, and full of sweets for us be air's mid-region.

   May the Field's Lord for us be full of sweetness, and may we follow after him uninjured.

4. Happily work our steers and men, may the plough furrow happily.

   Happily be the traces bound; happily may he ply the goad.

5. Suna and Sira, welcome ye this laud, and with the milk which ye have made in heaven

   Bedew ye both this earth of ours.

6. Auspicious Sita, come thou near : we venerate and worship thee

   That thou mayst bless and prosper us and bring us fruits abundantly.

7. May Indra press the furrow down, may Pusan guide its course aright.

   May she, as rich in milk, be drained for us through each succeeding year.

8. Happily let the shares turn up the ploughland, happily go the ploughers with the oxen.

   With meath and milk Parjanya make us happy.Grant us prosperity, Suna and Sira.

(IV/57)

Vastospati: Guardian of the House

Vasishtha

Vastospati is the Genius or tutelary God of the house. In this hymn he is addressed also as Indu, another name of Soma the Moon-God.

वास्तोष्पते प्रति जानीह्यस्मान् त्वविशो अनमीवो भवा नः।
यत् त्वेमहे प्रति तन्नो जुषस्व शं नो भव द्विपदे शं चतुष्पदे॥
वास्तोष्पते प्रतरणो न एधि गयस्फानो गोभिर श्वेभिरिन्दो।
अजरासस्ते सख्ये स्याम पितेव पुत्रान् प्रति नो जुषस्व॥
वास्तोष्पते शग्मया संसदा ते सक्षीमहि रण्वया गातुमत्या।
पाहि क्षेम उत योगे वरं नो यूयं पात स्वस्तिभिः सदा नः॥

1. Acknowledge us, O Guardian of the Homestead: bring no disease, and give us happy entrance.

   Whate'er we ask of thee, be pleased to grant it, and prosper thou quadrupeds and bipeds.

2. Protector of the Home, be our promoter: increase our wealth in kine and steeds, O Indu.

   May we be ever-youthful in thy friendship: be pleased in us as in his sons a father.

3. Though thy dear fellowship that bringeth welfare, may we be victors, Guardian of the Dwelling!

   Protect our happiness in rest and labour. Preserve us evermore, ye Gods, with blessings.

(VII/54)

Kesin: The Hairy Ones

-.-

Jutih

The Kesins, *Kesinah,* wearers of long loose hair, are Agni, Vayu, and Surya.

केश्यऽग्नि केशी विषं केशी बिभर्ति रोदसी।
केशी विश्वं स्वर्दृशे केशीदं ज्योतिरुच्यते॥
मुनयो वातरशनाः पिशङ्गा वसते मला।
वातस्यानु ध्राजिं यन्ति यद्देवासो अविक्षत॥
उन्मदिता मौनेयेन वाताँ आ तस्थिमा वयम्।
शरीरदेस्माकं यूयं मर्तासो अभि पश्यथ॥
अन्तरिक्षेण पतति विश्वा रूपावचाकशत्।
मुनिर्देवस्यदेवस्य सौकृत्याय सखा हितः॥
वातस्याश्वो वायोः सखा ऽथो देवेषितो मुनिः।
उभौ समुद्रावा क्षेति यश्च पूर्व उतापरः॥
अप्सरसां गन्धर्वाणां मृगाणां चरणे चरन्।
केशी केतस्य विद्वान् त्सखा स्वादुर्मदिन्तमः॥
वायुरस्मा उपामन्थत् पिनष्टि स्मा कुनन्नमा।
केशी विषस्य पात्रेण यद्रुद्रेणापिबत् सह॥

1. He with the long loose locks supports Agni, and moisture, heaven, and earth:

   He is all sky to look upon: he with long hair is called this light.

2. The Munis, girdled with the wind, wear garments soiled of yellow hue.

   They, following the wind's swift course go where the Gods have gone before.

3. Transported with our Munihood we have pressed on into the winds:

   You therefore, mortal men, behold our natural bodies and no more.

4. The Muni, made associate in the holy work of every God,

   Looking upon all varied forms flies through the region of the air.

5. The Steed of Vata, Vayu's friend, the Muni, by the Gods impelled,

   In both the oceans hath his home, in eastern and in western sea.

6. Treading the path of sylvan beasts, Gandharvas, and Apsarases,

   He with long locks, who knows the wish, is a sweet most delightful friend.

7. Vayu hath churned for him: for him he poundeth things most hard to bend,

   When he with long loose locks hath drunk, with Rudra, water from the cup.

   (X/136)

Havirdhanas: Oblation-bearers

-.-

Angiras

The deities are the two Sakatas, small carts or barrows used at sacrifices to carry the materials, especially the Soma-plant, hence called Havirdhanas, oblation-bearers.

युजे वां ब्रह्म पूर्व्यं नमोभिर्विं श्लोक एतु पथ्येव सूरे:।
शृण्वन्तु विश्वे अमृतस्य पुत्रा आ ये धामानि दिव्यानि तस्थु:॥
यमे इव यतमाने यदैतं प्र वां भरन् मानुषा देवयन्त:।
आ सीदतं स्वमु लोकं विदनि स्वासस्थे भवतमिन्दवे न:॥
पञ्च पदानि रुपो अन्वरोहं चतुष्पदीमन्वेमि व्रतेन।
अक्षरेण प्रति मिम एतामृतस्य नाभावधि सं पुनामि॥
देवेभ्य: कमवृणीत मृत्युं प्रजायै कममृतं नावृणीत।
बृहस्पति यज्ञमकृण्वत ऋषिं प्रियां यमस्तन्वं१ प्रारिरेचीत्॥
सप्त क्षरन्ति शिशवे मरुत्वते पित्रे पुत्रासो अप्यवीवतन्नृतम्।
उभे इदस्योभयस्य राजत उभे यतेते उभयस्य पुष्यत:॥

1. I yoke with prayer your ancient inspiration: may the laud rise as on the prince's pathway.

    All Sons of Immortality shall hear it, all the possessors of celestial natures.

2. When speeding ye came nigh us like twin sisters, religious-hearted votaries brought you forward.

    Take your place, ye who know your proper station: be near, be very near unto our Soma.

3. Five paces have I risen from Earth: I follow her who hath four feet with devout observance.

    This by the Sacred Syllable have I measured: I purify in the central place of Order.

4. He, for God's sake, chose death to be his portion. He chose not, for men's good, a life eternal.

    They sacrificed Brihaspati the Rishi. Yama delivered up his own dear body.

5. The Seven flow to the Youth on whom the Maruts wait: the Sons unto the Father brought the sacrifice.

Both these are his, as his they are the Lords of both; both toil; belonging unto both they prosper well.

(X/13)

Raja: The King

-.-

Abhivarta

The subject is the benediction of a newly-elected king.

अभीवर्तेन हविषा येनेन्द्रो अभिवावृते।
तेनास्मान् ब्रह्मणस्पते ऽभि राष्ट्राय वर्तय॥
अभिवृत्य सपत्नानभि या नो अरातयः।
अभि पृतन्यन्तं तिष्ठाऽभि यो न इरस्यति।
अभि त्वा देवः सविता ऽभि सोमो अवीवृतत्॥
अभि त्वा विश्वा भूतान्यभीवर्तो यथाससि।
येनेन्द्रो हविषा कृत्व्यभवद् द्युम्न्युत्तमः॥
इदं तदकि देवा असपत्नः किलाभुवम्।
असपत्नः सपत्नहा ऽभिराष्ट्रो विषासहिः॥
यथाहमेषां भूतानां विराजानि जनस्य च।

1. With offering for success in fight whence Indra was victorious.

    With this, O Brahmanaspati, let us attain to royal sway.

2. Subduing those who rival us, subduing all malignities,

Withstand the man who menaces, withstand the man who angers us.

3. Soma and Savitar the God have made thee a victorious King.

All elements have aided thee, to make thee general conqueror.

4. Oblation, that which Indra gave and thus grew glorious and most high,—

This have I offered, Gods! and hence now, verily, am rivalless.

5. Slayer of rivals, rivalless, victorious, with royal sway,

Over these beings may I rule, may I be Sovran of the folk.

(X/174)

Yajna: Sacrifice

-.-

Angiras

The subject of the Hymn is the origin and institution of sacrifice, first established by Agni under the authority of Varuna, Sacrifice is the path which leads the Gods from Heaven to Earth and the way through heaven is made visible for the sacrificial fire.

वृषा वृष्णे दुदुहे दोहसा दिव: पयांसि यह्वो अदितेरदाभ्य:।
विश्वं स वेद वरुणो यथा धिया स यज्ञियो यजतु यज्ञियाँ ऋतून्।।
रपद्गन्धर्वीरप्या च योषणा नदस्य नादे परि पातु मे मन:।
इष्टस्य मध्ये अदितिर्नि धातु नो भ्राता नो ज्येष्ठ: प्रथमो वि वोचति।।

सो चिन्नु भद्राँ क्षुमती यशस्वत्युषा उवास मनवे स्वर्वती।
यदीमुशन्तमुशतामनु क्रतुमग्निं होतारं विदथाय जीजनन्।।
अध त्यं द्रप्सं विभ्वं विचक्षणं विराभरदिषितः श्येनो अध्वरे।
यदी विशो वृणते दस्ममार्या अग्निं होतारमध धीरजायत।।
सदासि रण्वो यवसेव पुष्यते होत्राभिरम्ने मनुषः स्वध्वरः।
विप्रस्य वा यच्छशमान उक्थ्यंश् वाजं ससवाँ उपयासि भूरिभिः।।
उदीरय पितरा जार आ भगमियक्षति हर्यतो हृत्त इष्यति।
विवक्ति वह्निः स्वपस्यते मखस्तविष्यते असुरो वेपते मती।।
यस्ते अग्ने सुमतिं मर्तो अक्षत् सहसः सूनो अति स प्र शृण्वे।
इषं दधानो वहमानो अश्वैरा स द्युमाँ अमवान् भूषति द्यून्।।
यदग्न एषा समितिर्भवाति देवी देवेषु यजता यजत्र।
रत्ना च यद्विभजासि स्वधावो भागं नो अत्र वसुमन्तं वीतात्।।
श्रुधी नो अग्ने सदने सधस्थे युक्ष्वा रथममृतस्य द्रवित्नुम्।
आ नो वह रोदसी देवपुत्रे माकिर्देवानामप भूरिह स्याः।।

1. The Bull hath yielded for the Bull the milk of heaven:
   the Son of Aditi can never be deceived.

   According to his wisdom Varuna knoweth all: may
   he, the Holy, hallow times for sacrifice.

2. Gandharvi spake: may she, the Lady of the flood,
   amid the river's roaring leave my heart untouched.

   May Aditi accomplish all that we desire, and may
   our eldest Brother tell us this as Chief.

3. Yea, even this blessed Morning, rich in store of food,
   splendid, with heavenly lustre, hath shone out for
   man,

   Since they, as was the wish of yearning Gods,
   brought forth that yearning Agni for the assembly
   as the Priest.

4. And the fleet Falcon brought for sacrifice from afar this flowing Drop most excellent and keen of sight,

   Then when the Aryan tribes chose as Invoking Priest Agni the Wonder-Worker, and the hymn rose up.

5. Still art thou kind to him who feeds thee as with grass, and, skilled in sacrifice, offers thee holy gifts.

   When thou, having received the sage's strengthening food with lauds, after long toil, comest with many more.

6. Urge thou thy Parents, as a lover, to delight: the Lovely One desires and craves it from his heart.

   The priest calls out, the sacrificer shows his skill, the Asura tries his strength, and with the hymn is stirred.

7. Far-famed is he, the mortal man, O Agni, thou Son of Strength, who hath obtained thy favour.

   He, gathering power, borne onward by his horses, makes his days lovely in his might and splendour.

8. When, Holy Agni, the divine assembly, the sacred synod mid the Gods, is gathered,

   And when thou, Godlike One, dealest forth treasures, vouchsafe us, too, our portion of the riches.

9. Hear us, O Agni, in your common dwelling: harness thy rapid car of Amrita.

   Bring Heaven and Earth, the Deities' Parents, hither: stay with us here, nor from the Gods be distant.

(X/11)

Agnimanthan: Lighting the Fire

Gathi

अस्तीदमधिमन्थनमस्ति प्रजननं कृतम्।
एतां विश्पत्नीमा भरामिनं मन्थाम पूर्वथा।।

अरण्योर्निहितो जातवेदा गर्भ इव सुधितो गर्भिणीषु।
दिवेदिव ईड्यो जागृवद्भिर्हविष्मद्भिर्मनुष्योभिरग्निः।।

उत्तानायामव भरा चिकित्वान् त्सद्यः प्रवीता वृषणं जजान।
अरुषस्तूपो रुशदस्य पाज इळायास्पुत्रो वयुनेऽजनिष्ट।।

इळायास्त्वा पदे वयं नाभा पृथिव्या अधि।
जातवेदो नि धीमह्याग्ने हव्याय वोळ्हवे।।

मन्थता नरः कविमद्द्रयन्तं प्रचेतसममृतं सुप्रतीकम्।
यज्ञस्य केतुं प्रथमं पुरस्तादग्निं नरो जनयता सुशेवम्।।

यदी मन्थन्ति बहुभिर्वि रोचतेऽश्वो न वाज्यरुषो वनेष्वा।
चित्रो न यामन्नश्वनोरनिवृतः परि वृणक्त्यश्मनस्तृणा दहन्।।

जातो अग्नी रोचते चेकितानो वाजी विप्रः कविशस्तः सुदानुः।
यं देवास ईड्यं विश्वविदं हव्यवाहमदधुरध्वरेषु।।

सीद होतः स्व उ लोके चिकित्वान् त्सादया यज्ञं सुकृतस्य योनौ।
वेबाबीर्देबान् हविषा यजास्यग्ने बृहद् यजमाने वयो धाः।।

कृणोत धूमं वृषणं सखायोऽस्रेधन्त इतन वाजमच्छ।
अयमग्निः पृतनाषाद् सुवीरो येन देवासो असहन्त दस्यून्।।

अयं ते योनिर्ऋत्वियो यतो जातो अरोचथाः।
तं जानन्नग्न आ सीदाथा नो वर्धया गिरः।।

तनूनपादुच्यते गर्भ आसुरो नराशंसो भवति यद् विजायते।
मातरिश्वा यदमिमीत मातरि वातस्य सर्गो अभवत् सरीमणि।।

सुनिर्मथा निर्मथितः सुनिधा निहितः कविः।
अग्ने स्वध्वरा कृणु देवान् देवयते यज ॥
अजीजनन्नग्नमृतं मर्त्यासो ऽस्रेमाणं तरणिं वीळुजम्भम्।
दश स्वसारो अग्रुवः समीचीः पुमांसं जातमभि सं रभन्ते॥
प्र सप्तहोता सनकादरोचत मातुरुपस्थे यदशोचदूधनि।
न नि मिषति सुरणो दिवेदिवे यदसुरस्य जठरादजायत॥
अमित्रायुधो मरुतामिव प्रयाः प्रथमजा ब्रह्मणो विश्वमिद् विदुः।
द्युम्नवद् ब्रह्म कुशिकास एरिर एकएको दमे अग्निं समीधिरे॥
यदद्य त्वा प्रयति यज्ञे अस्मिन् होतश्चिकित्वोऽवृणीमहीह।
ध्रुवमया ध्रुवमुताशमिष्ठाः प्रजानन् विद्वाँ उप याहि सोमम्॥

1. Here is the gear for friction, here tinder made ready
   for the spark.

   Bring thou the Matron: we will rub Agni in ancient
   fashion forth.

2. In the two fire-sticks Jatavedas lieth, even as the
   well-set germ in pregnant women,

   Agni who day by day must be exalted by men
   who watch and worship with oblations.

3. Lay this with care on that which lies extended: straight
   hath she borne the Steer when made prolific.

   With his red pillar—radiant is his splendour—in
   our skilled task is born the Son of Ila.

4. In Ila's place we set thee down, upon the central
   point of earth,

   That, Agni Jatavedas, thou mayst bear our offerings
   to the Gods.

5. Rub into life, ye men, the Sage, the guileless,
   Immortal, very wise and fair to look on.

O men, bring forth the most propitious Agni, first ensign of the Sacrifice to eastward.

6. When with their arms they rub him straighthe shineth forth like a strong courser, red in colour, in the wood.

   Bright, checkless, as it were upon the Asvins' path, he passeth by the stones and burneth up the grass.

7. Agni shines forth when born, observant, mighty, bountiful, the Singer praised by sages;

   Whom, as adorable and knowing all things, Gods set at solemn rites as offering-bearer.

8. Set thee, O Priest, in thine own place, oblation: lay down the sacrifice in the home of worship.

   Thou, dear to Gods, shalt serve them with oblation: Agni, give long life to the sacrificer.

9. Raise ye a mighty smoke, my fellow-workers! Ye shall attain to wealth without obstruction.

   This Agni is the battle-winning Hero by whom the Gods have overcome the Dasyus.

10. This is thine ordered place of birth whence sprung to life thou shonest forth.

    Knowing this, Agni, sit thee down, and prosper thou the songs we sing.

11. As Germ Celestial he is called Tanunapat, and Narasamsa born diffused in varied shape.

    Formed in his Mother he is Matarisvan; he hath, in his course, become the rapid flight of wind.

12. With strong attrition rubbed to life, laid down with careful hand, a Sage,

    Agni, make sacrifices good, and for the pious bring the Gods.

13. Mortals have brought to life the God Immortal, the

Conqueror with mighty jaws, unfailing.

The sisters ten, unwedded and united, togeth r grasp the Babe, the new-born Infant.

14. Served by the seven priests, he shone forth from ancient time, when in his Mother's bosom, in her lap, he glowed.

Giving delight each day he closeth not his eye, since from the Asura's body he was brought to life.

15. Even as the Maruts' onslaughts who attack the foe, those born the first of all knew the full power of prayer.

The Kusikas have made the glorious hymn ascend, and, each one singly in his home, have kindled fire.

16. As we, O Priest observant, have elected thee this day, what time the solemn sacrifice began,

So surely hast thou worshipped, surely hast thou toiled: come thou unto the Soma, wise and knowing all.

(III/29)

Yajman-patni: Sacrificer and His Wife

Prajavana

The deiteis are the Sacrificer, his Wife, and the Hotar priest.

अपश्यं त्वा मनसा चेकितानं तपसो जातं तपसो विभूतम्।
इह प्रजामिह रयिं रराण: प्र जायस्व प्रजया पुत्रकाम॥
अपश्यं त्वा मनसा दीध्यानां स्वायां तनू ऋत्व्ये नाधमानाम्।

उप मामुच्चा युवर्तिर्बभूया: प्र जायस्व प्रजया पुत्रकामे॥

अहं गर्भमदधामोषधीष्वहं क्विश्वेषु भुवनेष्वन्त:।

अहं प्रजा अजनयं पृथिव्यामहं जनिभ्यो अपरीषु पुत्रान्॥

1. I saw thee meditating in thy spirit what sprang from
   Fervour and hath thence developed.

   Bestowing offspring here, bestowing riches, spread
   in thine offspring, thou who cravest children.

2. I saw thee pondering in thine heart, and praying that
   in due time thy body might be fruitful.

   Come as a youthful woman, rise to meet me:
   spread in thine offspring, thou who cravest children.

3. In plants and herbs, in all existent beings I have
   deposited the germ of increase.

   All progeny on earth have I engendered, and sons
   in women who will be hereafter.

(X/183)

Grivanah: Press-stones

-.-

Sarpa Airavat

आ व ऋञ्जस ऊर्जां व्युष्टिष्विन्द्रं मरुतो रोदसी अनक्तन।

उभे यथा नो अहनी सचाभुवा सद: सदो वरिवस्यात उद्भिदा॥

तदु श्रेष्ठं सवनं सुनोतनाऽत्यो न हस्तयतो अद्रि: सोतरि।

विदद्द्वयश्र्यो अभिभूति पौंस्यं महो राये चित् तरुते यदर्वत:॥

अदिद्ध्यस्य सवनं विवेरपो यथा पुरा मनवे गातुमश्रेत्।

सवर्णसि त्वाष्ट्रे अश्विनिर्णिजि प्रेमध्वरेष्वध्वराँ अशिश्रयुः॥

अप हत रक्षसो भङ्गुरावतः स्कभायत निर्ऋतिं सेधतामतिम्।

आ नो रयिं सर्ववीरं सुनोतन देवाव्यं भरतर श्लोकमद्रयः॥

दिवश्चिदा वोऽमवत्तरेभ्यो विभ्वना चिदश्वपस्तरेभ्यः।

वायोश्चिदा सोमरभस्तरेभ्यो ऽग्नेश्चिदर्च पितुकृत्तरेभ्यः॥

भुरन्तु नो यशसः सोत्वन्धसो ग्रावाणो वाचा दिविता दिवित्मता।

नरो यत्र दुहते काम्यं मध्वाघोषयन्तो अभितो मिथस्तुरः॥

सुन्वन्ति सोमं रथिरासो अद्रयो निरस्य रसं गविषो दुहन्ति ते।

दुहन्त्यूधरुपसेचनाय कं नरो हव्या न मर्जयन्त आसभिः॥

एते नरः स्वपसो अभूतन य इन्द्राय सुनुथ सोममद्रयः।

वामंवामं वो दिव्याय धाम्ने वसुवसु वः पार्थिवाय सुन्वते॥

1. I grasp at you when power and strength begin to dawn: bedew ye, Indra and the Maruts, Heaven and Earth,

   That Day and Night, in every hall of sacrifice, may wait on us and bless us when they first spring forth.

2. Press the libation out, most excellent of all: the Pressing- stone is grasped like a hand-guided steed.

   So let it win the valour that subdues the foe, and the fleet courser's might that speeds to ample wealth.

3. Juice that this Stone pours out removes defect of ours, as in old time it brought prosperity to man.

   At sacrifices they established holy rites on Tvastar's milk-blent juice bright with the hue of steeds.

4. Drive ye the treacherous demons far away from us: keep Nirriti afar and banish penury.

   Pour riches forth for us with troops of hero sons, and bear ye up, O Stones, the song that visits Gods.

5. To you who are more mighty than the heavens themselves who, finishing your task with more than Vibhvan's speed,

   More rapidly than Vayu seize the Soma juice, better than Agni give us food, to you I sing.

6. Stirred be the glorious Stones: let it press out the juice, the Stone with heavenly song that reaches up to heaven,

   There where the men draw forth the meath for which they long, sending their voice around in rivalry of speed.

7. The Stones press out the Soma, swift as car-borne men, and, eager for the spoil, drain forth the sap thereof.

   To fill the beaker, they exhaust the udder's store, as the men purify oblations with their lips.

8. Ye, present men, have been most skilful in your work, even ye, O Stones who pressed Soma for Indra's drink.

   May all ye have of fair go to the Heavenly Race, and all your treasure to the earthly worshipper.

                                                      (X/76)

Ghrita: Clarified Butter

-.-

Vamadeva

The hymn is in praise of Ghrita, Ghee or clarified butter used in sacrifices.

समुद्रादूर्मिर्मधुमाँ उदारदुपांशुना सममृतत्वमानट।
घृतस्य नाम गुह्यं यदस्ति जिह्वा देवानाममृतस्य नाभि:॥

वयं नाम प्र ब्रवामा घृतस्याऽस्मिन् यज्ञे धारयामा नमोभि:।
उप ब्रह्मा शृणवच्छस्यमानं चतु:शृङ्गोऽवमीद् गौर एतत्॥

चत्वारि शृङ्गा त्रयो अस्य पादा द्वे शीर्षे सप्त हस्तासो अस्य।
त्रिधा बद्धो वृषभो रोरवीति महो देवो मर्त्याँ आ विवेश॥

त्रिधा हितं पणिभिर्गुह्यमानं गवि देवासो घृतमन्वविन्दन्।
इन्द्र एकं सूर्य एकं जजान वेनादेकं स्वधया निष्टतक्षु:॥

एता अर्षन्ति हृद्यात् समुद्राच्छतव्रजा रिपुणा नावचक्षे।
घृतस्य धाराअभि चाकशीमि हिरण्ययो वेतसो मध्य आसाम्॥

सम्यक् स्रवन्ति सरितो न धेना अन्तर्हुदा मनसा पूयमाना:।
एते अर्षन्त्यूर्मयो घृतस्य मृगा इव क्षिपणोरीषमाणा:॥

सिन्धोरिव प्राध्वने शूघनासो वातप्रमिय: पतयन्ति यह्वा:।
घृतस्य धारा अरुषो न वाजी काष्ठा भिन्दन्नूर्मिभि: पिन्वमान:॥

अभि प्रवन्त समनेव योषा: कल्याण्य१: स्मयमानासो अग्निम्।
घृतस्य धारा: समिधो नसन्त ता जुषाणो हर्यति जातवेदा:॥

कन्या इव वहतुमेतवा उ अञ्ज्यञ्जाना अभि चाकशीमि।
यत्र सोम: सूयते यत्र यज्ञो घृतस्य धारा अभि तत् पवन्ते॥

अभ्यर्षत सुष्टुतिं गव्यमाजिमस्मासु भद्रा द्रविणानि धत्त।
इमं यज्ञं नयत देवता नो घृतस्य धारा मधुमत् पवन्ते॥

धामन् ते विश्वं भुवनमधि श्रितमन्त: समुद्रे हृद्यन्तरायुषि।
अपामनीके समिथे य आभृतस्तमश्याम मधुमन्तं त ऊर्मिम्॥

1. Forth from the ocean sprang the wave of sweetness:
   together with the stalk it turned to Amrita,

   That which is holy oil's mysterious title: but the
   Gods' tongue is truly Amrta's centre.

2. Let us declare aloud the name of Ghrita, and at this
   sacrifice hold it up with homage.

   So let the Brahmin hear the praise we utter. This

hath the four-horned Buffalo emitted.

3. Four are his horns, three are the feet that bear him; his heads are two, his hands are seven in number.

   Bound with a triple bond the Steer roars loudly: the mighty God hath entered into mortals.

4. That in triple shape the Gods discovered laid down within the Cow, concealed by Panis.

   Indra produced one shape, Surya another: by their own power they formed the third from Vena.

5. From inmost reservoir in countless channels flow down these rivers which the foe beholds not.

   I look upon the streams of oil descending, and lo! the Golden Reed is there among them.

6. Like rivers our libations flow together, cleansing themselves in inmost heart and spirit.

   The streams of holy oil pour swiftly downward like the wild beasts that fly before the bowman.

7. As rushing down the rapids of a river, flow swifter than the wind the vigorous currents,

   The streams of oil in swelling fluctuation like a red courser bursting through the fences.

8. Like women at a gathering fair to look on and gently smiling, they incline to Agni.

   The streams of holy oil attain the fuel, and Jatavedas joyfully receives them.

9. As maidens deck themselves with gay adornment to join the bridal feast, I now behold them.

   Where Soma flows and sacrifice is ready, thither the streams of holy oil are running.

10. Send to our eulogy a herd of cattle: bestow upon us excellent possessions.

Bear to the Gods the sacrifice we offer: the streams of oil flow pure and full of sweetness.

11. The universe depends upon thy power and might within the sea, within the heart, within all life.

May we attain that sweetly-flavoured wave of thine, brought, at its gathering, o'er the surface of the floods.

(IV/58)

Danastuti: Praising Charity

-·-

Kakshivana

This hymn is a dialogue between a wandering priest and a pious liberal prince, Svanaya.

प्राता रत्नं प्रातरित्वा दधाति तं चिकित्वान् प्रतिगृह्या नि धत्ते।
तेन प्रजां वर्धयमान आयू रायस्पोषेण सचते सुवीर:॥
सुगुरसत् सुहिरण्य: स्वश्वो बृहदस्मै वय इन्द्रो दधाति।
यस्त्वायन्तं वसुना प्रातरित्वो मुक्षीजयेव पदिमुत्तिसनाति॥
आयमद्य सुकृतं प्रातरिच्छन्निष्टे: पुत्रं वसुमता रथेन।
अंशो: सुतं पायय मत्सरस्य क्षयद्वीरं वर्धय सूनृताभि:॥
उप क्षरन्ति सिन्धवो मयोभुव ईजानं च यक्ष्यमाणं च धेनव:।
पृणन्तं च पपुरिं च श्रवस्यवो घृतस्य धारा उप यन्ति विश्वत:॥
नाकस्य पृष्ठे अधि तिष्ठति श्रितो य: पृणाति स ह देवेषु गच्छति।
तस्मा आपो घृतमर्षन्ति सिन्धवस्तस्मा इयं दक्षिणा पिन्वते सदा॥
दक्षिणावतामिदिमानि चित्रा दक्षिणावतां दिवि सूर्यास:।
दक्षिणावन्तो अमृतं भजन्ते दक्षिणावन्त: प्र तिरन्त आयु:॥

मा पृणन्तो दुरितमेन आरन् मा जारिषुः सूरयः सुव्रतासः।
अन्यस्तेषां परिधिरस्तु कश्चिदपृणन्तमभि सं यन्तु शोकाः॥

1. Coming at early morn he gives his treasure; the prudent one receives and entertains him.

   Thereby increasing still his life and offspring, he comes with brave sons to abundant riches.

2. Rich shall he be in gold and kine and horses. Indra bestows on him great vital power,

   Who stays thee, as thou comest, with his treasure, like game caught in the net, O early comer.

3. Longing, I came this morning to the pious, the son of sacrifice, with car wealth-laden.

   Give him to drink juice of the stalk that gladdens; prosper with pleasant hymns the Lord of Heroes.

4. Health-bringing streams, as milch-cows, flow to profit him who hath worshipped, him who now will worship.

   To him who freely gives and fills on all sides full streams of fatness flow and make him famous.

5. On the high ridge of heaven he stands exalted, yea, to the Gods he goes, the liberal giver.

   The streams, the waters flow for him with fatness: to him this guerdon ever yields abundance.

6. For those who give rich meeds are all these splendours, for those who give rich meeds suns shine in heaven.

   The givers of rich meeds are made immortal; the givers of rich fees prolong their lifetime.

7. Let not the liberal sink to sin and sorrow, never decay the pious chiefs who worship!

Let every man besides be their protection, and
let affliction fall upon the niggard.

(I/125)

Nairrat Kapota: Bird of Ill Omen

-.-

Nairrata Kapota

A dove, regarded as an ill-omened bird and the messenger
of Death, has flown into the house. (Similarly, in North-Lin-
colnshire, 'If a pigeon is seen sitting on a tree, or comes into
the house, or from being wild suddenly becomes tame, it is
a sign of death.')

देवा: कपोत इषितो यदिच्छन् दूतो निर्ऋंत्या इदमाजगाम।
तस्मा अर्चाम कृणवाम निष्कृतिं शं नो अस्तु द्विपदे शं चतुष्पदे॥
शिव: कपोत इषितो नो अस्त्वनागा देवा: शकुनो गृहेषु।
अग्निर्हि विप्रो जुषतां हविर्न: परि हेति: पक्षिणी नो वृणक्तु॥
हेति: पक्षिणी न दभात्यस्मानाष्ट्र्यां पदं कृणुते अग्निधाने।
शं नो गोभ्यश्च पुरुषेभ्यश्चास्तु मा नो हिंसीदिह देवा: कपोत:॥
यदुलूको वदति मोघमेतद्यत् कपोत: पदमग्नौ कृणोति।
यस्य दूत: प्रहित एष एतत् तस्मै यमाय नमो अस्तु मृत्यवे॥
ऋचा कपोतं नुदत प्रणोदमिषं मदन्त: परि गां नयध्वम्।
संयोपयन्तो दुरितानि विश्वा हित्वा न ऊर्जं प्र पतात् पतिष्ठ:॥

1. Gods, whatsoe'er the Dove came hither seeking, sent
   to us as the envoy of Destruction,

   For that let us sing hymns and make atonement.
   Well be it with our quadrupeds and bipeds.

2. Auspicious be the Dove that hath been sent us, a harmless bird, ye Gods, within our dwelling.

   May Agni, Sage, be pleased with our oblation, and may the Missile borne on wings avoid us.

3. Let not the Arrow that hath wings distract us: beside the fire-place, on the hearth is settles.

   May it bring welfare to our men and cattle: here let the Dove, ye Gods, forbear to harm us.

4. The screeching of the owl is ineffective; and when beside the fire the Dove hath settled,

   To him who sent it hither as an envoy, to him be reverence paid, to Death, to Yama.

5. Drive forth the Dove, chase it with holy verses: rejoicing, bring ye hither food and cattle,

   Barring the way against all grief and trouble. Let the swift bird fly forth and leave us vigour.

   (X/165)

Rakshoha: Charm against Miscarriage

-.-

Brahma

ब्रह्मणाग्रि: संविदानो रक्षोहा बाधतामित:।
अमीवा यस्ते गर्भं दुर्णामा योनिमाशये॥
यस्ते गर्भममीवा दुर्णामा योनिमाशये।
अग्निष्टं ब्रह्मणा सह निष्क्रव्यादमनीनशत्॥
यस्ते हन्ति पतयन्तं निषत्स्नुं य: सरीसृपम्।
जातं यस्ते जिघांसति तमितो नाशयामसि॥

यस्त ऊरू विहरत्यन्तरा दंपती शये।
योनिं यो अन्तरारेब्लिह तमितो नाशयामसि॥
यस्त्वा भ्राता पतिर्भूत्वा जारो भुत्वा निपद्यते।
प्रजां यस्ते जिघांसति तमितो नाशयामसि॥
यस्त्वा स्वप्नेन तमसा मोहयित्वा निपद्यते।
प्रजां यस्ते जिघांसति तमितो नाशयामसि॥

1. May Agni, yielding to our prayer, the Raksas-slayer, drive away

   The malady of evil name that hath beset thy labouring womb.

2. Agni, concurring in the prayer, drive off the eater of thy flesh,

   The malady of evil name that hath attacked thy babe and womb.

3. That which destroys the sinking germ, the settled, moving embryo,

   That which will kill the babe at birth,—even this will we drive far away.

4. That which divides thy legs that it may lie between the married pair,

   That penetrates and licks thy side,—even this will we exterminate.

5. What rests by thee in borrowed form of brother, lover, or of lord,

   And would destroy thy progeny,—even this will we exterminate.

6. That which through sleep or darkness hath deceived thee and lies down by thee,

   And will destroy thy progeny,—even this will we exterminate.

(X/162)

Sapatni-badhanam: Charm against a Rival Wife

-.-

Indrani

The hymn is a spell to rid a jealous wife of a more favoured rival. The Rishi is Indrani, the consort of Indra.

इमां खनाम्योषधिं वीरुधं बलवत्तमाम्।
यया सपत्नीं बाधते यया संविन्दते पतिम्॥
उत्तानपर्णे सुभगे देवजूते सहस्वति।
सपत्नीं मे परा धम पतिं मे केवलं कुरु॥
उत्तराहमुत्तर   उत्तरेदुत्तराभ्य:।
अथा सपत्नी या ममाऽधरा साधराभ्य:॥
नह्यस्या नाम गृभ्णामि नो अस्मिन् रमते जने।
परामेव परावतं सपत्नीं गमयामसि॥
अहमस्मि सहमाना ऽथ त्वमसि सासहि:।
उभे सहस्वती भूत्वी सपत्नीं मे सहावहै॥
उप तेऽधां सहमानामभि त्वाधां सहीयसा।
मामनु प्र ते मनो वत्सं गौरिव धावतु
                पथा वारिव धावतु॥

1. From out of the earth I dig this plant, a herb of most effectual power,

    Wherewith one quells the rival wife and gains the husband for oneself.

2. Auspicious, with expanded leaves, sent by the Gods, victorious plant,

    Blow thou the rival wife away, and make my husband only mine.

3. Stronger am I, O Stronger One, yea, mightier than the mightier;

   And she who is my rival wife is lower than the lowest dames.

4. Her very name I utter not: she takes no pleasure in this man.

   Far into distance most remote drive we the rival wife away.

5. I am the conqueror, and thou, thou also act victorious:

   As victory attends us both we will subdue my fellow-wife.

6. I have gained thee for vanquisher, have grasped thee with a stronger spell.

   As a cow hastens to her calf, so let thy spirit speed to me, hasten like water on its way.

(X/145)

Duhswapna-nashaham: Charm against Evil Dreams

-.-

Pracheta

अपेहि मनसस्पते ऽप क्राम परश्चर।
परो निर्ऋत्या आ चक्ष्व बहुधा जीवतो मन:॥
भद्रं वै वरं वृणते भद्रं युञ्जन्ति दक्षिणम्।
भद्रं वैवस्वते चक्षुर्बहुत्रा जीवतो मन:॥
यदाशसा नि:शसाभिशसो पारिम जाग्रतो यत् स्वपन्त:।
अग्निर्वि श्वान्यप दुष्कृतान्यजुष्टान्यारे अस्मद् दधातु॥

यदिन्द्र ब्रह्मणस्पते ऽभिद्रोहं चरामसि।

प्रचेता न आङ्गिरसो द्विषतां पात्वंहस:॥

अजैष्माद्याासनाम चाऽभूमानागसो वयम्।

जाग्रत्स्वप्र: संकल्प पापो यं द्विष्मस्तं स ऋच्छतु यो

नो द्वेष्टि तमृच्छतु।

1. Avaunt, thou Master of the mind! Depart, and vanish far away.

   Look on Destruction far from hence. The live man's mind is manifold.

2. A happy boon do men elect, a mighty blessing they obtain.

   Bliss with Vaivasvata they see. The live man's mind seeks many a place.

3. If by address, by blame, by imprecation we have committed sin, awake or sleeping,

   All hateful acts of ours, all evil doings may Agni bear away to distant places.

4. When, Indra, Brahmanaspati, our deeds are wrongful and unjust,

   May provident Angirasa prevent our foes from troubling us.

5. We have prevailed this day and won: we are made free from sin and guilt.

   Ill thoughts, that visit us awake or sleeping, seize the man we hate, yea, seize the man who hateth us.

(X/164)

Yaksma-nashanam: Charm against Tuberculosis

-.-

Vivraha

अक्षीभ्यां ते नासिकाभ्यां कर्णाभ्यां छुबुकादधि।
यक्ष्मं शीर्षण्यं मस्तिष्काज्जिह्वाया वि वृहामि ते।
ग्रीवाभ्यस्त उष्णिहाभ्य: कीकसाभ्यो अनूक्यात्।
यक्ष्मं दोषण्य१ँमंसाभ्वां बाहुभ्यां वि वृहामि ते॥
आन्त्रेभ्यस्ते गुदाभ्यो वनिष्ठोर्हृदयादधि।
यक्ष्मं मतस्नाभ्यां यक्र: प्लाशिभ्यो वि वृहामि ते॥
ऊरुभ्यां ते अष्ठीवद्ध्दयां पार्ष्णिभ्यां प्रपदाभ्याम्।
यक्ष्मं श्रोणिभ्यां भासदाद्ध्दंससो वि वृहामि ते॥
मेहनाद्वनंकरणाखोमभ्यस्ते   नखेभ्य:।
यक्ष्मं सर्वस्मादात्मनस्तमिदं वि वृहामि ते॥
अङ्गादङ्गाखम्नोलोम्नो जातं पर्वणिपर्वणि।
यक्ष्मं सर्वस्मादात्मनस्तमिदं वि वृहामि ते॥

1. From both thy nostrils, from thine eyes, from both thine ears and from thy chin.

   Forth from thy head and brain and tongue I drive thy malady away.

2. From the neck-tendons and the neck, from the breast-bones and from the spine,

   From shoulders, upper, lower arms, I drive thy malady away.

3. From viscera and all within, forth from the rectum, from the heart,

From kidneys, liver, and from spleen, I drive thy
malady away.

4. From thighs, from knee-caps, and from heels, and
   from the forepart of the feet,

   From hips, from stomach, and from groin I drive
   thy malady away.

5. From what is voided from within, and from thy hair,
   and from   they nails,

   From all thyself from top to toe, I drive thy malady
   away.

6. From every member, every hair, disease that comes
   in every joint,

   From all thyself, from top to toe, I drive thy malady
   away.

(X/163)

Alakshmighuam: Removal of Misfortune

-.-

Shirimbitha

The subject of the hymn is the averting or removal of mis-
fortune. Arayi: 'The stingy,' one of a class of malevolent she-
fiends. Ever-screeching: allied with Danus, Danavas, or
demons.

अरायि काणे विकटे गिरिं गच्छ सदान्वे।
शिरिम्बिठस्य सत्वभिस्तेभिख्वा चातयामसि॥
चत्तो इतश्चत्तामुत: सर्वा भ्रूणान्यारुषी।
अराय्यं ब्रह्मणस्पते तीक्ष्णशृङ्गोदृषत्रिहि॥

अदो यद्वारु प्लव सिन्धो: पारे अपूरुषम्।
तदा रभस्व दुर्हणो तेन गच्छ परस्तरम्॥
यद्ध प्राचीरजगन्तोरो मण्डूरधाणिकी:।
हता इन्द्रस्य शत्रव: सर्वे बुद्बुदयाशव:॥
परीमे गामनेषत पर्यग्निमहृषत।
देवेष्वक्रत श्रव: क इमाँ आ दधर्षति॥

1. Arayi, one-eyed limping hag, fly, ever-screeching, to
   the hill.

   We frighten thee away with these, the heroes of
   Shrimbitha.

2. Scared from this place and that is she, destroyer
   of each germ unborn.

   Go, sharp-horned Brahmanaspti and drive Arayi
   far away.

3. Yon log that floats without a man to guide it on the
   river's edge,—

   Seize it, thou thing with hideous jaws, and go thou
   far away thereon.

4. When foul with secret stain and spot, ye hastened
   onward to the breast,

   All Indra's enemies were slain and passed away
   like froth and foam.

5. These men have led about the cow, have duly carried
   Agni round,

   And raised their glory to the Gods. Who will attack
   them with success?

   (X/155)

Sapatnaghnam: Destruction of Rivals

Rishabha

The subject is the Destruction of Rivals.

ऋषभं मा समानानां सपत्नानां विषासहिम्।
हन्तारं शत्रूणां कृधि विराजं गोपतिं गवाम्॥
अहमस्मि सपत्नहेन्द्र इवारिष्टो अक्षतः।
अधः सपत्ना मे पदोरिमे सर्वे अभिष्ठिताः॥
अत्रैव वोऽपि नह्याम्युभे आर्त्नी इव ज्यया।
वाचस्पते निषेधेमान् यथा मदधरं वदान्॥
अभिभूरहमागमं वि श्वकर्मेण धाम्रा।
आ वश्चित्तमा वो व्रतमा वोऽहं समितिं ददे॥
योगक्षेमं व आदायाऽहं भूयासमुत्तम आ वो मूर्धानमक्रमीम्।
अधस्पदान्म उद्वदत मण्डूका इवोदकान्मण्डूका उदकादिव॥

1. Make me a bull among my peers, make me my rivals' conqueror:

   Make me the slayer of my foes, a sovran ruler, lord of kine.

2. I am my rivals' slayer, like Indra unwounded and unhurt,

   And all these enemies of mine are vanquished and beneath my feet.

3. Here, verily, I bind you fast, as the two bow-ends with the string.

   Press down these men, O Lord of Speech, that they may humbly speak to me.

4. Hither I came as conqueror with mighty all-effecting power,

   And I have mastered all your thought, your synod, and your holy work.

5. May I be highest, having gained your strength in war, your skill in peace: my feet have trodden on your heads.

   Speak to me from beneath my feet, as Frogs from out of the water croak, as frogs from out of the water croak.

   (X/166)

Mrityu: Death

-.-

Sankusu

Mrtyu, the God of Death, is distinct from Yama, the judge and ruler of the departed.

परं मृत्यो अनु परेहि पन्थां यस्ते स्व इतरो देवयानात्।
चक्षुष्मते शृण्वते ते ब्रवीमि मा न: प्रजां रीरिषो मोत वीरान्॥
मृत्यो: पदं योपयन्तो यदैत द्राघीय आयु: प्रतरं दधाना:।
आप्यायमाना: प्रजया धनेन शुद्धा: पूता भवत यज्ञियास:॥
इमे जीवा वि मृतैराववृत्रन्नभूद्भद्रा देवहूतिर्नो अद्य।
पाञ्चो अगाम नृतये हसाय द्राघीय आयु: प्रतरं दधानां॥
इमं जीवेभ्य: परिधिं दधामि मैषां नु गादपरो अर्थमेतम्।
शतं जीवन्तु शरद: पुरूचीरन्तर्मृत्युं दधतां पर्वतेन॥
यथाहान्यनुपूर्वं भवन्ति यथ ऋतव ऋतुभिर्यन्ति साधु।

यथा न पूर्वमपरो जहात्येवा धातरायूषि कल्पयैषाम्॥
आ रोहतायुर्जरसं वृणाना अनुपूर्वं यतमाना यति ष्ठ।
इह त्वष्टा सुजनिमा सजोषा दीर्घमायुः करति जीवसे वः॥
इमा नारीरविधवाः सुपत्नीराञ्जनेन सर्पिषा सं विशन्तु।
अनश्रवोऽनमीवाः सुरत्ना आ रोहन्तु जनयो योनिमग्रे॥
उदीर्ष्व नार्यभि जीवलोकं गतासुमेतमुप शेष एहि।
हस्तग्राभस्य दिधिषोस्तवेदं पत्युर्जनित्वमभि सं बभूथ॥
धनुर्हस्तादाददानो मृतस्याऽस्मे क्षत्राय वर्चसे बलाय।
अत्रैव त्वमिह वयं सुवीरा विश्वाः स्पृधो अभिमातीर्जयेम॥
उप सर्प मातरं भूमिमेता मुरुव्यचसं पृथिवीं सुशेवाम्।
ऊर्णम्रदा युवतिर्दक्षिणावत एषा त्वा पातु निर्ऋतेरुपस्थात्॥
उच्छृञ्चस्व पृथिवि मा नि बाधथाः सूपायनास्मै भव सूपवञ्चना।
माता पुत्रं यथा सिचा ऽभ्येनं भूम ऊर्णुहि॥
उच्छ्वञ्चमाना पृथिवी सु तिष्ठतु सहस्रं मित उप हि श्रयन्ताम्।
ते गृहासो घृतश्रुतो भवन्तु वि श्वाहास्मै शरणाः सन्त्वत्र॥
उत् ते स्तभ्नामि पृथिवीं त्वत् परीमं लोगं निदधन्मो अहं रिषम्।
एतां स्थूणां पितरो धारयन्तु तेऽत्रा यमः सादना ते मिनोतु॥
प्रतीचीने मामहनीष्वाः पर्णमिवा दधुः।
प्रतीचीं जग्रभा वाचमश्वं रशनया यथा॥

1. Go hence O Death, pursue thy special pathway apart from that which Gods are wont to travel.

   To thee I say it who hast eyes and hearest: Touch not our offspring, injure not our heroes.

2. As ye have come effacing Mrityu's footstep, to further times prolonging your existence,

   May ye be rich in children and possessions. cleansed, purified, and meet for sacrificing.

3. Divided from the dead are these, the living: now be our calling on the Gods successful.

   We have gone forth for dancing and for laughter, to further times prolonging our existence.

4. Here I erect this rampart for the living; let none of these, none other, reach this limit.

   May they survive a hundred lengthened autumns, and may they bury Death beneath this mountain.

5. As the days follow days in close succession, as with the seasons duly come the seasons,

   As each successor fails not his foregoer, so form the lives of these, O great Ordainer.

6. Live your full lives and find old age delightful, all of you striving one behind the other.

   May Tvastar, maker of fair things, be gracious and lengthen out the days of your existence.

7. Let these unwidowed dames with noble husbands adorn themselves with fragrant balm and unguent.

   Decked with fair jewels, tearless, free from sorrow, first let the dames go up to where he lieth.

8. Rise, come unto the world of life, O woman: come, he is lifeless by whose side thou liest.

   Wifehood with this thy husband was thy portion, who took thy hand and wooed thee as a lover.

9. From his dead hand I take the bow he carried, that it may be our power and might and glory.

   There art thou, there; and here with noble heroes may we'oercome all hosts that fight against us.

10. Betake thee to the lap of Earth the Mother, of Earth far-spreading, very kind and gracious.

Young Dame, wool-soft unto the guerdon giver, may she preserve thee from Destruction's bosom.

11. Heave thyself, Earth, nor press thee downward heavily : afford him easy access, gently tending him.

Cover him, as a mother wraps her skirt about her child, O Earth.

12. Now let the heaving earth be free from motion: yea, let a thousand clods remain above him.

Be they to him a home distilling fatness, here let them ever be his place of refuge.

13. I stay the earth from thee, while over thee I place this piece of earth. May I be free from injury.

Here let the Fathers keep this pillar firm for thee, and there let Yama make thee an abiding-place.

14. Even as an arrow's feathers, they have set me on a fitting day.

The fit word have I caught and held as 'twere a courser with the rein.

(X/18)

Yama: Ruler of the Dead

-.-

Yama

The hymn is a funeral address, partly to Yama, the God of the Dead, and partly to the soul of the departed whose body is being consumed on the pile. Yama: the deified Lord of the Dead: originally the first who died and so showed the souls of his successors the way to the home of the departed.

परेयिवांसं प्रवतो महीरनु बहुभ्यः पन्थामनुपस्पशानम्।
वैवस्वतं संगमनं जनानां यमं राजानं हविषा दुवस्य।।

यमो नो गातुं प्रथमो विवेद नैषा गव्यूतिरपभर्तवा उ।
यत्रा नः पूर्वे पितरः परेयुरेना जज्ञानाः पथ्या३ अनु स्वाः।।

मातली कव्यैर्यमो अङ्गिरोभिर्बृहस्पतिर्ऋक्वभिवावृधानः।
याँश्च देवा वावृधुर्ये च देवान् त्स्वाहान्ये स्वधयान्ये मदन्ति।।

इमं यम प्रस्तरमा हि सीदाऽङ्गिरोभिः पितृभिः संविदानः।
आ त्वा मन्त्राः कविशस्ता वहन्त्वेना राजन् हविषा मादयस्व।।

अङ्गिरोभिरा गहि यज्ञियेभिर्यम वैरूपैरिह मादयस्व।
विवस्वन्तं हुवे यः पिता ते अस्मिन् यज्ञे बर्हिष्या निषद्य।।

अङ्गिरसो नः पितरो नवग्वा अथर्वाणो भृगवः सोम्यासः।
तेषां वयं सुमतौ यज्ञियानामपि भद्रे सौमनसे स्याम।।

प्रेहि प्रेहि पथिभिः पूर्व्येभिर्यत्रा नः पूर्वे पितरः परेयुः।
उभा राजाना स्वधया मदन्ता यमं पश्यासि वरुणं च देवम्।।

सं गच्छस्व पितृभिः सं यमेनेष्टापूर्तेन परमे व्योमन्।
हित्वायावद्यं पुनरस्तमेहि सं गच्छस्व तन्वा सुवर्चाः।।

अपेत वीत वि च सर्पतातोऽस्मा एतं पितरो लोकमक्रन्।
अहोभिरद्भिरक्तुभिर्व्यक्तं यमो ददात्यवसानमस्मै।।

अति द्रव सारमेयौ श्वानौ चतुरक्षौ शबलौ साधुना पथा।
अथा पितॄन्त्सुविदत्राँ उपेहि यमेन ये सधमादं मदन्ति।।

यौ ते श्वानौ यम रक्षितारौ चतुरक्षौ पथिरक्षी नृचक्षसौ।
ताभ्यामेनं परि देहि राजन् त्स्वस्ति चास्मा अनमीवं च धेहि।।

उरूणसावसुतृपा उदुम्बलौ यमस्य दूतौ चरतो जनाँ अनु।
तावस्मभ्यं दृशये सूर्याय पुनर्दातामसुमद्येह भद्रम्।।

यमाय सोमं सुनुत यमाय जुहुता हविः।
यमं ह यज्ञो गच्छत्यग्निदूतो अरंकृतः।।

यमाय घृतवद्धविर्जुहोत प्र च तिष्ठत।
स नो देवेष्वा यमद् दीर्घमायुः प्र जीवसे।।

यमाय मधुमत्तमं राज्ञे हव्यं जुहोतन।

इदं नम ऋषिभ्यः पूर्वजेभ्यः पूर्वेभ्यः पथिकृद्भ्यः॥
त्रिकद्रुकेभिः पतति पञ्चवीरकेमिद्धृहत।
त्रिष्टुब्गायत्री छन्दासि सर्वा ता यम आहिता॥

1. Honour the King with thine oblations, Yama, Vivasvan's Son, who gathers men together,

   Who travelled to the lofty heights above us, who searches out and shows the path to many.

2. Yama first found for us a place to dwell in: this pasture never can be taken from us.

   Men born on earth tread their own paths that lead them whither our ancient Fathers have departed.

3. Matali prospers there with Kavyas, Yama with Angiras' sons, Brihaspati with Rikvans:

   Exalters of the Gods, by Gods exalted, some joy in praise and some in our oblation.

4. Come, seat thee on this bed of grass, O Yama, in company with Angirases and Fathers.

   Let texts recited by the sages bring thee: O King, let this oblation make thee joyful.

5. Come, Yama, with the Angirases the Holy rejoice thee here with children of Virupa.

   To sit on sacred, grass at this our worship, I call Vivasvan, too, thy Father hither.

6. Our Fathers are Angirases, Navagvas, Atharvans, Bhrigus who deserve the Soma.

   May these, the Holy, look on us with favour, may we enjoy their gracious loving-kindness.

7. Go forth, go forth upon the ancient pathways whereon our sires of old have gone before us.

There shalt thou look on both the Kings enjoying their sacred food, God Varuna and Yama.

7. Meet Yama, meet the Fathers, meet the merit of free or ordered acts, in highest heaven.

    Leave sin and evil, seek anew thy dwelling, and bright with glory wear another body.

8. Go hence, depart ye, fly in all directions: this place for him the Fathers have provided.

    Yama bestows on him a place to rest in adorned with days and beams of light and waters.

9. Run and outspeed the two dogs, Sarama's offspring, brindled, four-eyed, upon thy happy pathway.

    Draw nigh then to the gracious-minded Fathers where they rejoice in company with Yama.

10. And those two dogs of thine, Yama, the watchers, four-eyed, who look on men and guard the pathway,—

    Entrust this man, O King, to their protection, and with prosperity and health endow him.

11. Dark-hued, insatiate, with distended nostrils, Yama's two envoys roam among the people;

    May they restore to us a fair existence here and today, that we may see the sunlight.

12. To Yama pour the Soma, bring to Yama consecrated gifts:

    To Yama sacrifice prepared and heralded by Agni goes.

13. Offer to Yama holy gifts enriched with butter, and draw near:

    So may he grant that we may live long day of life among the Gods.

14. Offer to Yama, to the King, oblation very rich in meath:

Bow down before the Rishis of the ancient times, who made this path in days of old.

15. Into the six Expanses flies the Great One in Trikadrukas.

The Gayatri, the Tristup, all metres in Yama are contained.

(X/14)

•

Kumar

The subject of the hymn appears to be the funeral ceremony of a boy (*kumara*, said by some to be the name of a man). According to Sayana, a youth named Nackiketas was sent by his father to the kingdom of Yama who treated him kindly and allowed him to return to this world. It seems to have been the basis of the discussion in the Taittiriya Brahmana and in the Katha Upanishad, respecting what becomes of the soul after death, in dialogues between Naciketas and Yama.

यस्मिन् वृक्षे सुपलाशे देवै: संपिबते यम:।
अत्रा नो विश्पति: पिता पुराणाँ अनु वेनति॥

पुराणाँ अनुवेनन्तं चरन्तं पापयामुया।
असूयन्नभ्यचाकशं तस्मा अस्पृहयं पुन:॥

यं कुमार नवं रथमचक्रं मनसाकृणो:।
एकेषं विश्वत: प्राञ्चमपश्यन्नधि तिष्ठसि॥

यं कुमार प्रावर्तयो रथं विप्रेभ्यस्परि।
तं सामानु प्रावर्तत समितो नाव्याहितम्॥

क: कुमारमजनयद्रथं को निरवर्तयत्।
क: स्वित् तदद्य नो ब्रूयादनुदेयी यथाभवत्॥

यथाभवदनुदेयी ततो अग्रमजायत।
पुरस्ताद्बुघ्न आततः पश्चान्निरयणं कृतम्॥
इदं यमस्य सादनं देवमानं यदुच्यते।
इयमस्य धम्यते नाळीरयं गीर्भिः परिष्कृतः॥

1. In the Tree clothed with goodly leaves where Yama drinketh with the Gods,

   The Father, Master of the house, tendeth with love our ancient Sires.

2. I looked reluctantly on him who cherishes those men of old,

   On him who treafd that evil path, and then I yearned for this again.

3. Thou mountest, though thou dost not see, O Child, the new and wheel-less car

   Which thou hast fashioned mentally, onepoled but turning every way.

4. The car which thou hast made to roll hitherward from the Sages, Child!

   This hath the Saman followed close, hence, laid together on a ship.

5. Who was the father of the child? Who made the chariot roll away?

   Who will this day declare to us how the funeral gift was made?

6. When the funeral gift was placed, straightway the point of flame appeared.

   A depth extended in the front: a passage out was made behind.

7. Here is the seat where Yama dwells, that which is
   called the Home of Gods:

   Here minstrels blow the flute for him: here he
   is glorified with songs.

   (X/135)

Bhavavrittam: Funeral Hymn

-.-

Yami Vaivasvati

The Rishi of this funeral hymn is Yami, sister of Yama. *To
those let him depart:* let the spirit of the dead go to the realm
of the blessed, to the Fathers who receive offerings of Soma
juice and clarified butter.

सोम एकेभ्य: पवते घृतमेक उपासते।
येभ्यो मधु प्रधावति ताँश्चिदेवापि गच्छतात्॥
तपसा ये अनाधृष्यास्तपसा ये स्वर्ययु:।
तपो ये चक्रिरे महस्ताँश्चिदेवापि गच्छतात्॥
ये युध्यन्ते प्रधनेषु शूरासो ये तनूत्यज:।
ये वा सहस्रदक्षिणास्ताँश्चिदेवापि गच्छतात्॥
ये चित् पूर्वं ऋतसाप ऋताँवान ऋताावृध:।
पितृन् तपस्वतो यम ताँश्चिदेवापि गच्छतात्॥
सहस्रणीथा: कवयो ये गोपायन्ति सूर्यम्।
ऋषीन् तपस्वतो यम तपोजाँ अपि गच्छतात्॥

1. For some is Soma purified, some sit by sacrificial
   oil:

To those for whom the meath flows forth, even to those let him depart.

2. Invincible through Fervour, those whom Fervour hath advanced to heaven,

   Who showed great Fervour in their lives,—even to those let him depart.

3. The heroes who contend in war and boldly cast their lives away,

   Or who give guerdon thousandfold,—even to those let him depart.

4. Yea, the first followers of Law, Law's pure and holy strengtheners,

   The Fathers, Yama! Fervour-moved,—even to those let him depart.

5. Skilled in a thousand ways and means, the sages who protect the Sun,

   The Rishis, Yama! Fervour-moved,—even to those let him depart.

(X/154)

Sudas Paijavan: The Sudas Story

-.-

Vasishtha

The hymn glorifies Indra as the protector of Sudas, the King of the Tritsus, and praises the liberality of that prince.

त्वे ह यत् पितरश्चिन्न इन्द्र क्षिवा वामा जरितारो असन्वन्।
त्वे गाव: सुदुघास्त्वे ह्र्श्वास्त्वं वसु देवयते वनिष्ठ:॥
राजेव हि जनिभि: क्षेष्येवाऽव द्युभिरभि विदुष्कवि: सन्।
पिशा गिरो मघवन् गोभिरश्वैस्त्वायत: शिशीहि राये अस्मान्॥
इमा उ त्वा पस्पृधानासो अत्र मन्द्रा गिरो देवयन्तीरुप स्थु:।
अर्वाची ते पथ्या राय एतु स्याम ते सुमताविन्द्र शर्मन्॥
धेनुं न त्वा सूयवसे दुदुक्षन्नुप ब्रह्माणि ससृजे वसिष्ठ:।
त्वामिन्मे गोपतिं विश्व आहा ऽऽन इन्द्र: सुमतिं गन्त्वच्छ॥
अर्णांसि चित् पप्रथाना सुदास इन्द्रो गाधान्यकृणोत् सुपारा।
शर्धन्त शिम्युमुचथस्य नव्य: शापं सिन्धूनामकृणोदशस्ती:॥
पुरोळा इत् तुर्वशो यक्षुरासीद् राये मत्स्यासो निशिता अपीव।
श्रुष्टि चक्रुर्भृगवो द्रुह्यव श्व सखा सखायमतरद् विषूचो:॥

आ पक्थासो भलानसो भनन्ता ऽलिनासो विषाणिनः शिवासः।
आ योऽनयत् सधमा आर्यस्य गव्या तृत्सुभ्यो अजगन् युधा नॄन्॥

दुराध्यो३ अदितिं स्रेवयन्तो ऽचेतसो वि जगृभ्रे परुष्णीम्।
मह्नाविव्यक् पृथिवीं पत्यमानः पशुष्कविरशयच्चायमानः॥

ईयुरर्थं न न्यर्थं परुष्णीमाशुश्चनेदभिपित्वं जगाम।
सुदास इन्द्रः सुतुकाँ अमित्रा नरन्धयन्मानुषे वध्रिवाचः॥

ईयुर्गावो न यवसादगोपा यथाकृतमभि मित्रं चितासः।
पृश्निगावः पृश्निनिप्रेषितासः श्रुष्टिं चक्रुर्नियुतो रन्तयश्च॥

एकं च यो विंशतिं च श्रवस्या वैकर्णयोर्जनान् राजा न्यस्तः।
दस्मो न सद्मन् नि शिशाति बर्हिः शूरः सर्गमकृणोदिन्द्र एषाम्॥

अध श्रुतं कवषं वृद्धमप्स्वनु दुह्यं नि वृणग्वज्रबाहुः।
वृणाना अत्र सख्याय सख्यं त्वायन्तो ये अभदन्नु त्वा॥

वि सद्यो विश्वा दृंहितान्येषामिन्द्रः पुरः सहसा सप्त दर्दः।
व्यानवस्य तृत्सवे गयं भाग्जेष्म पुरुं विदथे मृध्रवाचम्॥

नि गव्यवोऽनवो द्रुह्यवश्च षष्टिः शता सुषुपुः षट् सहस्रा।
षष्टिर्वीरासो अधि षड् दुवोयु क्ष्वेदिन्द्रस्य वीर्या कृतानि॥

इन्द्रेणैते तृत्सवो वेविषाणा आपो न सृष्टा अधवन्त नीचीः।
दुर्मित्रासः प्रकलविन्निममाना जहुर्विश्वानि भोजना सुदासे॥

अर्धं वीरस्य शृतपामनिन्द्रं परा शर्धन्तं नुनुदे अभि क्षाम्।
इन्द्रो मन्युं मन्युम्यो मिमाय भेजे पथो वर्तनिं पत्यमानः॥

आध्रेण चित् तद्वेकं चकार सिंह्यं चित् पेत्वेना जघान।
अव स्रक्तीर्वेश्यावृश्चदिन्द्रः प्रायच्छद् विश्वा भोजना सुदासे॥

शश्वन्तो हि शत्रवो रारधुष्टे भेदस्य चिच्छर्धतो विन्द रन्धिम्।
मर्ता एनः स्तुवतो यः कृणोति तिग्मं तस्मिन् नि जहि वज्रमिन्द्र॥

आवदिन्द्रं यमुना तृत्सवश्व प्रात्र भेदं सर्वताता मुषायत्।
अजासश्च शिग्रवो यक्षवश्च बलिं शीर्षाणि जभ्रुरश्वयानि॥

न त इन्द्र सुमतयो न राय: संचक्षे पूर्वा उपसो न नूत्ना:।
देवकं चिन्मान्यमानं जघन्थाऽव त्मना बृहत: शम्बरं भेत्॥

प्र ये गृहादममदुस्त्वाया पराशर: शतयातुर्वसिष्ठ:।
न ते भोजस्य सख्यं मृषन्ताऽधा सूरिभ्य: सुदिना व्युच्छान्॥

द्वे नप्तुर्देववत: शते गोद्रा रथा वधूमन्ता सुदास:।
अर्हन्नग्ने पैजवनस्य दानं होतेव सद्य पर्येमि रेभन्॥

चत्वारो मा पैजवनस्य दाना: स्मद्दिष्टय: कृशनिनो निरेके।
ऋज्रासो मा पृथिविष्ठा: सुदासस्तोकं तोकाय श्रवसे वहन्ति॥

यस्य श्रवो रोदसी अन्तरुर्वी शीर्ष्णेशीर्ष्णे विबभाजा विभक्ता।
सप्तेदिन्द्रं न स्रवतो गृणन्ति नि युध्यामधिमशिशादभीके॥

इमं नरो मरुत: सश्चतानु दिवोदासं न पितरं सुदास:।
अविष्टना पैजवनस्य केतं दूणाशं क्षत्रमजरं दुवोयु॥

1. All is with thee, O Indra, all the treasures which
   erst our fathers won who sang thy praises.

   With thee are milch-kine good to milk, and
   horses: best winner thou of riches for the pious.

2. For like a King among his wives thou dwellest: with
   glories, as a Sage, surround and help us.

   Make us, thy servants, strong for wealth, and
   honour our songs with kine and steeds and
   decoration.

3. Here these our holy hymns with joy and gladness
   in pious emulation have approached thee.

   Hitherward come thy path that leads to riches:
   may we find shelter in thy favour, Indra.

4. Vasistha hath poured forth his prayers, desiring to
   milk thee like a cow in goodly pasture.

   All these my people call thee Lord of cattle:

may Indra come unto the prayer we offer.

5. What though the floods spread widely, Indra made them shallow and easy for Sudas to traverse.

   He, worthy of our praises, caused the Simyu, foe of our hymn, to curse the rivers' fury.

6. Eager for spoil was Turvasa Purodas, fain to win wealth, like fishes urged by hunger.

   The Bhrigus and the Druhyus quickly listened: friend rescued friend mid the two distant peoples.

7. Together came the Pakthas, the Bhalanas, the Alinas, the Sivas, the Visanins.

   Yet to the Tritsus came the Arya's Comrade, through love of spoil and heroes' war, to lead them.

8. Fools, in their folly fain to waste her waters, they parted inexhaustible Parusni.

   Lord of the Earth, he with his might repressed them: still lay the herd and the affrighted herdsman.

9. As to their goal they sped to their destruction: they sought Parusni; e'en the swift returned not.

   Indra abandoned, to Sudas the manly, the swiftly flying foes, unmanly babblers.

10. They went like kine unherded from the pasture, each clinging to a friend as chance directed.

    They who drive spotted steeds, sent down by Prisni, gave ear, the Warriors and the harnessed horses.

11. The King who scattered one-and-twenty people of both Vaikarna tribes through lust of glory—

    As the skilled priest clips grass within the chamber, so hath the Hero Indra wrought their downfall.

12. Thou, thunder-armed, o'erwhelmedst in the waters famed ancient Kavasa and then the Druhyu.

    Others here claiming friendship to their friendship, devoted unto thee, in thee were joyful.

13. Indra at once with conquering might demolished all their strong places and their seven castles.

    The goods of Anu's son he gave to Tritsu. May we in sacrifice conquer scornful Puru.

14. The Anavas and Druhyus, seeking booty, have slept, the sixty hundred, yea, six thousand,

    And six-and-sixty heroes. For the pious were all these mighty exploits done by Indra.

15. These Tritsus under Indra's careful guidance came speeding like loosed waters rushing downward.

    The foemen, measuring exceeding closely, abandoned to Sudas all their provisions.

16. The hero's side who drank the dressed oblation, Indra's denier, far o'er earth he scattered.

    Indra brought down the fierce destroyer's fury. He gave them various roads, the path's Controller.

17. E'en with the weak he wrought this matchless exploit: e'en with a goat he did to death a lion.

    He pared the pillar's angles with a needle. Thus to Sudas Indra gave all provisions.

18. To thee have all thine enemies submitted: e'en the fierce Bheda hast thou made thy subject.

    Cast down thy sharpened thunderbolt, O Indra, on him who harms the men who sing thy praises.

19. Yamuna and the Tritsus aided Indra. There he

stripped Bheda bare of all his treasures.

The Ajas and the Sigrus and the Yaksus brought in to him as tribute heads of horses.

20. Not to be scorned, but like Dawns past and recent, O Indra, are thy favours and thy riches.

Devaka, Manyamana's son, thou slewest, and smotest Sambara from the lofty mountain.

21. They who, from home, have gladdened thee, thy servants Parasara, Vasistha, Satayatu,

Will not forget thy friendship, liberal Giver. So shall the days dawn prosperous for the princes.

22. Priest-like, with praise, I move around the altar, earning Paijavana's reward, O Agni,

Two hundred cows from Devavan's descendant, two chariots from Sudas with mares to draw them.

23. Gift of Paijavana, four horses bear me in foremost place, trained steeds with pearl to deck them.

Sudas's brown steeds, firmly-stepping, carry me and my son for progeny and glory.

24. Him whose fame spreads between wide earth and heaven, who, as dispenser, gives each chief his portion,

Seven flowing Rivers glorify like Indra. he slew Yudhyamadhi in close encounter.

25. Attend on him O ye heroic Maruts, as on Sudas's father Divodasa.

Further Paijavana's desire with favour. Guard faithfully his lasting firm dominion.

(VII/18)

Sarama Panayosurah: Sarama and the Panis

-.·-.·-.·-.·-.·-.·-.·-.·-.·-.·-.·-.·-.·-.·-.·-.·-.·-.·-

Panis and Sarama

The hymn is a colloquy between Sarama, the mesenger of the Gods or of Indra, and the Panis or envious demons who have carried off the cows or rays of light which Indra wishes to recover.

The Panis address Sarama who has found her way to the rocky stronghold in which the stolen cows are imprisoned. The Panis speak the uneven stanzas, with the exception of stanza II, and Sarama the even. Rasa is in this place a mythical stream that flows round the atmosphere and the earth. Rasa appears to be a river of the Punjab, probably an affluent of the Indus.

किमिच्छन्ती सरमा प्रेदमानड् दूरे ह्यध्वा जगुरि: पराचै:।
कास्मेहिति: का परितक्म्यासीत् कथं रसाया अतर: पयांसि।।
इन्द्रस्य दूतीरिषिता चरामि मह इच्छन्ती पणयो निधीन् व:।
अतिष्कदो भियसा तन्न आवत् तथा रसाया अतरं पयासि।।
कीदृङिदन्द्र सरमे का दृशीका यस्येदं दूतीरसर: पराकात्।
आ च गच्छान्मित्रमेना दधामाऽथा गवां गोपतिर्नो भवाति।।
नाहं तं वेद दभ्यं दभत् स यस्येदं दूतीरसरं पराकात्।
न तं गूहन्ति स्रवतो गभीरा हता इन्द्रेण पणय: शयध्वे।।
इमा गाव: सरमे या ऐच्छ: परि दिवो अन्तान् सुभगे पतन्ती।
कस्त एना अव सृजादयुध्व्युतास्माकमायुधा सन्ति तिग्मा।।
असेन्या व: पणयो वंचास्य निषव्यास्तन्व: सन्तु पापी:।
अधृष्टो व एतवा अस्तु पन्था बृहस्पतिर्व उभया न मृळात्।।

अयं निधि: सरमे अद्रिबुध्नो गोभिरश्वेभिर्वसुभिर्न्यृष्ट:।
रक्षन्ति तं पणयो ये सुगोपा रेकु पदमलकमा जगन्थ॥
एह गमन्नृषय: सोमशिता अयास्यो अङ्गिरसो नवग्वा:।
त एतमूर्वं वि भजन्त गोनामथैतद्वच: पणयो वमन्त्रित्॥
एवा च त्वं सरम आजगन्थ प्रबाधिता सहसा दैव्येन।
स्वसारं त्वा कृणवै मा पुनर्गा अप ते गवां सुभगे भजाम॥
नाहं वेद भ्रातृत्वं नो स्वसृत्वमिन्द्रो विदुरङ्गिरसश्च घोरा:।
गोकामा मे अच्छदयन् यदायमपात इत पणयो वरीय:॥
दूरमित पणयो वरीय उद्गावो यन्तु मिनतीर्ऋतेन।
बृहस्पतिर्या अविन्दन्निगूळ्हा: सोमो ग्रावाण ऋषयश्व विप्रा:।

1. What wish of Sarama hath brought her hither? The
   path leads far away to distant places.

   What charge hast thou for us? Where turns thy
   journey? How hast thou made thy way o'er Rasa's
   waters.

2. I come appointed messenger of Indra, seeking your
   ample stores of wealth, O Panis.

   This hath preserved me from the fear of crossing:
   thus have I made my way o'er Rasa's waters.

3. What is that Indra like, what is his aspect whose
   envoy, Sarama, from afar thou comest?

   Let him approach, and we will show him
   friendship: he shall be made the herds man of our
   cattle.

4. I know him safe from harm : but he can punish
   who sent me hither from afar as envoy.

   Him rivers flowing with deep waters hide not.

Low will ye be, O Panis, slain by Indra.

5. These are the kine which, Sarama, thou seekest,
   flying, O Blest One, to the ends of heaven.

   Who will loose these for thee without a battle?
   Yea, and sharp-pointed are our warlike weapons.

6. Even if your wicked bodies, O ye Panis, were arrow-
   proof, your words are weak for wounding;

   And were the path to you as yet unmastered,
   Brihaspati in neither case will spare you.

7. Paved with the rock is this our treasure-chamber;
   filled full of precious things, of kine, and horses.

   These Panis who are watchful keepers guard it.
   In vain hast thou approached this lonely station.

8. Rishis will come inspirited with Soma, Angirases
   unwearied, and Navagvas.

   This stall of cattle will they part among them:
   then will the Panis wish these words unspoken.

9. Even thus, O Sarama, hast thou come hither, forced
   by celestial might to make the journey.

   Turn thee not back, for thou shalt be our sister:
   O Blest One, we will give thee of the cattle.

10. Brotherhood, sisterhood, I know not either: the dread
    Angirases and Indra know them.

    They seemed to long for kine when I departed.
    Hence, into distance, be ye gone, O Panis.

11. Hence, far away, ye Panis! Let the cattle lowing
    come forth as holy Law commandeth, Kine which
    Brihaspati, and Soma, Rishis, sages, and pressing-
    stones have found when hidden.

(X/108)

Vrisakapi: The Strong Ape

-·-

Indra

Vrisakapi is said to have monopolized the offerings that should have been presented to Indra. *Vrisakapi*—literally 'the strong ape.' or 'the male ape'—appears to be a sort of intermediate being between a demigod and a demon.

He is also said to be the setting sun, and the sun who draws up vapour and irrigates with mist. According to M. Bergaigne, he was a mythical sacrificer.

वि   हि   सोतोरसृक्षत्   नेन्द्रं   देवममंसत।

यत्रामददृषाकपिग्यः पुष्टेषु मत्सखा वि श्वस्मादिन्द्र उत्तरः॥

परा   हीन्द्र   धावसि   वृषाकपेरति   व्यथिः।

नो अह प्र विन्दस्यन्यत्र सोमपीतये वि श्वस्मादिन्द्र उत्तरः॥

किमयं   त्वां   वृषाकपिश्चकार   हरितो   मृगः।

यस्मा इरस्यसीदु न्वर्यो वा पुष्टिमद्वसु वि श्वस्मादिन्द्र उत्तरः॥

यमिमं   त्वं   वृषाकपिं   प्रियमिन्द्राभिरक्षसि।

श्वा न्वस्य जम्भिषदपि कर्णं वराहयुर्वि श्वस्मादिन्द्र उत्तरः॥

प्रिया   तष्टानि   मे   कपिर्व्यक्ता   व्यदृदुषत्।

शिरो न्वस्य राविषं न सुरां दुष्कृते भुवं वि श्वस्मादिन्द्र उत्तरः॥

न मत् स्त्री सुभसत्तरा न सुयाशुतरा भुवत्।

न मत् प्रतिच्यवीयसी न सक्थ्युद्यमीयसी वि श्वस्मादिन्द्र उत्तरः॥

उवे   अम्ब   सुलाभिके   यथेवाङ्ग   भविष्यति।

भसन्मे अम्ब सक्थि मे शिरो मे वीव हृष्यति विश्वस्मादिन्द्र उत्तरः॥

किं   सुबाहो   स्वङ्गुरे   पृथुष्टो   पृथुजाघने।

किं शूरपत्नि नस्त्वमभ्यमीपि वृषाकपि वि श्वस्मादिन्द्र उत्तरः॥

अवीरामिव   मामयं   शरारुरभि   मन्यते।

उताहमस्मि वीरिणीन्द्रपत्नी मरुत्सखा वि श्वस्मादिन्द्र उत्तरः॥

संहोत्रं स्म पुरा नारी समनं वाव गच्छति।

वेधा ऋतस्य वीरिणीन्द्रपत्नी महीयते वि श्वस्मादिन्द्र उत्तर:॥

इन्द्राणीमासु नारिषु सुभगामहमश्रवम्।

नह्यस्या अपरं चन जरसा मरते पतिर्वि श्वस्मादिन्द्र उत्तर:॥

नाहमिन्द्राणि रारण सख्युर्वृषाकपेर्ऋते।

यस्येदमप्यं हवि: प्रियं देवेषु गच्छति वि श्वस्मादिन्द्र उत्तर:॥

वृषाकपायि रेवति सुपुत्र आदु सुस्नुपे।

घसत त इन्द्र उक्षण: प्रियं काचित्करं हविर्वि श्वस्मादिन्द्र उत्तर:॥

उक्ष्णो हि मे पञ्चदश साकं पचन्ति विंशतिम्।

उताहमद्मि पीव इदुभा कुक्षी पृणन्ति मे वि श्वस्मादिन्द्र उत्तर:॥

वृषभो न तिग्मशृङ्गो ऽन्तर्यूथेषु रोरुवत्।

मन्थस्त इन्द्र शं हृदे यं ते सुनोति भावयुर्वि श्वस्मादिन्द्र उत्तर:॥

न सेशे यस्य रम्बते ऽन्तरा सक्थ्या३ कपृत्।

सेदीशे यस्य रोमशं निषेदुषो विजृम्भते वि श्वस्मादिन्द्र उत्तर:॥

न सेशे यस्य रोमशं निषेदुषो विजृम्भते।

सेदीशे यस्य रम्बते ऽन्तरा सक्थ्या३ कपृद् वि श्वस्मादिन्द्र उत्तर:॥

अयमिन्द्र वृषाकपि: परस्वन्तं हतं विदत्।

असिं सूनां नवं चरुमादेधस्यान आचितं वि श्वस्मादिन्द्र उत्तर:॥

अयमेमि विचाकशद् विचिन्वन् दासमार्यम्।

पिबामि पाकसुत्वनो ऽभि धीरमचाकशं वि श्वस्मादिन्द्र उत्तर:॥

धन्व च यत् कृन्तत्रं च कति स्वित् ता वि योजना।

नेदीयसो वृषाकपे ऽस्तमेहि गृहाँ उप वि श्वस्मादिन्द्र उत्तर:॥

पुनरेहि वृषाकपे सुविता कल्पयावहै।

य एष स्वप्ननंशनो ऽस्तमेषि पथा पुनर्वि श्वस्मादिन्द्र उत्तर:॥

यदुदञ्चो वृषाकपे गृहमिन्द्राजगन्तन।

क्व१स्य पुल्वधो मृग: कमगञ्जनयोपनो विश्वस्मादिन्द्र उत्तर:॥

पर्शुर्हं नाम मानवी साकं ससूव विंशतिम्।

भद्रं भल त्यस्या अभूद् यस्या उदरमामयद् वि श्वस्मादिन्द्र उत्तर:॥

1. Men have abstained from pouring juice: they count not Indra as a God.

   Where at the votary's store my friend Vrisakapi hath drunk his fill. Supreme is Indra over all.

2. Thou, Indra, heedless passest by the ill Vrisakapi hath wrought;

   Yet nowhere else. thou findest place wherein to drink the Soma juice. Supreme is Indra over all.

3. What hath he done to injure thee, this tawny beast Vrisakapi,

   With whom thou art so angry now? What is the votary's foodful store? Supreme is Indra over all.

4. Soon may the hound who hunts the boar seize him and bite him in the ear,

   O Indra, that Vrisakapi whom thou protectest as a friend. Supreme is Indra over all.

5. Kapi hath marred the beauteous things, all deftly wrought, that were my joy.

   In pieces will I rend his head; the sinner's protion shall be woe. Supreme is Indra over all.

6. No Dame hath ampler charms than I, or greater wealth of love's delights.

   None with more ardour offers all her beauty to her lord's embrace. Supreme is Indra over all.

7. Mother whose love is quickly won, I say what verily will be.

   My breast, O Mother, and my head and both my hips seem quivering. Supreme is Indra over all.

8. Dame with the lovely hands and arms, with broad hair-plaints add ample hips,

    Why, O thou Hero's wife, art thou angry with our Vrisakapi? Supreme is Indra over all.

9. This noxious creature looks on me as one bereft of hero's love,

    Yet Heroes for my sons have I, the Maruts' Friend and Indra's Queen. Supreme is Indra ove all.

10. From olden time the matron goes to feast and general sacrifice.

    Mother of Heroes, Indra's Queen, the rite's ordainer is extolled. Supreme is Indra over all.

11. So have I heard Indrani called most fortunate among these Dames,

    For never shall her Consort die in future time through length of days. Supreme is Indra over all.

12. Never, Indrani, have I joyed without my friend Vrisakapi,

    Whose welcome offering here, made pure with water, goeth to the Gods. Supreme is Indra over all.

13. Wealthy Vrisakapayi, blest with sons and consorts of thy sons,

    Indra will eat thy bulls, thy dear oblation that effecteth much. Supreme is Indra over all.

14. Fifteen in number, then, for me a score of bullocks they prepare,

    And I devour the fat thereof: they fill my belly full with food. Supreme is Indra over all.

15. Like as a bull with pointed horn, loud bellowing amid the herds,

    Sweet to thine heart, O Indra, is the brew which she who tends thee pours. Supreme is Indra over all.

16. O Indra this Vrisakapi hath found a slain wild animal,

    Dresser, and new-made pan, and knife, and wagon with a load of wood. Supreme is Indra over all.

17. Distinguishing the Dasa and the Arya viewing all, I go.

    I look upon the wise, and drink the simple votary's Soma juice. Supreme is Indra over all.

18. The desert plains and steep descents, how many leagues in length they spread!

    Go to the nearest houses, go unto thine home, Vrsakapi. Supreme is Indra over all.

19. Turn thee again Vrisakapi: we twain will bring thee happiness.

    Thou goest homeward on thy way along this path which leads to sleep. Supreme is Indra over all.

20. When, Indra and Vrisakapi, ye travelled upward to your home,

    Where was that noisome beast, to whom went it, the beast that troubles man? Supreme is Indra over all.

21. Daughter of Manu, Parshu vare a score of children at birth,

    Her portion verily was bliss although her burthen caused her grief.

(X/86)

Asamati: Subandhu's Recall to Life

-.-

Bandhu

According to Sayana, Asamati is the name of a king. But the word is more probably an adjective, as in stanza 5 qualifying ratham, car, and signifying unequalled.

आ जनं त्वेषसंदृशं माहीनानामुपस्तुतम्। अगन्म बिभ्रतो नमः।
असमातिं नितोशनं त्वेषं नियायिनं रथम्। भजेरथस्य सत्पतिम्॥
यो जनान् महिषाँ इवाऽतितस्थौ पवीरवान्। उतापवीरवान् युधा।
यस्येक्ष्वाकुरुप व्रते रेवान् मराय्येधते। दिवीव पञ्च कृष्टयः॥
इन्द्र क्षत्रासमातिषु रथाप्रोष्ठेषु धारय। दिवीव सूर्यं दृशे।
अगस्त्यस्य नद्धय: सप्ती युनक्षि रोहिता॥
पणीन् न्यक्रमीरभि वि श्वान् राजन्नराधसः।
अयं माताय पिता ऽयं जीवातुरागमत्॥
इदं तव प्रसर्पणं सुबन्धवेहि निरिहि।
यथा युगं वरत्रया नह्यन्ति धरुणाय कम्॥
एवा दाधार ते मनो जीवातवे न मृत्यवे ऽथो अरिष्टतातये।
यथेयं पृथिवी मही दाधारेमान् वनस्पतीन्॥
एवा दाधार ते मनो जीवातवे न मृत्यवे ऽथों अरिष्टतातये।
यमादहं वैवस्वतात् सुबन्धोर्मन आभरम्॥
जीवातवे न मृत्यवे ऽथो अरिष्टतातये।
न्यग्वातोऽव वाति न्यक् तपति सूर्यः॥
नीचीनमघ्या दुहे न्यग्भवतु ते रपः।
अयं मे हस्तो भगवा नयं मे भगवत्तरः॥
अयं मे वि श्वभेषजो ऽयं शिवाभिमर्शनः।

1. Bringing our homage we have come to one magnificent in look.

   Glorified of the mighty Gods;

2. To Asamati, spring of gifts, lord of the brave, a radiant car,

   The conqueror of Bhajeratha;

3. Who, when the spear hath armed his hand, or even weaponless o'erthrows

4. Men strong as buffaloes in fight; Him in whose service flourishes iksvaku, rich and dazzling-bright.

   As the Five Tribes that are in heaven.

5. Indra, support the princely power of Rathaprosthas matched by none,

   Even as the Sun for all to see.

6. Thou for Agastya's sister's Sons yokest thy pair of ruddy steeds.

   Thou troddest niggards under foot, all those, O King, who brought no gifts.

7. This is the mother, this the sire, this one hath come to be thy life.

   What brings thee forth is even this. Now come, Subandhu, get thee forth.

8. As with the leather thong they bind the chariot yoke to hold it fast,

   So have I held thy spirit fast, held it for life and not for death held it for thy security.

9. Even as this earth, the mighty earth, holds fast the monarchs of the wood.

   So have I held thy spirit fast, held it for life and not for death, held it for thy security.

10. Subandhu's spirit I have brought from Yama, from Vivasvan's Son,

   Brought it for life and not for death, yea, brought it for security.

11. The wind blows downward from on high, downward the Sun-God sends his heat,

   Downward the milch-cow pours her milk: so downward go thy pain and grief.

12. Felicitous is this mine hand, yet more feticitous is this,

   This hand containing all healing balms, and this makes whole with gentle touch.

(X/60)

Shachi Paulomi: Shachi's Exultation over Her Rival Wives

-.-
Shachi Paulomi

Shachi Paulomi, called also Indrani, the consort of Indra, is also the Rishi of the hymn. 'Literally, this is a song of exultation by Shachi over her rival wives: but *saci* means also an "act", "exploit," and this hymn is metaphorically the praise of Indra's glorious acts.

उदसौ सूर्यो अगादुदयं मामको भग:।
अहं तद्विद्वला पतिमभ्यसाक्षि विषासहि:॥
अहं केतुरहं मूर्धा ऽहमुग्रा विवाचनी।

नमेदनु क्रतुं पति: सेहानाया उपाचरेत्॥
मम पुत्रा: शत्रुहणो ऽथो मे दुहिता विराट्।
उताहमस्मि संजया पत्यौ मे श्लोक उत्तम:॥
येनेन्द्रो हविषा कृत्व्यभवद् द्युम्न्युत्तम:।
इदं तदक्रि देवा असपत्ना किलाभुवम्॥
असपत्ना सपत्नघ्नी जयन्त्यभिभूवरी।
आवृक्षमन्यासां वर्चो राधो अस्थेयसामिव॥
समजैषमिमा अहं सपत्नीरभिभूवरी।
यथाहमस्य वीरस्य विराजानि जनस्य च॥

1. Yon Sun hath mounted up, and this my happy fate hate mounted high.

    I knowing this, as conqueror have won my husband for mine own.

2. I am the banner and the head, a mighty arbitress am I:

    I am victorious, and my Lord shall be submissive to my will.

3. My Sons are slayers of the foe, my Daughter is a ruling Queen:

    I am victorious : o'er my Lord my song of triumph is supreme.

4. Oblation, that which Indra gave and thus grew glorious and most high,—

    This have I offered, O ye Gods, and rid me of each rival wife.

5. Destroyer of the rival wife, Sole Spouse, victorious, conqueror,

    The others' glory have I seized as 'twere the wealth of weaker Dames.

6. I have subdued as conqueror these rivals, these my fellow-wives,

That I may hold imperial sway over this Hero and the folk.

(X/159)

Suryavivaha: Surya's Marriage

-.--

Savitri Surya

The main subject of this composite hymn, is the ceremony of marriage in general and more especially the wedding of Surya, the daughter of the Sun, another form of Dawn, who is regarded as the typical bride.

सत्येनोत्तभिता भूमिः सूर्येणोत्तभिता द्यौः।
ऋतेनादित्यास्तिष्ठन्ति दिवि सोमो अधि श्रितः॥
सोमेनादित्या बलिनः सोमेन पृथिवी मही।
अथो नक्षत्राणामेषामुपस्थे सोम आहितः॥
सोमं मन्यते पपिवान् यत् संपिषन्त्योषधिम्।
सोमं यं ब्रह्माणो विदुर्न तस्याश्नाति कश्चन॥
आच्छद्विधानैर्गुपितो बार्हतैः सोम रक्षितः।
प्राव्णामिच्छृण्वम् तिष्ठसि न ते अश्नाति पार्थिवः॥
यत् त्वा देव प्रतिबन्ति तत आ प्यायसे पुनः।
वायुः सोमस्य रक्षिता समानां मास आकृतिः॥
रैभ्यासीदनुदेयी नाराशंसी न्योचनी।
सूर्याया भद्रमिद्वासो गाथयैति परिष्कृतम्॥
चित्तिरा उपबर्हणं चक्षुरा अभ्यञ्जनम्।

द्यौर्भूमिः कोश आसीद् यदयात् सूर्या पतिम्।।
स्तोमा आसन् प्रतिधयः कुरीरं छन्द ओपशः।
सूर्याया अश्विना वरा अग्निरासीत् पुरोगवः।।
सोमो वधूयुरभवदश्विनास्तामुभा वरा।
सूर्यां यत् पत्ये शंसन्तीं मनसा सविताददात्।।
मनो अस्या अन आसीद् द्यौरासीदुत च्छदिः।
शुक्रावनडुवाहावास्तां यदयात् सूर्या गृहम्।।
ऋक्सामाभ्यामभिहितौ गावौ ते सामनाविते।
श्रोतं ते चक्रे आस्तां दिवि पन्थाश्चराचरः।।
शुची ते चक्रे यात्या व्यानो अक्ष आहतः।
अनो मनस्मयं सूर्या ऽऽरोहत् प्रयती पतिम्।।
सूर्यायाः बहतुः प्रागात् सविता यमवासृजत।
अघासु हन्यन्ते गावो ऽर्जुन्योः पर्युह्यते।।
यदश्विना पृच्छमानावयातं त्रिचक्रेण बहतुं सूर्यायाः।
विश्वे देवा अनु तद्वामजानन् पुत्रः पितराववृणीत पूषा।।
यदयातं शुभस्पती वरेयं सूर्यामुप।
क्वैकं चक्रं वामासीत् क्वं देष्ट्राय तस्थथुः।।
द्वे ते चक्रे सूर्ये ब्रह्माण ऋतुथा विदुः।
अथैकं चक्रं यद्गुहा तदद्धातय इद्विदुः।।
सूर्यायै देवेभ्यो मित्राय वरुणाय च।
ये भूतस्य प्रचेतस इदं तेभ्योऽकरं नमः।।
पूर्वापरं चरतो माययैतौ शिशू क्रीळन्तौ परि यातो अध्वरम्।
विश्वान्यन्यो भुवनाभिचष्ट ऋतूँरन्यो विदधज्जायते पुनः।।
नवोनवो भवति जायमानो ऽह्नां केतुरुषसामेत्यग्रम्।
भागं देवेभ्यो वि दधात्यायन् प्र चन्द्रमास्तिरते दीर्घमायुः।।
सुकिंशुकं शल्मलिं विश्वरूपं हिरण्यवर्णं सुवृतं सुचक्रम्।
आ रोह सूर्ये अमृतस्य लोकं स्योनं पत्ये वहतुं कृणुष्व।।
उदीर्ष्वातः पतिवती ह्येषा विश्वावसुं नमसा गीर्भिरीळे।
अन्यामिच्छ पितृषदं व्यक्तां स ते भागो जनुषा तस्य विद्धि।।

उदीष्वाॅतो वि श्वावसो नमसेळामहे त्वा।
अन्यामिच्छ प्रफर्व्यं१ सं जायां पत्या सृज।।
अनृक्षरा ऋतवः सन्तु पन्था येभिः सखायो यन्ति नो वरेयम्।
समर्यमा सं भगो नो निनीयात् सं जास्पत्यं सुयममस्तु देवाः।।
प्र त्वा मुञ्चामि वरुणस्य पाशाद् येन त्वाबध्नात् सविता सुशेवः।
ऋतस्य योनौ सुकृतस्य लोके ऽरिष्टां त्वा सह पत्या दधामि।।
प्रेतो मुञ्चामि नामुतः सुबद्धाममुतस्करम्।
यथेयामिन्द्र मीढ्वः सुपुत्रा सुभगासति।।
पूषा त्वेतो नयतु हस्तगृह्याऽश्विना त्वा प्र वहतां रथेन।
गृहान् गच्छ गृहपत्नी यथासो वशिनी त्वं विदथमा वदासि।।
इह प्रियं प्रजया ते समृध्यतामस्मिन् गृहे गार्हपत्याय जागृहि।
एना पत्या तन्वं सं सृजस्वाधा जिव्री विदथमा वदाथः।।
नीललोहितं भवति कृत्यासक्तिर्व्यज्यते।
एधन्ते अस्या ज्ञातयः पतिर्बन्धेषु बध्यते।।
परा देहि शामुल्यं ब्रह्मभ्यो वि भजा वसु।
कृत्यैषा पद्वती भूत्वा जाया विशते पतिम्।।
अश्रीरा तनूर्भवति रुशती पापयामुया।
पतिर्यद्वध्वो३ वाससा स्वमङ्गमभिधित्सते।।
ये वध्वश्वन्तं वहतुं यक्ष्मा यन्ति जनादनु।
पुनस्तान् यज्ञिया देवा नयन्तु यत आगताः।।
मा विदन् परिपन्थिनो य आसीदन्ति दंपती।
सुगेभिर्दुर्गमतीतामप द्रान्त्वरातयः।।
सुमङ्गलीरियं वधूरिमां समेत पश्यत।
सौभाग्यमस्यै दत्त्वायाॅथास्तं वि परेतन।।
तृष्टमेतत् कटुकमेतदपाष्ठवद्विषवन्नैतदत्तवे।
सूर्यां यो ब्रह्मा विद्यात् स इद्वाधूयमर्हति।।
आशासनं विशसनमथो अधिविकर्तनम्।
सूर्यायाः पश्य रूपाणि तानि ब्रह्मा तु शुन्धति।।
गृभ्णामि ते सौभगत्वाय हस्तं मया पत्त्वा जरदष्टिर्यथासः।

भर्गो अर्यमा सविता पुरंधिर्महां त्वादुर्गार्हपत्याय देवाः॥

तां पूषञ्छिवतमामेरयस्व यस्यां बीजं मनुष्या३ वपन्ति।

या नं ऊरू उशती विश्रयाते यस्यामुशन्तः प्रहराम शेपम्॥

तुभ्यमग्रे पर्यवहन् त्सूर्यां वहतुना सह।

पुनः पतिभ्यो जायां दा अग्ने प्रजया सह॥

पुनः पत्नीमग्निरदादायुषा सह वर्चसा।

दीर्घायुरस्या यः पतिर्जीवाति शरदः शतम्॥

सोमः प्रथमो विविदे गन्धर्वो विविद उत्तरः।

तृतीयो अग्निष्टे पतिस्तुरीयस्ते मनुष्यजाः॥

सोमो ददद्गन्धर्वाय गन्धर्वो दददग्नये।

रयिं च पुत्राँ शर्चादादग्निर्मह्यमथो इमाम्॥

इहैव स्तं मा वि यौष्टं वि श्वमायुर्व्यश्नुतम्।

क्रीळन्तौ पुत्रैर्नप्तृभिर्मोदमानौ स्वे गृहे॥

आ नः प्रजां जनयतु प्रजापतिराजरसाय समनक्त्वर्यमा।

अदुर्मङ्गलीः पतिलोकमा विश शं नो भव द्विपदे शं चतुष्पदे॥

अघोरचक्षुरपतिघ्न्येधि शिवा पशुभ्यः सुमनाः सुवर्चाः।

वीर सूदेवकामा स्योना शं नो भव द्विपदे शं चतुष्पदे॥

इमां त्वमिन्द्र मीढ्वः सुपुत्रां सुभगां कृणु।

दशास्यां पुत्राना धेहि पतिमेकादशं कृधि॥

सम्राज्ञी श्वशुरे भव सम्राज्ञी श्वश्वां भव।

ननान्दरि सम्राज्ञी भव सम्राज्ञी अधि देवृषु॥

समञ्जन्तु वि श्वे देवाः समापो हृदयानि नौ।

सं मातरिश्वा सं धाता समु देष्ट्री दधातु नौ॥

1. Truth is the base that bears the earth; by Surya are the heavens sustained.

   By Law the Adityas stand secure, and Soma holds his place in heaven.

2. By Soma are the Adityas strong, by Soma mighty is the earth.

Thus Soma in the midst of all these constellations hath his place.

3. One thinks, when they have brayed the plant, that he hath drunk the Soma's juice;

   Of him whom Brahmins truly know as Soma no one ever tastes.

4. Soma, secured by sheltering rules, guarded by hymns in Brihati,

   Thou standest listening to the stones: none tastes of thee who dwells on earth.

5. When they begin to drink thee then, O God, thou swellest out again.

   Vayu is Soma's guardian God. The Moon is that which shapes the years.

6. Raibhi was her dear bridal friend, and Narasamsi led her home.

   Lovely was Surya's robe: she came to that which Gatha had adorned.

7. Thought was the pillow of her couch, sight was the unguent for her eyes:

   Her treasury was earth and heaven when Surya went unto her Lord.

8. Hymns were the cross bars of the pole, Kurira-metre decked the car:

   The bridesmen were the Asvin Pair: Agni was leader of the train.

9. Soma was he who wooed the maid: the groomsmen were both Asvins, when

   The Sun-God Savitar bestowed his willing Surya on her Lord.

10. Her spirit was the bridal car; the covering thereof was heaven:

    Bright were both Steers that drew it, when Surya approached her husband's home.

11. Thy Steers were steady, kept in place by holy verse and Sama-hymn:

    All ear were thy two chariot wheels: thy path was tremulous in the sky,

12. Clean, as thou wentest, were thy wheels: wind was the axle fastened there.

    Surya, proceeding to her Lord, mounted a spirit-fashinoned car.

13. The bridal pomp of Surya, which Savitar started, moved along.

    In Magha days are oxen slain, in Arjunis they wed the bride.

14. When on your three-wheeled chariot, O Asvins, ye came as wooers unto Surya's bridal,

    Then all the Gods agreed to your proposal: Pusan as Son elected you as Fathers.

15. O ye Two Lords of lustre, then when ye to Surya's wooing came,

    Where was one chariot wheel of yours? Where stood ye for the Sire's command?

16. The Brahmins, by their seasons, know, O Surya, those two wheels of thine:

    One kept concealed, those only who are skilled in highest truths have learned.

17. To Surya and the Deities, to Mitra and to Varuna.

    Who know aright the thing that is, this adoration have I paid.

18. By their own power these Twain in close succession move;

> They go as playing children round the sacrifice.

> One of the Pair beholdeth all existing things; the other ordereth seasons and is born again.

19. He, born afresh, is new and new for ever: ensign of days he goes before the Mornings.

> Coming, he orders for the Gods their portion. The Moon prolongs the days of our existence.

20. Mount this, all-shaped, gold-hued, with strong wheels, fashioned of Kimsuka and Salmali, light-rolling,

> Bound for the world of life immortal, Surya: make for thy lord a happy bridal journey.

21. Rise up from hence: this maiden hath a husband. I laud Visvavasu with hymns and homage.

> Seek in her father's home another fair one, and find the portion from of old assigned thee.

22. Rise up from hence, Visvavasu: with reverence we worship thee.

> Seek thou another willing maid, and with her husband leave the bride.

23. Straight in direction be the paths, and thornless, whereon our fellows travel to the wooing.

> Let Aryaman and Bhaga lead us: perfect, O Gods, the union of the wife and husband.

24. Now from the noose of Varuna I free thee, wherewith Most Blessed Savitar hath bound thee.

> In Law's seat, to the world of virtuous action, I give thee up uninjured with thy consort.

25. Hence, and not thence, I send thee free. I make thee softly fettered there.

That, Bounteous Indra, she may live blest in her fortune and her sons.

26. Let Pusan take thy hand and hence conduct thee; may the two Asvins on their car transport thee.

    Go to the house to be the household's mistress and speak as lady to thy gathered people.

27. Happy be thou and prosper with thy children here: be vigilant to rule thy household in this home.

    Closely unite thy body with this man, thy lord. So shall ye, full of years, address your company.

28. Her hue is blue and red: the fiend who clingeth close is driven off.

    Well thrive the kinsmen of this bride: the husband is bound fast in bonds.

29. Give thou the woolen robe away: deal treasure to the Brahmin priests.

    This female fiend hath got her feet, and as a wife attends her lord.

30. Unlovely is his body when it glistens with this wicked fiend,

    What time the husband wraps about his limbs the garment of his wife.

31. Consumptions, from her people, which follow the bride's resplendent train,—

    These let the Holy Gods again bear to the place from which they came.

32. Let not the highway thieves who lie in ambush find the wedded pair.

    By pleasant ways let them escape the danger, and let foes depart.

33. Signs of good fortune mark the bride: come all of you and look at her.

Wish her prosperity, and then return unto your homes again.

34. Pungent is this, and bitter this, filled, as it were, with arrow-barbs, Empoisoned and not fit for use.

The Brahmin who knows Surya well deserves the garment of the bride.

35. The fringe, the cloth that decks her head, and then the triply parted robe,—

Behold the hues which Surya wears: these doth the Brahmin purify.

36. I take thy hand in mine for happy fortune that thou mayst reach old age with me thy husband.

Gods, Aryaman, Bhaga, Savitar, Purandhi, have given thee to be my household's mistress.

37. O Pusan, send her on as most auspicious, her who shall be the sharer of my pleasures;

Her who shall twine her loving arms about me, and welcome all my love and mine embraces.

38. For thee, with bridal train, they, first, escorted Surya to her home.

Give to the husband in return, Agni, the wife with progeny.

39. Agni hath given the bride again with splendour and with ample life.

Long lived be he who is her lord; a hundred autumns let him live.

40. Soma obtained her first of all; next the Gandharva was her lord.

Agni was thy third husband: now one born of

woman is thy forth.

41. Soma to the Gandharva, and to Agni the Gandharva gave:

   And Agni hath bestowed on me riches and sons and this my spouse.

42. Be ye not parted; dwell ye here; reach the full time of human life.

   With sons and grandsons sport and play, rejoicing in your own abode.

43. So may Prajapati bring children forth to us; may Aryaman adorn us till old age come nigh.

   Not inauspicious enter thou thy husband's house: bring blessing to our bipeds and our quadrupeds.

44. Not evil-eyed, no slayer of thy husband, bring weal to cattle, radiant, gentle-hearted;

   Loving the Gods, delightful, bearing heroes, bring blessing to our quadrupeds and bipeds.

45. O Bounteous Indra, make this bride blest in her sons and fortunate.

   Vouchsafe to her ten sons, and make her husband the eleventh man.

46. Over thy husband's father and thy husband's mother bear full sway.

   Over the sister of thy lord, over his brothers rule supreme.

47. So may the Universal Gods, so may the Waters join our hearts.

   May Matarisvan, Dhatar, and Destri together bind us close.

(X/85)

Pururava-Urvashi: A Love Story

-.‿

Pururava and Urvashi

The hymn is a dialogue between Pururava and Urvashi, contains the germs of a legend which is related in the *Satapatha Brahmana*, reappears in the *Mahabharata* and *Purunas*, and forms the plot of the wellknown drama, *Vikramorvashi*. According to this legend, Urvashi, an Apsaras or Nymph of heaven, has been banished to earth where she consents to live with King Pururava on condition that he takes care of her two pet rams, and that she never sees him unclothed.

She lives with Pururava for four years, when the Gandharvas, heavenly minstrels, resolve to bring her back. They steal one of the rams by night. Pururava springs from his bed; the Gandharvas send on him a flash of magic lightning, and Urvashi sees her husband naked. One of the conditions of the continuance of their union is broken, and the nymph instantly vanishes. Pururava meets her afterwards and in vain implores her to return. At last she relents, and in due time a son is born to them.

हये जाये मनसा तिष्ठ घोरे वचांसि मिश्रा कृणवावहै नु।
न नौ गन्त्रा अनुदितास एते मयस्करन् परतरे चनाहन्॥
किमेता वाचा कृणवा तवाहं प्राक्रमिषमुषसामग्रियेव।
पुरूरवः पुनरस्तं परेहि दुरापना वात इवाहमस्मि॥
इषुर्न श्रिय इषुधेरसना गोषाः शतसा न रंहिः।
अवीरे क्रतौ वि दविद्युतन्नोरा न मायुं चितयन्त धुनयः॥
सा वसु दधती श्वशुराय वय उषो यदि वष्ट्यन्तिगृहात्।
अस्तं ननक्षे यस्मिञ्चाकन् दिवा नक्तं श्रथिता वैतसेन॥
त्रिः स्म माह्नः श्रथयो वैतसेनोत स्म मेऽव्यत्यै पृणासि।

पुरूरवोऽनुते केतमायं राजा मे वीर तन्व१स्तदासी:॥
या सुजूर्णि: श्रेणि: सुम्नआपिर्ह्रदेचक्षुर्न ग्रन्थिनी चरण्यु:।
ता अञ्जयोऽरुणयो न सस्रु: श्रिये गावो न धेनवोऽनवन्त॥
समस्मिञ्जायमान आसत् ग्ना उतेमवर्धन् नद्य१: स्वगूर्ता:।
महे यत् त्वा पुरूरवो रणाया ऽवर्धयन् दस्युहत्याय देवा:॥
सचा यदासु जहतीष्वत्क ममानुषीष्षु मानुषो निषेवे।
अप स्म मत् तरसन्ती न भुज्युस्ता अत्रसन् रथस्पृशो नाश्वा:॥
यदासु मर्तो अमृतासु निस्पृक् सं क्षोणीधि: क्रतुभिर्न पृङ्क्ते।
ता आतयो न तन्व: शुम्भत स्वा अश्वासो न क्रीळयो दन्दशाना:॥
विद्युन्न या पतन्ती दविद्योद्धरन्ती में अप्या काम्यानि।
जनिष्टो अपो नर्य: सुजात: प्रोर्वशी तिरत दीर्घमायु:॥
जज्ञिष इत्था गोपीथ्याय हि दधाथ तत् पुरूरवो म ओज:।
अशासं त्वा विदुषी सस्मिन्नहन् न म आशृणो: किमभुग्वदासि॥
कदा सूनु: पितरं जात इच्छाच्चक्रन्नाश्रु वर्तयद्विजानन्।
को दंपती समनसा वि यूयोदध यदग्नि:श्वशुरेषु दीदयत्॥
प्रति ब्रवाणि वर्तयते अश्रु चक्रन् न क्रन्ददाध्ये शिवायै।
प्र तत् ते हिन्वा यत् ते अस्मे परेह्यस्तं नहि भूर मापः:॥
सुदेवो अद्य प्रपतेदनावृत् परावतं परमां गन्तवा उ।
अधा शयीत नि ॠतेरुपस्थे ऽधैनं वृका रभसासो अद्यु:॥
पुरूरवो मा मृथा मा प्र पप्तो मा त्वा वृकासो अशिवास उ क्षन्।
न वै स्त्रैणानि सख्यानि सन्ति सालावृकाणां हृदयान्येता॥
यद्विरूपाचरं मर्त्येष्ववसं रात्री: शरदश्चतम्र:।
घृतस्य स्तोकं सकृदह्न आश्नां तादेवेदं तातृपाणा चरामि॥
अन्तरिक्षप्रां रजसो विमानीमुप शिक्षाम्युर्वशीं वसिष्ठ:।
उप त्वा राति: सुकृतस्य तिष्ठात्रि वर्तस्व हृदयं तप्यते में॥
इति त्वा देवा इम आहुरैळ यथेमेतद्भवसि मृत्युबन्धु:।
प्रजा ते देवान् हविषा यजाति स्वर्ग उ त्वमपि मादयासे॥

1. Ho there, my consort! Stay, thou fierce-souled lady,
and let us reason for a while together.

Such thoughts as these of ours, while yet unspoken in days gone by have never brought us comfort.

2. What am I now to do with this thy saying? I have gone from thee like the first of Mornings.

    Pururava, return thou to thy dwelling: I, like the wind, am difficult to capture.

3. Like a shaft sent for glory from the quiver, or swift steed winning cattle winning hundreds.

    The lightning seemed to flash, as cowards planned it. The minstrels bleated like a lamb in trouble.

4. Giving her husband's father life and riches, from the near dwelling, when her lover craved her,

    She sought the home wherein she found her pleasure, accepting day and night her lord's embraces.

5. Thrice in the day didst thou embrace thy consort, though coldly she received thy fond caresses.

    To thy desires, Pururava, I yielded: so wast thou king, O hero, of my body.

6. The maids Sujurni, Sreni, Sumne-api, Charanyu, Granthini, and Hradechaksus,—

    These like red kine have hastened forth, the bright ones, and like milch-cows have lowed in emulation.

7. While he was born the Dames sat down together, the Rivers with free kindness gave him nurture;

    And then, Pururavas, the Gods increased thee for mighty battle, to destroy the Dasyus.

8. When I, a mortal, wooed to mine embraces these heavenly nymphs who laid aside their raiment,

Like a scared snake they fled from me in terror,
like chariot horses when the car has touched them.

9. When, loving these Immortal Ones, the mortal hath
   converse with the nymphs as they allow him.

   Like swans they show the beauty of their bodies,
   like horses in their play they bite and nibble.

10. She who flashed brilliant as the falling lightning
    brought me delicious presents from the waters.

    Now from the flood be born a strong young
    hero! May Urvashi prolong her life for ever!

11. Thy birth hath made me drink from earthly milch-
    kine: this power, Pururavas, hast thou vouchsafed
    me.

    I knew, and, warned thee, on that day. Thou
    wouldst not hear me. What sayest thou, when naught
    avails thee?

12. When will the son be born and seek his father?
    Mourner-like, will he weep when first he knows him?

    Who shall divide the accordant wife and husband,
    while fire is shining with thy consort's parents?

13. I will console him when his tears are falling: he
    shall not weep and cry for care that blesses.

    That which is thine, between us, will I send
    thee. Go home again, thou fool; thou hast not won
    me.

14. Thy lover shall flee forth this day for ever, to seek,
    without return, the farthest distance.

    Then let his bed be in Destruction's bosom,
    and there let fierce rapacious wolves devour him.

15. Nay, do not die, Pururava, nor vanish: let not the
    evil-omened wolves devour thee.

With women there can be no lasting friendship:
hearts of hyenas are the hearts of women.

16. When amid men in altered shape I sojourned, and
through four autumns spent the nights among them,

I tasted once a day a drop of butter; and even
now with that am I contented.

17. I, her best love, call Urvashi to meet me, her who
fills air and measures out the region.

Let the gift brought by piety approach thee. Turn
thou to me again: my heart is troubled.

18. Thus speak these Gods to thee, O son of Ila: As
death hath verily got thee for his subject,

Thy sons shall serve the Gods with their oblation,
and thou, moreover, shalt rejoice in Svarga.

(X/95)

Yama and Yami: A Dialogue between Twins

-.-

Yama and Yami

Yama and Yami, son and daughter of Vivasvan, is a dialogue
between them. They are, as their names denote, twin brother
and sister, and are the first human pair, the originators of
the race. As the Hebrew conception closely connected the
parents of mankind by making the woman formed from a
portion of the body of the man, so by the Indian tradition
they are placed in the relationship of twins.

Max Muller, on the other hand, says: 'There is a curious
dialogue between her and her brother, where she (the night)

implores her brother (the day) to make her his wife, and where he declines her offer, "because", as he says, "they have called it a sin that a brother should marry his sister." Again, there is not a single word in the Veda pointing to Yama and Yami as the first couple of mortals, the Indian Adam and Eve...If Yama had been the first created of men, surely the Vedic poets, in speaking of him, could not have passed this over in silence.

ओ चित् सखायं सख्या ववृत्यां तिर: पुरू चिदर्णवं जगन्वान्।
पितुर्नपातमा दधीत वेधा अधि क्षमि प्रतरं दीध्यान:॥

न ते सखा सख्यं वष्ट्येतत् सलक्ष्मा यद्विषुरूपा भवाति।
महस्पुत्रासो असुरस्य वीरा दिवो धर्तार उर्विया परि ख्यन्॥

उशन्ति घा ते अमृतास एतदेकस्य चित् त्यजसं मर्त्यस्य।
नि ते मनो मनसि धाय्यस्मे जन्यु: पतिस्तन्व१मा विविश्या:॥

न यत् पुरा चकृमा कद्ध नूनमृता वदन्तो अनृतं रपेम।
गन्धर्वो अप्स्वप्या च योषा सा नो नाभि: परमं जामि तन्नौ॥

अर्मे नु नौ जनिता दंपती कर्देवस्त्वष्टा सविता क्विश्वरूप:।
नाकिरस्य प्र मिनन्ति व्रतानि वेद नावस्य पृथिवी उत द्यौ:॥

को अस्य वेद प्रथमस्याह: क ई ददर्श क इह प्र वोचत्।
बृहन्मित्रस्य वरुणस्य धाम कदु ब्रव आहनो वीच्या नृन्॥

यमस्य मा यम्यं१ काम आगन् त्समाने योनौ सहशेय्याय।
जायेव पत्ये तन्वं रिरिच्यां वि चिद्वृहेव रथ्येव चक्रा॥

न तिष्ठन्ति न नि मिषन्त्येते देवानां स्पश इह ये चरन्ति।
अन्येन मदाहनो याहि तूयं तेन वि वृह रथ्येव चक्रा॥

रात्रीभिरस्मा अहभिर्दशस्येत् सूर्यस्य चक्षुर्मुहुरुन्निमीयात्।
दिवा पृथिव्या मिथुना सबन्धू यमीर्यमस्य बिभृयादजामि॥

आ घा ता गच्छानुत्तरा युगानि यत्र जामय: कृणवन्नजामि।
उप बर्बृहि वृषभाय बाहुमन्यमिच्छस्व सुभगे पतिं मत्॥

किं भ्रातासद्यदनाथं भवाति किमु स्वसा यन्निर्ऋतिर्निगच्छात्।
काममूता बह्वेत३द्रपामि तन्वा मे तन्वं१ सं पिपृग्धि॥

न वा उ ते तन्वा तन्वं१ सं पपृच्यां पापमाहुर्य: स्वसारं निगच्छात्।

अन्येन मत् प्रमुद: कल्पयस्व न ते भ्राता सुभगे वष्टयेतत्॥
बतो बतासि यम नैव ते मनो हृदयं चाविदाम।
अन्या किल त्वां कक्ष्येव युक्तं परि ष्वजाते लिबुजेव वृक्षम्॥
अन्यमू षु त्वं यम्यन्य उ त्वां परि ष्वजाते लिबुजेव वृक्षम।
तस्य वा त्वं मन इच्छा स वा तवाऽधा कृणुष्व संविदं सुभद्राम्॥

1. Fain would I win my friend to kindly friendship.
   So may the Sage, come through the air's wide ocean,

   Remembering the earth and days to follow,
   obtain a son, the issue of his father.

2. Thy friend loves not the friendship which considers
   her who is near in kindred as a stranger.

   Sons of the mighty Asura, the Heroes, supporters
   of the heavens, see far around them.

3. Yea, this the Immortals seek of thee with longing,
   progeny of the sole existing mortal.

   Then let thy soul and mine be knit together,
   and as a loving husband take thy consort.

4. Shall we do now what we ne'er did aforetime? We
   who spake righteously now talk impurely?

   Gandharva in the floods, the Dame of Waters—
   such is our bond, such our most lofty kinship.

5. Even in the womb God Tvastar, Vivifier, shaping
   all forms, Creator, made us consorts.

   None violates his holy ordinances: that we are
   his the heavens and earth acknowledge.

6. Who knows that earliest day whereof thou speakest?
   Who hath beheld it? Who can here declare it?

   Great is the Law of Varuna and Mitra. What,
   wanton! wilt thou say to men to tempt them?

7. I, Yami, am possessed by love of Yama, that I may
    rest on the same couch beside him.

    I as a wife would yield me to my husband. Like
    car-wheels let us speed to meet each other.

8. They stand not still, they never close their eyelids,
    those sentinels of Gods who wander round us.

    Not me—go quickly, wanton, with another, and
    hasten like a chariot wheel to meet him.

9. May Surya's eye with days and nights endow him,
    and ever may his light spread out before him.

    In heaven and earth the kindred Pair commingle.
    On Yami be the unbrotherly act of Yama.

10. Sure there will come succeeding times when brothers
    and sisters will do acts unmeet for kinsfolk.

    Not me, O fair one,—seek another husband, and
    make thine arm a pillow for thy consort.

11. Is he a brother when no lord is left her? Is she
    a sister when Destruction cometh?

    Forced by my love these many words I utter.
    Come near, and hold me in thy close embraces.

12. I will not fold mine arms about thy body: they call
    it sin when one comes near his sister.

    Not me,—prepare thy pleasures with another:
    thy brother seeks not this from thee, O fair one.

13. Alas! thou art indeed a weakling, Yama; we find
    in thee no trace of heart or spirit.

    As round the tree the woodbine clings, another
    will cling about thee girt as with a girdle.

14. Embrace another, Yami; let another, even as the
    woodbine rings the tree, enfold thee.

Win thou his heart and let him win thy fancy,
and he shall form with thee a blest alliance.

(X/10)

Ghosha: The Call of a Sick Woman

-·-

Ghosha

This famous hymn describes the travails of Ghosha, daughter
of Kakshivan, who could not marry because of leprosy.
Growing old at home, she requests the healer gods to cure
her.

यो वां परिज्मा सुवृदश्विना रथो दोषामुषासो हव्यो हविष्मता।
शश्वत्तमासस्तमु वामिदं वयं पितुर्न नाम सुहवे हवामहे॥

चोदयतं सूनृता: पिन्वत धिय उत् पुरंधीरीरयतं तदुश्मसि।
यशसं भागं कृणुतं नो अश्विना सोमं न चारु मघवस्त्सु नस्कृतम्॥

अमाजुरश्चिद्भवथो युवं भगो ऽनाशोश्चिदवितारापमस्य चित्।
अन्धस्य चिन्नासत्या कृशस्य चिद्युवामिदाहुर्भिषजा रुतस्य चित्॥

युवं च्यवानं सनयं यथा रथं पुनर्युवानं चरथाय तक्षथु:।
निष्टौग्यमूहथुरद्भ्यस्परि वि श्वेत् ता वां सवनेषु प्रवाच्या॥

पुराण॥ व। वीर्या३ प्र ब्रया जगे ऽथो हाराथुर्भिषज्ञा मयोभुवा।
ता वां नु नव्याववसे करामहे ऽयं नासत्या श्रदरियथा दधेत्॥

इयं वामह्वे शृणुतं में अश्विना पुत्रायेव पितरा मह्य शिक्षतम्।
अनापिरज्ञा असजात्यामति: पुरा तस्या अभिशस्तेरव स्मृतम्॥

युवं रथेन विमदाय शुन्ध्युवं न्यूहथु: पुरुमित्रस्य योषणाम्।
युवं हवं वध्रिमत्या अगच्छतं युवं सुषुतिं चक्रथु: पुरंधये॥

युवं विप्रस्य जरणामुपेयुष: पुन: कलेरकृणुतं युवद्वय:।
युवं वन्दनमृश्यदादुदूपथुर्युवं सद्यो विश्पलामेतवे कृथ:॥

युवं ह रेभं वृषणा गुहा हितमुदैरयतं ममृवांसमश्विना।
युवमृबीसमुत तप्तसमत्रय ओमन्वन्तं चक्रथु: सप्तवध्रये॥
युवं श्वेतं पेदवेऽश्विनश्वं नवभिर्वाजैर्नवती च वाजिनम्।
चर्कृत्यं ददथुर्द्रवयत्सखं भगं न नृभ्यो हव्यं मयोभुवम्॥
न तं राजानावदिते कुतश्चन नांहो अश्रोति दुरितं नकिर्भयम्।
यमश्विना सुहवा रुद्रवर्तनी पुरोरथं कृणुथ: पत्न्या सह॥
आ तेन यातं मनसो जवीयसा रथं यं वामृभक्षवकुरश्विना।
यस्य योगे दुहिता जायते दिव उभे अहनी सुदिने विवस्वत:॥
ता वर्तिर्यातं जयुषा वि पर्वतमपिन्वतं शयवे धेनुमश्विना।
वृकस्य चिद्वर्तिकामन्तरास्याद्युवं शचीभिर्ग्रसिताममुञ्चतम्॥
एतं वां स्तोममश्विनावकर्मातक्षाम भृगवो न रथम्।
न्यमृक्षाम योषणां न मर्ये नित्यं न सूनुं तनयं दधाना:॥

1. As 'twere the name of father, easy to invoke, we all assembled here invoke this Car of yours,

    Asvins, your swiftly-rolling circumambient Car which he who worships must invoke at eve and dawn.

2. Awake all pleasant strains and let the hymns flow forth: raise up abundant fulness: this is our desire.

    Asvins, bestow on us a glorious heritage, and give our princes treasure fair as Soma is.

3. Ye are the bliss of her who groweth old at home, and helpers of the slow although he linger last.

    Men call you too, Nasatyas, healers of the blind, the thin and feeble, and the man with broken bones.

4. Ye made Chyavana, weak and worn with length of days, young again, like a car, that he had power to move.

    Ye lifted up the son of Tugra from the floods. At our libations must all these your acts be praised.

5. We will declare among the folk your ancient deeds heroic; yea, ye were Physicians bringing health.

   You, you who must be lauded, will we bring for aid, so that this foe of ours, O Asvins, may believe.

6. Listen to me, O Asvins; I have cried to you. Give me your aid as sire and mother aid their son.

   Poor, without kin or friend or ties of blood am I. Save me before it be too late, from this my curse.

7. Ye, mounted on your chariot brought to Vimada the comely maid of Purumitra as a bride.

   Ye, came unto the calling of the weakling's dame, and granted noble offspring to the happy wife.

8. Ye gave again the vigour of his youthful life to the sage Kali when old age was coming nigh.

   Ye rescued Vandana and raised him from the pit, and in a moment gave Vishpala power to move.

9. Ye Asvins Twain, endowed with manly strength, brought forth Rebha when hidden in the cave and well-nigh dead,

   Freed Saptavadhri, and for Atri caused the pit heated with fire to be a pleasant resting-place.

10. On Pedu ye bestowed, Asvins, a courser white, mighty with nine and-ninety varied gifts of strength,

    A horse to be renowned, who bore his friend at speed, joy-giving, Bhaga-like to be invoked of men.

11. From no side, ye Two Kings, whom none may check or stay, doth grief, distress, or danger come upon the man

    Whom, Asvins swift to hear, borne on your

glowing path, ye with your consort make the foremost in the race.

12. Come on that Chariot which the Ribhus wrought for you, the Chariot, Asvins, that is speedier than thought.

At harnessing whereof Heaven's Daughter springs to birth, and from Vivasvan come auspicious Night and Day.

13. Come, Conquerors of the sundered mountain, to our home, Asvins who made the cow stream milk for Sayu's sake,

Ye who delivered even from the wolf's deep throat and set again at liberty the swallowed quail.

14. We have prepared this laud for you, O Asvins, and, like the Bhrigus, as a car have framed it,

Have decked it as a maid to meet the bridegroom, and brought it as a son, our stay for ever.

(X/39)

Apala: Indra Cures Her

-.-

Apala

A maiden named Apala was afflicted with a cutaneous disease and was consequently repudiated by her husband. She was cured by Indra. Indra dragged her through the wide hole of his chariot, the narrower hole of the cart and the small hole of the yoke, and she cast off three skins. The first skin became a hedgehog, the second an alligator, the third a chamleon.

कन्या३ वारवायती सोममपि स्तुताविदत्।
अस्तं मरन्त्यब्रवीदिन्द्राय सुनवै त्वा शक्राय सुनवै त्वा॥
असौ य एषि धीरको गृहंगृहं विचाकशत्।
इमं जम्मसुतं पिब धानावन्तं करम्भिणमपूयवन्तमुक्थिनम्॥
आ चन त्वा चिकित्सामो ऽधि चन त्वा नेमसि।
शनैरिव शनकैरिवेन्द्रयिन्दो परि स्रव॥
कुविच्छकत् कुवित् करत् कुविन्नो वस्यसस्करत्।
कुवित् पतिद्विषो यती रिन्द्रेण संगमामहै॥
इमानि त्रीणि विष्टपा तानीन्द्र वि रोहय।
शिरस्ततस्योर्वरामादिदं म उपोदरे।
असौ च या न उर्वरादिमां तन्वं३ मम।
अथो ततस्य यच्छिरः सर्वा ता रोमशा कृधि॥
खे रथस्य खेऽनसः खे युगस्य शतक्रतो।
अपालामिन्द्र त्रिष्पूत्व्यकृणोः सूर्यत्वचम्॥

1. Down to the stream a maiden came, and found
   the Soma by the way.

   Bearing it to her home she said, For Indra will
   I press thee out, for Sakra will I press thee out.

2. Thou roaming yonder, little man, beholding every
   house in turn,

   Drink thou this Soma pressed with teeth, accompanied with grain and curds, with cake of meal
   and song of praise.

3. Fain would we learn to know thee well, nor yet
   can we learn to know thee well, nor yet can we
   attain to thee.

   Still slowly and in gradual drops, O Indu, unto

Indra flow.

4. Will he not help and work for us? Will he not make
    us wealthier?

    Shall we not, hostile to our lord, unite ourselves
    to Indra now?

5. O Indra, cause to sprout again three places, these
    which I declare,—

    My father's head, his cultured field, and this
    the part below my waist.

6. Make all of these grow crops of hair, you cultivated
    field of ours,

    My body, and my father's head.

7. Cleansing Apala, Indra! thrice, thou gavest sunlike
    skin to her,

    Drawn, Satakratu! through the hole of car, of
    wagon, and of yoke.

                                        (VIII/80)

Aksha: A Gambler's Repent

-·-

Kavash Ailush

प्रावेपा मां बृहतो मादयन्ति प्रवातेजा इरिणेववृताना:।
सोमस्येव मौजवतस्य भक्षो विभीदको जागृविर्महयमच्छान्
न मां मिमेथ न जिहीळ एषा शिवा सखिभ्य उत महयमासीत।
अक्षस्याहमेकपरस्य हेतोरनुव्रतामप जायामरोधम्
द्वेष्टि श्वश्रूरप जाया रुणद्धि न नाथितो विन्दते मर्दितारम्।

अश्वस्येव जरंतो वस्न्यस्य नाहं विन्दामि कितवस्य भोगम्
अन्ये जायां परिं मृशन्त्यस्य यस्यागृधद्वेदने वाज्यपक्षः।
पिता माता भ्रातर एनमाहुर्न जानीमो नयता बद्धमेतम्
यदादीध्ये न दविषाण्येभिः परायद्भयोऽवं हीये सखिभ्यः।
न्युप्ताश्च बभ्रवो वाचमक्रतँ एमीदेषां निष्कृतं जारिणीव
सभामेति कितवः पृच्छभानो जेप्याभीति तन्वाइ शूशुजानः।
अक्षासो अस्य वि तिरन्ति कामे प्रतिदीव्ने दधत आ कृतानि
अक्षास इदङ्कुशिनो नितोदिनो निकृत्वानस्तपनास्तापयिण्णवे:।
कुमारदेष्णा जयतः पुनर्हणो भध्वा संपृक्ताः कितवस्यं बर्हणा
त्रिपञ्चाशः क्रीळति व्रात एषां देव इव सविता सत्यधर्मा।
उग्रस्यं चिन्मन्यवे ना नमन्ते राजा चिदेभ्यो नभ इत् कृणोति
नीचा वर्तन्त उपरिं स्फुरन्त्यहस्तासो हस्तवन्तं सहन्ते।
दिव्या अङ्गारा इरिणे न्युप्ताः शीताः सन्तो हृदयं निर्दहन्ति
जाया तप्यते कितवस्यं हीना माता पुत्रस्य चरं कं स्वित।
ऋणावा विभ्यद्धनमिच्छमानो न्येषामस्तमुप नक्तमेति
स्त्रियं दृष्टाव्य कितवं ततापान्येषां जायां सुकृतं च योनिम्।
पूर्वाह्णे अश्वान् युजुजे हि बभ्रून् त्सो अग्नेरन्ते वृषलः पपाद
यो वः सेनानीर्महतो गणस्य राजा व्रातस्य प्रथमो बभूव।
तस्मै कृणोभि न धना रुणध्मि दशाहं प्राचीस्तदूहं वंदमि
अक्षैर्मा दीव्यः कृषिमित् कृषस्व वित्ते रमस्व बहु मन्यमानः।
तत्र गावः कितव तत्र जाया तन्मे वि चष्टे सवितायभर्यः
मित्रं कृणुध्वं खलु मृळता नो मा नो घोरेण चरताभि धृष्णु।
नि वो नुः मन्युर्विंशताभरातिरन्यो बभूणां प्रसितौ न्वस्तु

1. Sprung from tall trees on windy heights, these rollers transport me as they turn upon the table.

   Dearer to me the die that never slumbers than the deep draught of Mujavan's own Soma.

2. She never vexed me nor was angry with me, but to my friends and me was ever gracious.

For the die's sake, whose single point is final, mine own devoted wife I alienated.

3. My wife holds me aloof, her mother hates me: the wretched man finds none to give him comfort.

   As of a costly horse grown old and feeble, I find not any profit of the gamester.

4. Others caress the wife of him whose riches the die hath coveted, that rapid courser:

   Of him speak father, mother, brothers saying, We know him not: bind him and take him with you.

5. When I resolve to play with these no longer, my friends depart from me and leave me lonely.

   When the brown dice, thrown on the board, have rattled, like a fond girl I seek the place of meeting.

6. The gamester seeks the gambling-house, and wonders, his body all afire, Shall I be lucky?

   Still do the dice extend his eager longing, staking his gains against his adversary.

7. Dice, verily, are armed with goads and driving-hooks, deceiving and tormenting, causing grievous woe.

   They give frail gifts and then destroy the man who wins, thickly anointed with the player's fairest good.

8. Merrily sports their troop, he three-and-fifty, like Savitar the God whose ways are faithful.

   They bend not even to the mighty's anger: the King himself pays homage and reveres them.

9. Downward they roll, and then spring quickly upward, and, handless, force the man with hands to serve them.

Cast on the board, like lumps of magic charcoal, though could themselves they burn the heart to ashes.

10. The gambler's wife is left forlorn and wretched: the mother mourns the son who wanders homeless.

In constant fear, in debt, and seeking riches, he goes by night unto the home of others.

11. Sad is the gambler when he sees a matron, another's wife, and his well-ordered dwelling.

He yokes the brown steeds in the early morning, and when the fire is cold sinks down and outcuast.

12. To the great captain of your mighty army, who hath become the host's imperial leader,

To him I show my ten extended fingers: I speak the truth. No wealth am I withholding.

13. Play not with dice: no, cultivate thy corn-land. Enjoy the gain, and deem that wealth sufficient.

There are thy cattle, there thy wife, O gambler. So this this good Savitar himself hath told me.

14. Make me your friend: show us some little mercy. Assail us not with your terrific fierceness.

Appeased be your malignity and anger, and let the brown dice snare some other captive.

(X/34)

■ ■ ■

THE WYE VALLEY

From Ross to Chepstow

Chris Morris

TANNER'S YARD PRESS

First published 2013 by Tanners Yard Press

Tanners Yard Press Church Road Longhope GL17 0LA
www.tannersyardpress.co.uk

Designed by Paul Manning

Printed and bound in Poland

British Library Cataloguing in Publication Data
A catalogue record for this book is available from the British Library

ISBN 978 0 9564 3584 2

Front cover: The Wye from Symonds Yat Rock.
Back cover: Watercolourist Mariana Robinson painting at Bigsweir Bridge.
Previous page: a wintry view of Welsh Bicknor from Symonds Yat Rock

CONTENTS

FOREWORD

This photographic book celebrates the history and culture of the lower course of the River Wye and its valley, from Ross to Chepstow. This section of the river has not been chosen arbitrarily: famous for its wild landscapes, it has been the destination of countless tourists from the mid-eighteenth century until the present, and it was here that the leisured classes first enjoyed the concept of organised tourism.

The photographs follow the river from Backney, just north of Ross, to Chapel Rock, south of Chepstow, where the Wye meets the Severn. The river is well known for its fishing and as a haven for painters, and these subjects recur in a random way throughout our progress downstream.

Most of the locations featured in the book lie within the Wye Valley 'Area of Outstanding Natural Beauty' (AONB). Several of the historic sites pictured were renovated in 2012 as part of the 'Overlooking the Wye' conservation project.

Facing page: Dog-walking by the river at Ross-on-Wye

THE LOWER WYE

A RIVER FRONTIER

The lower reaches of the River Wye have served as a frontier since pre-history. Evidence of its defensive role include hillforts, Offa's Dyke and later stone-built castles. The wide, swift river runs south from Ross and separates, protects and isolates the high ground of the Forest of Dean to the east. Although it was possible to cross the river by ferry, the only bridges in the lower valley were at Ross, Monmouth and Chepstow until the turnpike road arrived in 1828, crossing the river at Bigsweir.

Today the river is only a loose guide to the border between England and Wales, as is Offa's Dyke.

TRADE AND INDUSTRY

The Wye Valley and the Forest of Dean on its eastern flank were very early areas of British industry, the woodlands providing charcoal for iron-smelting, and the fast-moving side streams supplying the power to drive waterwheels and bellows for the furnaces. In the vanguard of this industrial activity were the monks of Tintern, who controlled a network of furnaces and forges up the Angiddy Valley specialising in wire production. Upstream, Redbrook had its own niche industries of copper and tinplating.

As the main highway for transport of raw materials and products, the river had a huge part to play in the development of the region. From Chepstow,

Facing page: Chepstow Castle.
Above: The ramparts of Little Doward Iron Age fort.

Above: Waterwheel at Abbey Mills, Tintern.

where seagoing vessels could dock, quays as far upriver as Ross catered for small flat-bottomed boats named trows which carried agricultural goods including lime for farming and sheep fleeces, as well as raw materials and products for local industries.

Traders who used the river to transport their goods co-existed uneasily with millers and fishermen, whose 'flash-weirs' were designed to keep water-level high but were breached each time a barge was hauled through (by teams of up to ten men!). The conflict between the navigation lobby and the millers and fishermen would perhaps have been far more satisfactorily resolved if, instead of demolishing the weirs, the millers had kept them and added proper pound locks. The resulting higher water-level would surely have benefited all parties.

With the arrival of the turnpike roads in 1828, the river traffic went into decline, and was finished off when the Wye Valley railway opened in 1876. Today, commercial salmon fishing, for which the Wye was once famous, has totally stopped. Netting is banned and all fish are returned to the river. A fisherman is an unusual sight, and that of a fish rarer still!

THE BIRTH OF TOURISM

By the middle of the eighteenth century it was possible to hire a boat in Ross and to follow the river down to Monmouth and Chepstow expressly to wonder at the dramatic scenery. The Reverend William Gilpin, the man credited with inventing tourism, made this trip in 1770, but it was the publication of his account of his travels some twelve years later that proved to be inspirational. The middle classes of the Enlightenment queued to take the river tour, and amongst Gilpin's admirers were the painter J.M.W. Turner, the poet William Wordsworth and Lord Nelson.

Perhaps surprisingly, Gilpin's notions of topographical beauty were rather different from those of our own day. Far from complaining about the evidence of the rampant industries, he espoused the smoke of charcoal burners and the fiery glow of iron furnaces, feeling they added to the atmosphere. Gilpin, himself a painter, formulated a set of rules for admiring the river vistas: to qualify for his plaudit 'picturesque', the view must have a strong foreground, 'sidescreens' and an interesting skyline. He was very particular: in his view, Tintern Abbey could not be 'picturesque' as it had too many gables!

From the time of the earliest tours, landowners had begun to prettify their land. Just north of Chepstow at Piercefield, Valentine Morris made extensive 'improvements' to his estate, adding grottoes, viewpoints and follies linked by woodland walks along high cliffs. South of Ross, the ancient hillfort of Little Doward was 'improved' by its new owner, who cut a carriage drive straight through the ramparts!

Today all these historic influences blend together, the river cliffs softened by more extensive woodlands, and tourists can still enjoy a magnificent set of vistas, many of them best appreciated from a canoe on the river.

Above: The author with a print of J.M.W. Turner's watercolour at Tintern Abbey.

View of the Saracen's Head ferry at Symonds Yat, looking downstream

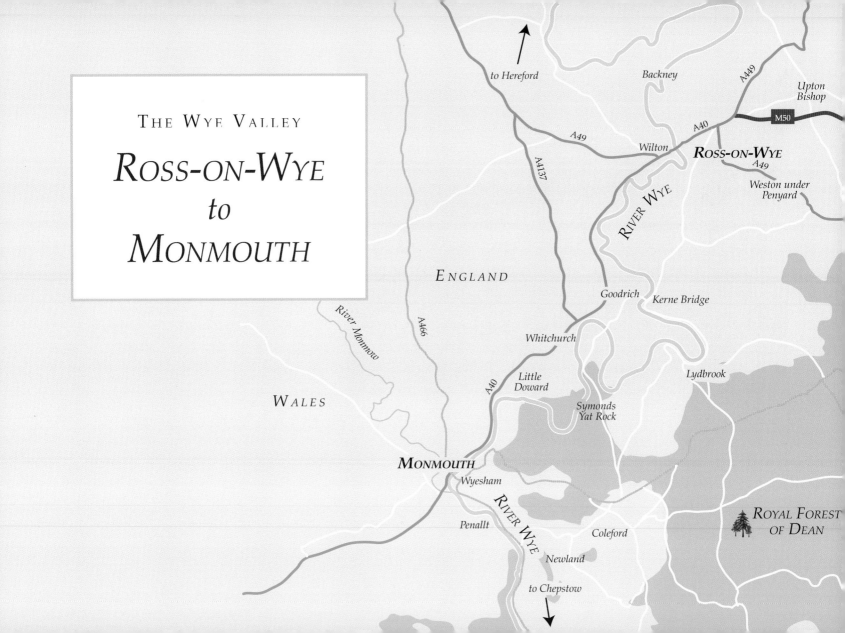

NORTH OF ROSS

The Wye flows south out of Herefordshire in a generally placid manner through a landscape of gentle hills, the meanders so wide that Brunel's railway had to cross the river four times between Hereford and Ross. Brunel built his bridges of timber on brick piers; the brick structure survives at Backney, just north of Ross (facing page).

Backney marks the start of the third day of the annual Hay to Huntsham raft race (left). Sadly, the days when a raft could be built of oil drums, planks and binder twine are long gone. Health and safety legislation now dictates that all entrants have to follow a strict specification.

ROSS-ON-WYE

*The 'valley' is so wide and flat at Ross that flooding is
endemic (above), but the town itself, and the landmark
church and spire, sit high on a bluff above a river bend.
The water meadows play host to riverside pubs, the
rowing club and an annual literary festival. The steel
sculpture of ducks which stands by the river (right)
is by Walenty Pytel.*

WILTON

Adjacent to Ross is the ancient settlement of Wilton, where a castle (facing page) guards the medieval red stone bridge. To the east, the high hill of Penyard (below) threatens an end to the wide vale, and marks the start of the steep-sided valley to come.

Left: Floodwater pouring under Wilton Bridge.

ROSS AND LITTLE DOWARD

*The landscape south of Ross, named by the
Romans for its red rock, is today dominated
by poly-tunnels growing asparagus (facing
page), while new ploughed fields stand out as
red corduroy (above). To the east the heights
of Little Doward are crowned by an Iron
Age earthwork, bisected here by a nineteenth-
century carriage drive (left).*

GOODRICH

Goodrich castle (left) dates back to the 11th century. During the Civil War it was held by both sides before being surrendered to the Parliamentarians. Today it guards nothing more significant than a set of barns and a famous salmon fishing beat at Goodrich Court. Just downstream is Kerne Bridge (above), built in 1828 as part of the new turnpike road linking Monmouth to Ross.

CORACLES

Tim Oakes is a coracle-maker, seen here carrying out repair work in his Lydbrook garden. A current project is the building of a seagoing coracle, based on archaeological finds in the Baltic, where evidence has been unearthed of ten-foot-long coracles with sails, in which the Vikings are believed to have reached western Europe. Coracles are traditional on the English/Welsh borders, but there is no evidence that Scandinavian marauders sailed up the Wye.

    Although the river is particularly prone to flood at Lydbrook, it is generally shallow enough at the old wharf to allow paddling (left).

RAILWAYS AT LYDBROOK

Lydbrook, today a two-mile-long village winding up from its old river quay, was once a hive of industry. Its most evocative landmark was a high rail viaduct taking the Severn and Wye line over the valley before dropping down to river level. Its siting took it directly over the Garden Café, a converted malthouse where Paul Hayes has lived and worked for twenty-five years. In his steep back garden, with a backdrop of the old viaduct's abutments, Paul shows a print of the viaduct being dismantled in 1966 (facing page).

The tracks of the Severn and Wye Railway joined the Monmouth-to-Ross line, crossed the river (above right) and almost immediately plunged into a tunnel through Welsh Bicknor (right) which cut off a big bend of river. Today the bridge is part of the Wye Valley walk, and in the past the blocked tunnel entrance has been kicked down to allow walkers to enjoy the same short cut. Be warned, you can enter, but the far end is blocked!

SYMONDS YAT ROCK

After Tintern Abbey, Symonds Yat Rock is probably the best known location in the valley. The name refers to a high rock pinnacle at a point where the river doubles back on itself. The village of Symonds Yat consists of settlements on both sides of the river and is located a mile downstream. The rock's viewing platform provides a vista to the north-east and is a must for birdwatchers observing nesting peregrine falcons.

SYMONDS YAT WEST

*Close to the A40 at Whitchurch,
Symonds Yat West boasts a
seaside-standard pleasure park,
with canoe hire and boat trips.
Just downstream at the Ferrie
Inn, viewed from the rock, is
the first of two 'hand' ferries
(see page 31).*

SYMONDS YAT EAST

The east side of Symond's Yat is more restrained in its offerings than the opposite bank, with hotels and pubs, a canoe-hire yard (facing page) and a second ferry (left) running from the Saracen's Head.

NEW WEIR

Just downstream from the summer bustle of Symonds Yat, a wide shallow stretch of rocks and shingle in the river marks the remains of New Weir. Other weirs on the lower river were removed by the navigation lobby, but New Weir and its lock were spared because a leat from the higher water level powered the bellows of New Weir furnace. The site has recently been renovated as part of the Wye Valley AONB (facing page), and an area of quieter water (above) may mark the site of the furnace pond.

Today the shallows provide sport for white water kayaks (right) and a frisson of excitement for canoe day-trippers on their way down to Monmouth.

THE KYMIN

The Kymin is a site high above the river on the Glouces-
tershire side, overlooking Monmouth, with two separate
historic structures dating from the late 18th century. The
Naval Temple is a memorial to admirals and their battles,
while the Round House, a set of banquetting rooms with
a view, was originally built by subscription as a private
dining club.

When Nelson came to visit in 1802, he was combining
business with pleasure: his business was inspecting Forest
oaks for the Navy, and his travelling companions were
Lord and Lady Hamilton.

MONMOUTH REGATTA

The modern A40 rushes along Monmouth's eastern edge, largely cutting the town off from its waterfront and leaving little of the myriad quays that once lined this stretch of the river. The annual two-day Monmouth Regatta (facing page) recreates the former bustle of the riverside and provides a home fixture for Monmouth Comprehensive's coxed four (above).

MONMOW BRIDGE

Monmouth's most striking architecture is the old gated bridge, crossing the River Monmow just before it joins the Wye.

Watercolourist Mariana Robinson, who has a gallery at St Briavels,
painting at Bigsweir Bridge

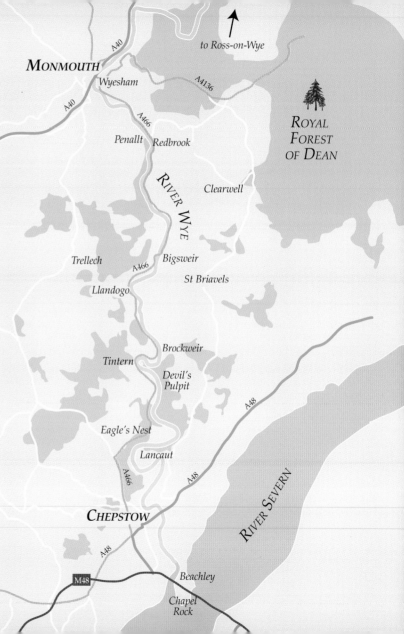

THE WYE VALLEY

MONMOUTH
to
CHEPSTOW

MONMOUTH

Wyesham

to Ross-on-Wye

ROYAL FOREST OF DEAN

Penallt Redbrook

Clearwell

RIVER WYE

Trellech Bigsweir

St Briavels

Llandogo

Brockweir

Tintern

Devil's Pulpit

Eagle's Nest

Lancaut

CHEPSTOW

RIVER SEVERN

Beachley

M48

Chapel Rock

A40 A4136 A466 A48

WYESHAM

Above: The old rail bridge at Wyesham is a favourite route for dog walkers.

Across the meadows downstream, it is a treat to see a boat on the river, as Ray Morris, ghillie for this beat, takes a client out on the river, hoping for salmon (right and facing page).

PENALLT

Penallt's riverside is best approached from Redbrook, along the pedestrian path slung alongside the old rail bridge (see next page). A walk along the river downstream from the Boat Inn leads eventually to the site where mill stones (right), manufactured in the quarries above, were rolled down to the river for loading. It is said that the ones that 'ran away' ended up in the river shallows, and there they are still.

The mill stones are made from a conglomerate rock looking like concrete, locally known as 'pudding stone' (below right); its suitability for grinding is disputed by Ray Morris, ghillie at Wyesham (previous page); in his view, the stones from the Penallt quarry were unfit for purpose, leaving a white powdery residue when put to use, which is why they lie abandoned on the river edge.

Facing page: What looks like a piece of an old weir extending into the river is a 'crib', a low breakwater extending into the river causing a back current attractive to the tired salmon. Ray Morris knows this location well, having built the 'crib' in the photo himself using stone dredged from the riverbed.

REDBROOK

*Susan Peterken (far right) shows her
painting of Redbrook Bridge at its
high viewpoint. Like many pictures of
the Wye at Redbrook, it exhibits strong
strong red tones – a memorial to the
iron ore and copper working for which
the village was famous.*

*Leading up the hill away from
the river, an unusual bridge built on
a steep gradient (above) is a remnant
of the inclined plane that led from the
river to the industrial workings above.*

CLEARWELL

There is little to show of Redbrook's past, but the lane under the incline bridge shown on page 48 eventually leads up to Clearwell, where the pre-Roman iron ore caves are still in business, albeit mostly for the benefit of tourists. A valuable sideline is ochre, important as a paint pigment, which Ray Wright (left) is scraping off the top surface of the cave to collect on the polythene sheet below.

Facing page: Clare Robertson – known locally as 'Miss Fire' – is Clearwell's resident blacksmith.

ST BRIAVELS & WHITECLIFF

*St Briavels Castle was built by
Edward I in 1292. Behind the splendid
twin-towered gatehouse (facing page),
the building is now a youth hostel.*

*At first glance coming down the lane
from Coleford you would be forgiven
for thinking Whitecliff (right) was the
ruin of another castle; in fact, it is a most
important ironworks. Built in 1798, it
was one of the earliest furnaces in the
Forest to use coke, not charcoal. After
various partnerships, by 1810 it was
run by David Mushet, famous for his
experimental work on the production
of steel.*

*Whitecliff has been restored by the
Dean Heritage Centre and more recently
by the Wye Valley AONB.*

ST BRIAVELS COMMON

In the 1790s, while Gilpin's tourists were floating past Bigsweir on their quest for the picturesque, the Gloucestershire woods above them were playing host to a totally different kind of social scene.

St Briavels Common was being gradually taken over by squatters, who enclosed and cleared small meadows, pushing down into the woodland above the Wye. As the going got rougher, the movement petered out, but on the ground today the meadow pattern remains. Although the woodland has re-asserted itself, it is still possible to see areas cleared of stone and intriguing remains of tiny stone-built cottages (facing page).

Dr George Peterken (right) lives on the cusp, where the woods meet the meadows; a forest ecologist with an interest in history, he has mapped twenty cottage sites. He feels that not enough has been done to conserve this unusual piece of social development.

Above: Mature trees grow out of piles of stone – two-hundred-year-old evidence that stumps were not removed at the time of clearance.

BIGSWEIR

Artist Mary Edwards (left) lives in an isolated farm a mile up a track from Bigsweir Bridge (facing page). Most of her paintings refer to her late husband and his work around the farm. The old railway station buildings (see next page) have been taken over by Bigsweir Fishery and a fisherman is often to be seen just below the bridge (above). On the Gloucestershire side of the river are both the Wye Valley and Offa's Dyke paths.

Wye Valley Railway

The Wye Valley railway is celebrated downstream at Tintern station, where the restored signal box is located, along with cafés and tourist information. But the flavour of the old route is better appreciated at the old halt by Bigsweir bridge, oddly named St Briavels. The waiting room is used by fishermen, but the abandoned goods shed (top centre), complete with its internal crane (top right), is worth a sneaky view.

CHARCOAL

Charcoal-burning was the basis for all the industrial endeavour in the Wye Valley, as the many flattened platforms on the wooded hillsides bear witness. The old method of covering the burning wood with turf is still demonstrated at Dean Heritage once a year, but the 'modern tradition' is to use a big iron cylinder kiln with a 'coolee hat' conical lid.

The Gwent Wildlife Trust manage Cross Robert wood, near Trellech, and the wood is coppiced to optimise both fauna and flora. Charcoal-burning is really a by-product of managing the woodland, but is also a business in its own right.

Fine-tuning the vents and chimneys of the kilns comes easily to Jan Kinchington (facing page), who has been making charcoal here for thirty years.

TRELLECH

A study of the map shows an old furnace located a mile from Trellech, but the village has a more unusual claim to fame with its three standing monoliths known as the Harald Stones (facing page). It also boasts a fine Celtic cross in the churchyard (left), and a 'holy well', dressed with flowers (above).

LLANDOGO

Llandogo has rather lost its connection with the river and is separated from it by a wide spread of water meadows. A couple of stones are all that remain of the once-thriving quays, boat-building yards and other riverside enterprises. In the twenty-first century, life here has a gentler pace. The village has two art galleries, and in the Wye Valley Arts converted chapel, Val Welham (far left of picture) organises a regular art class (above).

From the river looking back, the village seems to consist of houses thrown randomly against the hill (facing page). In fact a network of alleys and steps rise up, eventually taking the energetic to the Cleddon Falls high in the woods (above, right).

BROCKWEIR

Brockweir is truly a village of the river and was once the busiest port after Chepstow. A tiny lane winds up into the heart of the Forest, but until the bridge (facing page) was built in 1907, putting the ferry man out of business, the best access was by boat. The quay has been recently restored by the Wye Valley AONB.

Currently moored up above Brockweir waiting for high water is the 150 foot-long motor barge Wye Invader *(right), en route to Bristol from Hereford, where she was moored since 1990.*

With a reputation for drunkeness, law-breaking and cock-fighting on Sundays, Brockweir village had no church until a Moravian Chapel (stained-glass window, above) was built here in 1831.

TINTERN PARVA

As you approach the site of Tintern Abbey, the little hamlet (left) gives you time to reflect on the combination of tranquillity and industry that must have existed here before the dissolution of the monasteries in the mid-sixteenth century.

OFFA'S DYKE AND DEVIL'S PULPIT

Offa was an eighth-century king of Mercia who built his dyke on defensible high ground to keep the Welsh in their place. Today the Offa's Dyke footpath (left) is easy to locate, but does not always follow the original earthwork; in places, the Wye Valley AONB have deliberately separated the two to avoid erosion of the ancient monument.

The secluded viewpoint known as Devil's Pulpit can be reached by walking up through the woods from the bridge by Abbey Mills, or across the meadows from the St Briavels road. The best view is through a gap in the trees a hundred yards or so to the south (facing page). A few hundred metres further south, a substantial yew tree grows out of the centre of the rampart and ditch (above).

Tintern

The monks settled in Tintern for a quiet, secluded life, but turned the area into an industrial hotspot. They managed not only a traditional agricultural estate but a network of metal industry furnaces and forges around the abbey itself, as well as further up the valley.

TINTERN

*The original abbey site included what is now the
Anchor inn and spread through to the site of Abbey
Mills craft enterprises (see page 76). The arch (above)
was the abbey's water gate but today leads to the pub's
kitchen yard.*

ANGIDY

The Angidy Valley, running down to Tintern, was an integral part of the monks' industrial empire. The stream that ran through it fed ponds and leats which provided power for various furnaces, notably a wireworks, before tumbling into the Wye. It also drove two huge wheels at Abbey Mill forge, one of which remains on the site (see page 8). The stone bearers (facing page) supported the leat which drove the waterwheel at Abbey Tintern furnace.

The 'Eagle's Nest'

Between Tintern and Chepstow the valley seems to deepen, with the sides often forming sheer cliffs. The first of the viewpoints that Gilpin celebrated, high on Wyndcliff, is the 'Eagle's Nest' – carefully renovated by the Wye Valley AONB (see next page) to include nineteenth-century graffiti (above). From the lower car park on the main road, a famous flight of 365 steps (left) leads up to the heights. The view includes the woods of Piercefield, the grassy peninsular of Lancaut (see next pages) and, on the distant horizon, the Severn estuary (facing page).

PIERCEFIELD

In the mid-eighteenth century Valentine Morris, owner of the Piercefield estate, carried out what he considered improvements to his magnificent chunk of riverside landscape, adding follies, grottoes and creating viewpoints linked by paths through – be warned! – the very steeply sloping woods. At 'Lovers' Leap' pieces of original fence remain and it was here, while out planning his schemes, that Morris is reputed to have fallen down a 180-foot sheer cliff, only to be saved by landing in the branches of a tree.

Previous page: Riverside cliffs including 'Wintour's Leap', viewed from Lancaut.

LANCAUT

Lancaut is a huge isolated peninsular on the east bank of the river. From the end of the lane, walking down through the meadow past a huge lonely oak tree (above) brings you to the ruin of St James's chapel (left) – almost the only remains of the community that once thrived at the riverside. The cliffs downstream are partly the result of quarrying: sticking up from the mud is a piece of eroded timber (facing page) that confirms the presence of jetties for loading the stone.

The most prominent of the cliffs is known as 'Wintour's Leap', commemorating a probably mythical Civil War episode in which royalist Sir John Wintour, escaping a chasing posse of parliamentarians, rode his horse clear over the top of the cliffs to land in the river, and was able to swim to safety in Chepstow.

CHEPSTOW CASTLE

After Tintern Abbey and the soaring splendour of the river cliffs, Chepstow Castle provides a dramatic finale to the river trip. Dating back to 1067, this is the southernmost and oldest of the defensive line of castles on the English/Welsh borders.

CHEPSTOW RIVERSIDE

Chepstow was a busy port, where seagoing ships would berth to transfer cargoes to river trows. One quay known as the 'Packet Slip' is still in use, but the single small boat on the mud in front of the handsome road bridge (planned by John Rennie but constructed by John Rastrick) sums up the general lack of activity.

BOATS

Facing page: In an external gallery of Chepstow Museum built of black planking like a boatshed, curator Annie Lansbury displays the last remaining 'stop boat' used by salmon fishermen. The poles seen on the right of the picture were pushed down into the riverbed to allow nets to be slung between them; triangulated, they also fixed the boat in position against the current.

Above: With no such protection, on the quayside beside the railway bridge is one of the car ferries that crossed the Severn on the 'old passage' route before the first motorway bridge was built.

THE WYE MEETS THE SEVERN

This book began with the remains of a Brunel bridge, and ends with another. Chepstow provided the great engineer with a further development of his tubular suspension principle which climaxed in the Royal Albert Bridge at Saltash. Sadly, only the cast-iron piers remain (left), though a section of the suspension tube is located in a nearby engineering works (bottom left).

Facing page: From the walkway of the Wye bridge section of what is now named the M48, the river can be seen joining its country cousin the Severn at Chapel Rock (with the white light).

Index

Facing page: The author posing as Nelson at the Kymin (see page 36)

Further Reading

Gilpin, William: *Observations on the River Wye* (Pallas Athene, 200)

Kissack, Keith: *The River Wye* (Terence Dalton, 1982)

Peterken, Susan: *Landscapes of the Wye Tour* (Logaston Press, 2008)

Waycott, Ruth: *Overlooking the Wye* (Black Dwarf Publications, 2005)

Wye Valley AONB publish a set of very informative leaflets. These are available at tourist locations or via download from the AONB website, *www.aonb.org.uk*.

Acknowledgements

Thanks to all those who appear in the book and to:

Kate Biggs
Chepstow Museum
Adam Fisher
Gwent Wildlife Trust
Paul Manning
Monmouth Museum
Woody Morris
Wye & Usk Foundation
Wye Valley AONB
Wye Valley Arts

About the Author

Photographer Chris Morris lives and works in the Forest of Dean. He is the author of several books featuring documentary photographs of landscape and industrial history.

Canal Pioneers
978-0-9564358-3-5

The Stephensons: Railway Pioneers
978-0-9564358-0-4

Searching for Sir Humphrey
978-0-9542096-8-1

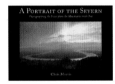

A Portrait of the Severn
978-0-9542096-5-0

Under Blorenge Mountain
978-0-9542096-1-2

Dean's Big Oaks
978-0-9542096-7-4